THE THREAT OF PEACE

The Threat of Peace

James F. Byrnes and the Council
of Foreign Ministers, 1945-1946

PATRICIA DAWSON WARD

The Kent State University Press

Library of Congress Cataloging in Publication Data

Ward, Patricia Dawson.
    The threat of peace.

    Bibliography: p.
    Includes index.
    1. Council of Foreign Ministers. 2. World War, 1939-1945—Peace.
3. United States—Foreign relations—1945-1953. 4. Byrnes, James Fran-
cis, 1879-1972.
I. Title.
D814.4.W37   940.53'22'0924   79-88604
ISBN 0-87338-233-1

For Devon

CONTENTS

PREFACE

In recent years historians of American foreign relations have vigorously pursued the origins of the cold war, but in their pursuit they have consistently overlooked the importance of the diplomacy of Secretary of State James F. Byrnes in the Council of Foreign Ministers. The heads of state at the Potsdam Conference created the Council of Foreign Ministers to write the treaties ending World War II, and Byrnes represented the United States on the council from September 1945 until January 1947. After resigning as secretary of state Byrnes wrote the only complete, if self-serving, account of his council negotiations, and historians subsequently have accepted Byrnes's analysis as accurate.

As secretary of state Byrnes suffered from a difficult relationship with President Harry Truman, lack of diplomatic experience, and independent work habits that led to his ignoring State Department expertise. Compounding these liabilities was the expectation of the American people that the treaties would not only be quickly written so that the troops could come home but also that the treaties would reflect American wartime goals of national self-determination, equal trade rights, and collective security.

Byrnes joined his colleagues on the Council of Foreign Ministers—V. M. Molotov of the USSR, Ernest Bevin of the United Kingdom, Georges Bidault of France, and Wang Shih-Chieh of China—with the benevolently arrogant expectation that American postwar military and economic superiority would allow the United States to dictate the type of treaties the American people wanted. At the first council meeting Byrnes learned that the Soviet Union wanted its status as a victorious Great Power acknowledged in treaties giving it control of the Balkans, reparations with which to rebuild, bases in the Mediterranean, a share in the control of Japan, and benefits for its client state, Yugoslavia.

This account details Byrnes's attempt to harmonize the conflicting Soviet and American positions at the six conferences of the Council of Foreign Ministers held during 1945 and 1946. These negotiations both influenced and were influenced by the growing American suspicion of USSR postwar intentions. The resulting American demand that the U.S. government get tough with the Soviet Union placed new strictures on Byrnes's efforts to write the peace treaties.

The secretary's solution was to pursue both a policy of public intransigence toward Soviet demands and a policy of private quid pro quo diplomacy within the Council of Foreign Ministers. This tactic eventually produced realistic treaties for Italy, Rumania, Bulgaria, Hungary, and Finland, but Byrnes's public-private diplomacy also placed him in the position of simultaneously abetting the impetus toward cold war while demonstrating an alternative to American-Soviet estrangement—continuous, realistic, persistent, face-to-face negotiation.

I wish to acknowledge the role of Robert A. Divine of the University of Texas in the preparation of this manuscript and to thank him for establishing the standard of scholarly and professional conduct which serves as my guide and goal. I also appreciate the valuable criticisms which W. W. Rostow, Harrison Wagner, and Robert Cotner, all of the University of Texas, have made of my work. At Baylor University I owe a special debt to E. Bruce Thompson who patiently and gently suggested revision after revision, to Herbert Reynolds who made possible the essential time and funds to research and write, and to Lynnette Geary who expertly and considerately helped me in the preparation of the manuscript. Equally as important to me as the scholarly guidance which I have received is the personal encouragement from my daughter, Devon; her grandparents, Cotton and Alleyne Ward; and my brother and sister-in-law, Dale and Gail Dawson. To them I offer my sincere thanks.

Patricia Dawson Ward

CHAPTER ONE

INTRODUCTION

James Francis Byrnes was the only person in
United States history to serve as congressman, senator,
Supreme Court justice, secretary of state, and governor.
During a political career that began in 1910 and ended in
1955, Byrnes served in the House of Representatives for
fourteen years, in the Senate for eleven years, on the
Supreme Court for sixteen months, in the State Department
for eighteen months, and in the South Carolina capitol for
four years. Byrnes's career reached its pinnacle after
America's entry into World War II when Franklin Roosevelt
named him his "assistant president" as director of economic
stabilization and then as director of war mobilization.
Anticipating more triumphs at the end of the war, James
Byrnes became the American secretary of state and expected
to facilitate the transition from war to peace. Faced with
tasks beyond his talents and forces beyond his control,
Byrnes's career faltered when he facilitated instead the
transition from World War II to the cold war.

Byrnes served as secretary of state from July 1945 to
January 1947, a period characterized by postwar confusion.
The death of Franklin Roosevelt after twelve years as
president and the succession of Harry Truman after four
months of serving as vice-president were major factors in
promoting disarray. By keeping decision making powers in
the White House and by dominating his administration to an
extent rarely equalled by other American presidents,

Roosevelt had been able to mobilize the cumbersome democratic processes against first the Depression and then the Axis powers. But by dominating his administration so completely, Roosevelt made the transition to a new administration after his death all the more difficult. Roosevelt left postwar America under the leadership of a notoriously uninformed vice-president who had conferred privately with the president only three times as vice-president and then only about trivial matters.

Harry Truman's liabilities were not confined to lack of knowledge about the Roosevelt administration. His biographers differ as to whether the presidency made Truman a great man, but most agree that he entered the White House with definite limitations.[1] During his ten years in the United States Senate, Truman had been a conscientious, hard worker, but he had not been a member of the leadership. He had had no voice in determining policy; he had merely had a good voting record on Roosevelt legislation. Truman had achieved national recognition with his Committee to Investigate the National Defense Fund, which made him an acceptable vice-presidential alternative for Roosevelt who was caught between factions promoting Henry Wallace and James F. Byrnes. At a time when the United States needed strong leadership, an experienced follower became president.

Truman entered the presidency with the narrow perspective of a good American patriot. Harry Truman was a simple man, not given to reflection, and when there was a problem to be solved, he listened to the information presented, adequate or not, and then made a decision. He prided himself on quick decisions, and he did not indulge in self-doubts once he had made the decision. He also prided himself on being patriotic, and wartime fervor, plus his own provincialism, had enhanced this characteristic. Truman looked at international affairs through strictly American eyes, finding it difficult, if not impossible, to understand another nation's perspective, especially if he considered the other nation's government immoral. Truman's inadequate knowledge, experience, and capabilities caused the State Department to doubt his ability to guide the nation's foreign affairs and contributed to the postwar confusion.[2]

Truman compounded this situation by selecting James F. Byrnes as his secretary of state. Byrnes was not politically limited, but his extensive political career had depended largely on his close personal friendship with Roosevelt. Their friendship had dated from Roosevelt's election as governor of New York in 1928 and had led to Byrnes's marshalling through the Senate much of the New Deal legislation that Truman had supported. Roosevelt had considered Byrnes as a vice-presidential possibility in 1940 but had appointed him to the Supreme Court instead. Shortly afterwards Roosevelt had talked Byrnes into resigning to become head of the Office of Economic Stabilization and then director of War Mobilization. In the latter position Byrnes's powers were so extensive that Roosevelt himself had referred to Byrnes as his "assistant president."[3]

Before Truman became president, he and Byrnes had had one significant encounter, which involved Roosevelt's choice of a vice-presidential nominee in 1944. Accounts of what happened vary, but they all agree that before the 1944 Democratic convention Byrnes had called Truman and had told him that Roosevelt wanted him (Byrnes) for vice-president. He had asked Truman to nominate him, and Truman had agreed, saying, "Why sure, Jimmy, if that's what the president wants I'll not only nominate you I'll work for you." Later when Truman had received Roosevelt's nod, he had called Byrnes and had asked to be relieved of his promise. Byrnes recorded no ill will toward Truman over the affair, only disappointment in Roosevelt, but Truman implied in his memoirs that Byrnes had known before Byrnes had called him that Roosevelt had wanted Truman, not Byrnes, as vice-president. Truman's daughter Margaret bluntly stated this charge years later and characterized Byrnes's action as "shrewdness—perhaps duplicity is a better word." Judge Samuel Rosenman, special counsel to Roosevelt and Truman, agreed with this assessment but added that Byrnes had not so much intended to eliminate Truman from consideration as to convince Roosevelt that Byrnes was a good liberal Democrat or Truman wouldn't support him. Another evaluation held that Truman did not reluctantly accept the vice-presidential spot but rather actively sought it through Democratic National Chairman

Bob Hannegan of St. Louis. This view presented Truman as being ambitious and joining "heartily in slitting Byrnes's throat." Whatever the motivation of the two men, there was no indication that the incident generated great personal ill will between them at the time, and even Margaret Truman said that her father didn't come to believe that Byrnes had deceived him until 1949. At best, though, the confrontation was awkward and raised the question of why President Truman would select Byrnes for his secretary of state.[4]

Byrnes had stayed on as director of the Office of War Mobilization after the 1944 election, but had told Roosevelt that he would resign after the war in Europe ended. Rumor had it that Byrnes had asked Roosevelt for the secretary of state post when Cordell Hunt had resigned, but was turned down in favor of Edward Stettinius. Perhaps as a gesture of reconciliation Roosevelt had taken Byrnes to the Yalta Conference with him in January 1945, but after their return Byrnes had ended his duties in Washington on schedule and had left for presumed retirement in Spartanburg, South Carolina, on 8 April. Roosevelt died four days later.[5]

Secretary of the Navy James Forrestal called Byrnes from the White House to say that he was sending a plane to bring Byrnes back to Washington. Truman received Byrnes warmly the next morning, although Margaret Truman later called Forrestal's actions "rather startling gestures wholly unauthorized." The former vice-president and the former "assistant president" went together to meet the train bringing Roosevelt's body to Washington and accompanied it to Hyde Park. The next day Truman told Byrnes that he wanted him for his secretary of state and strangely emphasized Byrnes's presence at the Yalta Conference as one of his main qualifications for the top cabinet post. At Yalta Byrnes had competed with Alger Hiss in insignificance, but unlike Hiss, he had occupied himself by keeping a shorthand record of the proceedings. Truman wanted a copy of this record and complained that it was ten days before he got it. Explaining Byrnes's appointment to South Carolina Senator Olin Johnston, the president said, "I'm doing it, Olin, because I think it is the only way I can be sure of knowing the facts of what went on at Yalta." Looking to

Byrnes as an expert on Yalta decisions when he had at his command men who were much better informed was indicative of Truman's ignorance of the Roosevelt administration.[6] Truman was also aware that the secretary of state was next in line for the presidency and believed that because Edward Stettinius, Roosevelt's new secretary of state, had never held elective office while Byrnes had had vast political experience, Byrnes was the man best qualified. George Allen, whom Truman delegated to tell Stettinius that Byrnes would replace him after the San Francisco Conference, said that Truman was worried about competition from Byrnes and didn't like Stettinius. By appointing Byrnes secretary of state he would keep Byrnes busy and make Congress happy while getting rid of Stettinius.[7]

Truman also mentioned a personal reason for choosing Byrnes, one that related to the vice-presidential affair. He said that Byrnes "undoubtedly was deeply disappointed and hurt" by that situation, and "I thought that my calling on him at this time might help balance things up." Although admirable, if true, the president's sentiments hardly amounted to a valid rationale for selecting the man who would guide the nation's foreign policy during this chaotic period. Though it was understandable that Truman, acutely conscious of his own shortcomings upon becoming president, should turn to Byrnes who had been much closer to Roosevelt and a leader in the Democratic Party, yet the choice was unfortunate. James F. Byrnes was as ignorant of foreign affairs as the president.[8]

Byrnes's political experience had been almost exclusively domestic and he was as provincial as Truman in his outlook. A product of South Carolina politics, Byrnes, born in 1879, was in Congress in 1910 and a member of the powerful House Appropriations Committee by World War I. A small, wiry extrovert, he soon became what *Time* magazine called a "politician's politician" and moved on to the Senate in 1930. His talents as a fixer led his enemies to consider him sly and his friends to characterize him as able. He was, like Truman, supremely self-confident and often believed that he had mastered an issue when he was just beginning to understand its complexity. However, unlike Truman, he was familiar with leadership. Having forged his leadership abilities in the political arena, he prided himself on being able to harmonize opposing factions and reach an agreement acceptable to both. On the surface this skill in compromise would appear to be a useful talent in diplomacy, but it did not always work out that way. His vast political experience led him to appreciate expediency, and he sometimes valued reaching an agreement above the substance of that agreement. He shared another characteristic with Truman, an impatience that led to his making quick decisions and expecting quick results, and in the slow moving field of diplomacy impatience was a liability. As a successful politician, Byrnes was also trained to keep a close eye on American public opinion, and he knew that the majority of Americans expected that since the war was over peace treaties reflecting the United States's postwar goals would be quickly written. Still politically ambitious, he wanted the credit for writing the treaties ending the war and foresaw little difficulty in writing into the treaties the American postwar vision.[9]

Roosevelt rhetoric had held that after the end of the great war America would forge a new world order designed to prevent future wars. Roosevelt had convinced the American people that if the United States learned the lessons of the past they would have peace in the future. The first of these lessons was that participation in an international organization was preferable to America's traditional foreign policy of noninvolvement. The United Nations was to be the United States's second chance at internationalism, and diplomats were to discard the approach of spheres of influence in favor of international cooperation. The advantages of national self-determination and multilateral trading policies were other lessons to be learned. Every nation was to have the right to choose its own form of government, and equal economic access was to replace preferential trading systems. Roosevelt believed in this diplomatic millennium because he was sure that the Grand Alliance, forged between the United States, Great Britain, and the Soviet Union to defeat the Axis threat, would continue after the war.[10]

Americans generally believed in Roosevelt's postwar dream and, significantly, so did the new president and his new secretary of state. Actually, there was little reason to believe that Roosevelt's dream of a postwar world with unity among the allies would ever be realized. Truman, who prided himself on his knowledge of history, should have realized that wartime coalitions traditionally tended to dissolve once the threat that united them disappeared. In 1815 the Quadruple Alliance that defeated Napoleon had almost ended in two simultaneous wars: one between Great Britain and France and the other between Russia and Prussia. Within recent memory the United States itself had aided the dissolution of the United Front of World War I by refusing to join the League of Nations. But this very example was the hallmark of the American determination to maintain the Grand Alliance. One of the most dubious lessons Americans learned was that World War II would not have occurred if the United States had joined the League. Perhaps it was the American determination to make up for past mistakes that caused much of the nation's leadership to take an unrealistic attitude toward peace. If they had expected that keeping the peace would be as difficult as winning the war, Americans might have responded differently to the Soviet pursuit of a policy contrary to expectation.

Even before the end of the war there was ample evidence that the USSR intended to take full advantage of its position as a victorious Great Power. Had the British been equal to the Soviets in strength, they undoubtedly would have done the same. Like the USSR, Great Britain never shared American illusions about the United Nations, self-determination, or a freer trade system, but, unlike the USSR, it ended the war economically dependent on the United States. The Soviet Union was hardly the equal of the United States after the war, but the Americans were slow to realize this. The strength of the Soviet Union lay in having definite territorial, economic, and political goals that it pursued with skilled diplomacy. These goals conflicted with American goals and brought the Soviet Union and the United States into postwar confrontation. Truman's, and especially Brynes's, responsibility was to negotiate this conflict of interest.

Historians have argued that Truman immediately and deliberately reversed Roosevelt's policy of cooperating with the Soviet Union.[11] This interpretation is overstated, because Truman entered the presidency determined to realize Roosevelt's aim of maintaining the Grand Alliance.[12] He soon found, however, that several of Roosevelt's key foreign policy advisers—Averell Harriman, William Leahy, John R. Deane, and James V. Forrestal—urged him to take a much stronger stand against Russia. Truman was immensely susceptible to the influence of his advisers during the first uncertain weeks of his administration, particularly in foreign policy, because he immediately had to prepare for a conference with the Soviet Foreign Minister V. M. Molotov. Initially these advisers, especially Harriman, appeared to have influenced Truman to change Roosevelt's policy. The new president fastened upon the idea that the Russians had not lived up to the Yalta agreement on Poland and began to talk about insisting on Soviet compliance. At the 23 April meeting with Molotov, Truman upbraided the foreign minister for Russia's failure to live up to its agreements. Truman's blunt, undiplomatic manner undoubtedly convinced both his advisers and Molotov that he was reversing his predecessor's attitude toward the alliance with Russia.[13]

The opposite conclusion could have easily been drawn, given Truman's temperament, his desire to appear decisive, and the information he had available. He assumed that Roosevelt's policy was embedded in the Yalta agreement on Poland, and that by insisting on Russian compliance, he was upholding the former president's policies. In fact, Roosevelt himself had been unhappy with the Yalta agreement on Poland but had thought it was the best compromise he could get at the time. He had by no means considered the issue closed and before his death had decided to use the same economic pressure on the Russians to gain acceptance of peacetime goals that he had been using on the British during the war. Truman carried out this Roosevelt policy, although in a more abrasive manner than Roosevelt would have done.[14]

The San Francisco Conference, which followed Truman's encounter with Molotov, publicized for the first time during the war the differences existing between the USSR and the U.S. Russia's efforts to seat representatives from the Lublin

Polish government and the arrest of the sixteen Polish underground leaders made Poland the symbol of the American-Soviet conflict. The accelerating deterioration of U.S.-USSR relations plus the glare of publicity caused Truman to reassess the situation. By this time other Roosevelt advisers—Henry Stimson, Joseph Davies, and Harry Hopkins—had warned Truman against unyielding confrontation with the Russians. The president decided to send Davies to London and Hopkins to Moscow to urge maintenance of the Big Three unity. Hopkins returned with a facesaving, if unsatisfactory, compromise on the Polish government that considerably defused that issue. Although Truman's statements about Russia continued to be intemperate, he did not consistently follow either an unyielding or a conciliatory policy toward Russia until March 1947 and his announcement of the Truman Doctrine. During the intervening year and one-half, late 1945–1946, the Truman administration, instead, negotiated the postwar conflict of American-Soviet interests in a series of Council of Foreign Ministers' meetings.[15]

Byrnes took credit for initiating the idea of a Council of Foreign Ministers to write the peace treaties after World War II, but this claim was only partially, if at all, accurate. On 19 June 1944, Under Secretary of State Stettinius had recommended to Roosevelt that the foreign ministers of the Great Powers write the first drafts of the treaties ending the war. Stettinius had added that the State Department wanted to avoid a Versailles-type general peace conference because such a meeting would be cumbersome and slow.[16] The next documented mention of peace settlement machinery came 9 June 1945, when Truman asked the State Department for its recommendations. Specifically, the president asked if the department would prefer a series of conferences or a Dumbarton-Oaks type meeting, "where under the leadership of responsible representatives of the great powers, continuous negotiation can proceed until different proposals for the European peace settlements can be agreed upon?" Before becoming secretary of state, Byrnes had sent a memorandum to President Truman on 11 June 1945, suggesting he do what Truman had just done, namely, to ask the State

Department for its views on the peace. Byrnes, too, wanted to know if the State Department preferred the treaties written at a series of conferences over a long period of time or at one general peace conference.[17]

On 19 June 1945, Edward Stettinius in San Francisco responded to the president's query by again warning against a "full-fledged peace conference," suggesting that "the problems concerned . . . be dealt with on an ad hoc basis by a council of Foreign Ministers." The State Department elaborated on its view in a "Briefing Book" dated 27 June 1945, which it had prepared for the Potsdam Conference. This memorandum listed the topics likely to be considered at Potsdam and gave a suggested statement of the position of the United States on each. In reference to the peace treaties, the department recommended that a council of the foreign ministers of Great Britain, the Soviet Union, China, France, and the United States be established to write the draft treaties instead of a general peace conference. The State Department planners wrote: "One of the most urgent problems in the field of foreign relations facing us today is the establishment of some procedure and machinery for the development of peace negotiations and territorial settlements without which the existing confusion, political uncertainty, and economic stagnation will continue to the serious detriment of Europe and the world." They cited Versailles as the prime example of an unwieldy general peace conference in which rival claims and counterclaims generated ill will and delay, but they also opposed a formal peace conference limited to the three Great Powers on the grounds that the smaller nations already had accused the Big Three of running the world without consideration of the interests of the lesser powers. To avoid these problems the State Department suggested a Council of Foreign Ministers of the permanent members of the United Nations Security Council. By limiting the council to these members the department believed that both Great Britain and the Soviet Union would be kept from trying to add nations sympathetic to their views.[18]

This last observation pointed to another planned purpose of the proposed Council of Foreign Ministers. The council was not intended solely to write treaties but also to keep the Soviet Union and Great Britain from hardening their spheres of influence. Until the U.N. began to function, the council was to serve as an interim collective security organization. The "Briefing Book" stated that: "Such a Council would tend to reduce the possibility of unilateral action by either the Russians or the British and would serve as a useful interim means through which the United States would work for the liquidation of spheres of influence."[19]

In his 1947 memoir, *Speaking Frankly*, Byrnes asserted that he sent a memorandum of his own to Truman suggesting the creation of a Council of Foreign Ministers before he became secretary of state. Byrnes's memorandum, which he said he wrote with the assistance of his major foreign policy adviser, Benjamin V. Cohen, cannot be found in the Byrnes Papers, the State Department archives, or those papers now open at the Truman Library. Byrnes said that he told Truman that the council should first consider the Italian and Balkan treaties "because these were the least controversial," and then take up Germany. The idea of dealing with lesser enemy states first was not in the State Department plan. He also envisioned the foreign ministers determining general principles for the European settlement and appointing deputies to do the actual drafting of the treaties. The State Department paper differed with Byrnes on this point also. It wanted a deputy to accompany each minister, though with the understanding "that the major work of preparation would be undertaken by the respective foreign offices." Another departure from the State Department memorandum was that Byrnes had a Dumbarton Oaks-San Francisco precedent in mind. Once the Big Three were in agreement on the treaties prepared by the foreign ministers, he wanted the drafts presented to all the United Nations at a general peace conference. Byrnes agreed that a conference without this preliminary work was a bad idea, because "the logrolling, the interplay of conflicting interests, plus the sheer number of issues and people, would result . . . in such conflict that the conference would last a year, if indeed, it could ever end successfully." Byrnes said that Truman approved his proposal for a Council of Foreign

Ministers and sent it on to the State Department for comment. He acknowledged that the department had been thinking along similar lines but insisted that the State Department approved his plan before he became the secretary of state. Whatever Byrnes's role in the original formulation, the idea of a Council of Foreign Ministers to write the treaties and handle postwar problems became official United States policy.[20]

There is no evidence in either the Byrnes Papers, the State Department archives, or the Truman Papers to support Gar Alperovitz's contention that Truman and Byrnes wanted a Council of Foreign Ministers as a forum for atomic diplomacy. The idea of a Council of Foreign Ministers originated within the State Department and was written into the Potsdam "Briefing Book" by men who knew nothing of the atomic project. Equally unsubstantial is Alperovitz's statement that the council was established to provide a forum for post-Potsdam negotiation because American officials expected "that there would be little likelihood of a settlement during the heads-of-government meeting." Although the State Department's rationale for creating a council was complex, Byrnes's was not, because he was thinking in terms of making his mark by successfully writing treaties. Neither Byrnes nor anyone else in the American leadership knew what the results of the first atomic test would be. The bomb was not the basis of American foreign policy at this juncture; Roosevelt's postwar expectations were.[21]

James F. Byrnes was sworn in as secretary of state at the White House on 3 July 1945, and three days later left with Truman for the Big Three conference at Potsdam. He prepared for the meeting on board the *Augusta* enroute to Antwerp. Hasty, frantic preparation became a staple of Byrnes's diplomacy and so did his conviction that his preparation was adequate. Byrnes worked during the crossing with Ben Cohen, H. Freeman Matthews, director of the Office of European Affairs, and Charles Bohlen, Soviet affairs expert. Ben Cohen, a small, quiet bachelor, achieved national prominence during the early days of the New Deal when he collaborated with Thomas J. Corcoran in drafting several controversial measures: the Securities and Exchange

Act, the Public Utilities Holding Company Act, and the Fair Labor Standards Act. Cohen also participated in the negotiations exchanging destroyers for bases in World War II and served as an adviser to the American delegation at the Bretton Woods Monetary Conference and at the Dumbarton Oaks Conference. Cohen moved next to Byrnes's small, elite War Mobilization staff where he established a close personal relationship with Byrnes, and when Byrnes went to the State Department, he named Cohen State Department counselor. Doc Matthews was an experienced career diplomat who began his service in the 1920s and first met Byrnes at the Yalta Conference. Chip Bohlen had served as first secretary of the Moscow Embassy from 1943 to 1944 and was chief of the Division of Eastern European Affairs. As Roosevelt's and now Truman's Russian interpreter, Bohlen also served as liaison between the president and the State Department. These four—Byrnes, Cohen, Matthews, and Bohlen—using State Department prepared briefing books, discussed issues with President Truman once a day during the seven-day crossing.[22]

At Potsdam Truman presided during the first plenary session with Joseph Stalin and Winston Churchill. The president's first proposal, and the first proposal made at Potsdam, was to create a Council of Foreign Ministers. Bohlen observed that Truman closely followed the position agreed upon on board the *Augusta* and even used the language cited above from the State Department working paper as the rationale for his proposal. Bohlen believed that everyone immediately liked the idea of a Council of Foreign Ministers, but Churchill suggested that the issue be referred for study to the foreign secretaries, Anthony Eden, Vyacheslav Molotov, and Byrnes. Stalin agreed, but questioned the inclusion of China of the grounds that it was a European peace that would be settled. Truman asked that the foreign secretaries discuss the question of China as a participant and report back, and the meeting moved to other issues. Just before the adjournment of this first plenary session, however, Stalin again brought up the proposed Council of Foreign Ministers and questioned for the second time China's inclusion. Truman replied that China was a member of the U.N. Security Council, but Churchill, agreeing with

Stalin that it complicated matters to let China participate, suggested that the foreign ministers consider whether the council should be composed of four or five members. "Or three members," Stalin quickly added, because he opposed French participation also. Churchill suggested excluding China at least until the defeat of Japan, and the president responded that he had no objection to excluding China if the foreign secretaries agreed that they should. Truman and Stalin thought that both the Yalta agreement for periodic meetings of foreign ministers, and the European Advisory Commission, would be superseded by the Council of Foreign Ministers, but Churchill disagreed. Stalin returned to the original agreement of referring the whole issue to the foreign ministers, and the others concurred.[23]

When the three secretaries met the next morning, Molotov wanted to restrict the participants in the Council of Foreign Ministers as much as possible and suggested alternating membership according to the treaty under discussion. Eden agreed and proposed that only the nations that signed the armistice with the enemy state under consideration attend. The ministers approved this significant amendment, although it meant eliminating China from all European discussions, and France from all except those about Germany. Contrary to Churchill's position the day before, Eden wanted to end the periodic meetings of the foreign ministers established at Yalta. Byrnes welcomed Eden's support, but Molotov, reversing the Soviet position at the first meeting, persuaded them to keep those meetings separate from the proposed council.[24]

That afternoon Churchill, Stalin, and Truman accepted this revised version of the Council of Foreign Ministers at their second plenary session. But this time Churchill questioned the necessity of submitting the draft treaties to the U.N., because he thought even this "would be a lengthy and laborious process." Byrnes told Truman that the 1 January 1942, Declaration of the United Nations required submission, and Stalin said, without elaboration, that presenting the drafts to the other allies would make no difference because "the three powers would represent the interests of all." Byrnes pointed out that the important consideration was that the Big Five Powers would have to agree among themselves first, and the discussion ended with that observation.[25]

When the foreign secretaries met the next day, Byrnes reopened the discussion of the composition of the council and argued that the French should have a voice in the Italian treaty because France, while not a signatory to the Italian armistice, did fight against Italy. Molotov agreed to French participation in the Italian settlement, but asked for Byrnes's views on French participation in matters concerning nations against which it had not declared war. Molotov's concern was for the Balkan nations since France had never declared war on them, and Byrnes responded that he wanted France present at the discussion of the treaties for Rumania, Hungary, and Bulgaria, but not in a decision making role. Specifically, he said that "if France were not at war with any country she would be present during any discussions but would not necessarily participate in the decisions." A U.S. delegation memorandum of this foreign ministers meeting stated more precisely that: "It was understood that if a member of the Council was not at war with a given state, it might participate in the *discussions* of the peace settlement concerning that state but would not participate in the *decisions* connected with that peace settlement." But the final text presented to the heads of state omitted reference to discussion privileges and stated only that: "For the purpose of the peace settlement for Italy, France shall be regarded as a signatory to the terms of surrender for Italy. Other members should be invited to participate when matters directly concerning them are under discussion." French and Chinese rights to discuss treaties for nations whose armistice they did not sign would surface again at the first meeting of the Council of Foreign Ministers.[26]

With little discussion of this last, imprecise revision, the heads of state made their first Potsdam decision, the creation of a Council of Foreign Ministers to hold its first meeting in September in London. The original State Department proposal advised against holding meetings in the capitals of the participants and suggested instead Brussels or Vienna. But both Churchill, and Labour Party leader Clement Attlee, argued in favor of London, because it was halfway between Moscow and Washington. When Attlee and Ernest Bevin replaced Churchill and Eden as Great Britain's new prime minister and foreign secretary, they approved the proposal for a Council of Foreign Ministers, and the conference continued.[27]

There is no evidence to support Charles Mee's dramatic assertion that Truman and Byrnes wanted a Council of Foreign Ministers to prepare for a peace conference that they never intended to convene, but to which they could defer issues they wanted unresolved. Mee, basing this conclusion on the Briefing Book itself, wrote: "What Stalin and Churchill did not know was that in Truman's briefing book it said 'It seems clear that it would be desirable to avoid the convocation of a full-fledged peace conference to deal with the major political problems that have arisen as a result of the termination of the war in Europe.' In short, Truman put off problems to a peace conference that would never be held." Neither Truman nor Byrnes were Machiavellian; their proposal to establish a Council of Foreign Ministers explicitly stated what Mee pictured as a subterranean plot hidden in their working papers. The American proposal read: "The experience at Versailles following the last war does not encourage the belief that a full formal peace conference without preliminary preparation on the part of the leading powers is the best procedure. Such a conference without such preparation would be slow and unwieldly, its sessions would be conducted in a heated atmosphere of rival claims and counterclaims and ratification of the resulting documents might be long delayed." The American proposal suggested as an alternative that the draft treaties prepared by the Council of Foreign Ministers be referred to the United Nations; and this referral process, in Truman's and Byrnes's understanding, would constitute a limited, controled peace conference analogous to the Dumbarton Oaks-San Francisco precedent.[28]

Byrnes and Truman were optimistic about the future success of the council. At a Potsdam luncheon with Molotov on 24 July, Byrnes discussed plans for the September meeting in London. He thought that the foreign ministers could agree within ten days on directives for their deputies and their staffs so work could begin on the drafts. Byrnes said: "We discussed the appointment of deputies, the relation of the Council to the United Nations and the desirability of beginning work on the Italian treaty upon our return home. On all these points we appeared to be in complete accord." Truman reported to the American people in a radio speech 9 August: "The Council is going to be the continuous meeting ground of the five principal governments, on which to reach common understanding regarding the peace settlements. . . . This preparation by the Council will make possible speedier, more orderly, more efficient and more cooperative peace settlements than could otherwise be obtained."[29]

The Joint Communiqué of the Potsdam conference, which defined the council's responsibilities, stated that its immediate task was to draw up draft treaties for Italy, Rumania, Bulgaria, Hungary, and Finland—and later Germany. The communique specified, however, that other matters might be referred to the council by agreement of the participating nations. The heads of state authorized the council to form a joint secretariat to be housed permanently in London and instructed each foreign minister to appoint a high ranking deputy who would have the authority to act in the absence of his minister. Each deputy was to have a small staff of technical advisers. The ministers could decide on other sites for later meetings, adopt its own rules of procedure, and invite representatives of other nations to participate if desired.[30]

Thus the Grand Alliance, almost casually, established the machinery for handling the threat of peace. Byrnes took a State Department idea and changed it significantly. The British and the Russians quickly accepted his concept of a Council of Foreign Ministers, because it merely enlarged on the Yalta agreement that the foreign ministers would meet regularly to handle postwar problems. He based his optimism about the success of the council on its speedy acceptance by the other powers. A more experienced diplomat might have noticed that at Potsdam the heads of state had followed the wartime tradition of postponing decisions on controversial subjects for later consideration— in this case, by the new Council of Foreign Ministers. But the council would not have the luxury of postponing decisions; it would become instead the showcase for Allied division.[31]

CHAPTER TWO

THE LONDON CONFERENCE OF THE COUNCIL OF FOREIGN MINISTERS
11 September–2 October 1945

Events of major importance came so quickly in 1945 that even if the United States had been blessed with an experienced secretary of state, he would have had difficulty mastering them. James Byrnes returned to Washington from the Potsdam Conference on 7 August. By then the United States had used the first atomic bomb on Hiroshima, and the second was to explode over Nagasaki on 9 August. The Soviet Union entered the war against Japan on 8 August, and by 10 August Washington received a message concerning surrender from the Japanese. Japan formally surrendered on 14 August with decisions about the occupation and administration of Japan to follow. Byrnes was also busy with changes within the State Department staff necessitated by a new secretary and with the transition of the department from a wartime to peacetime status. There were discussions about the Lend-Lease termination of 21 August and a visit by General Charles de Gaulle on 22 August. New efforts to unite the Nationalist and Communist Chinese competed for Byrnes's attention, and President Truman presented him with the Distinguished Service Medal. Not surprisingly then, Byrnes spent little time preparing for the first conference of the Council of Foreign Ministers. He had been secretary of state for two months and back in Washington for twenty-eight days when he left for London on 5 September.

The Potsdam Protocol specified 1 September as the council's opening date, but on 15 August British Foreign Secretary Bevin suggested postponing the meeting until 3 September. Byrnes preferred an even later date, and the foreign ministers agreed on 11 September. There was little communication among the Allied governments prior to the London meeting. As host, Bevin assumed the initiative by suggesting as the agenda: first the Italian treaty; then treaties for Hungary, Rumania, Bulgaria and Finland; withdrawal of troops from Iran; Italian colonies; international waterways; and Japan.[1]

On this voyage Byrnes sailed on the *Queen Elizabeth*, but the preparation was as frantic and as inadequate as before. He left with American policy still undecided on several issues to be discussed at London, but said that "on the boat we started to work in earnest." Again he held daily sessions with his small delegation: Ben Cohen, James C. Dunn, Charles Bohlen, and John Foster Dulles. Dunn had headed the Office of European Affairs until Stettinius had promoted him to assistant secretary of state, and at Potsdam Dunn had served as Byrnes's political adviser; on this trip he was Byrnes's deputy. Byrnes had replaced Bohlen as liaison between the White House and the State Department, because he wanted to deal directly with the president; Bohlen's rank on this trip was special assistant to the secretary.[2]

John Foster Dulles was the new addition to Byrnes's team; again trying to learn from the past, Byrnes wanted a bipartisan peace. Dulles, the grandson and nephew of secretaries of state, had served as foreign affairs adviser to the Republican nominee for president, Thomas Dewey, in the 1944 campaign and was on good terms with Senator Arthur Vandenberg, the ranking Republican member of the Foreign Relations Committee. The harried secretary of state did not ask Dulles to accompany him until a 22 August luncheon at Blair House. Byrnes told Dulles that he was "peculiarly qualified" to act as his personal adviser, but Dulles made it clear that he did not want to be "merely scenery." Byrnes agreed to a "limited engagement" for the two of them to see if, as Dulles put it, their "minds worked along similar lines." When Dulles asked if Truman approved of his going to

London, Byrnes replied that "he had not discussed it with
President Truman because it was definitely understood
between them that in all such matters he would have the
right to act as he saw fit." At Dulles's insistence, Byrnes
asked the president about a bipartisan approach and his
choice of Dulles in particular before leaving for London.
Truman approved of both.[3]

Byrnes left for the first conference of the Council of
Foreign Ministers without any other directions from the
president or advice from the State Department. As director of
the Office of War Mobilization, he had relied on his own
abilities and a small group of advisers, and, given his self-
confident personality, he considered it natural to continue
this plan of operation. Truman was partly responsible for
allowing his secretary of state to assume almost total control
of American foreign policy, because he, like Byrnes, was
overwhelmed with a variety of problems and was relieved to
have Byrnes take charge of this arena. Byrnes had not, and
would not, gain control of the State Department bureaucra-
cy, and wanting independence from career diplomats as well
as the White House, he chose not to utilize the vast resources
of the department. Accordingly, the American delegation to
the London Conference worked without the assistance of a
State Department planning book while they hastily determined the United States' position on the treaties ending
World War II.[4]

Byrnes considered the American bargaining position
much stronger at London than at Potsdam. The United
States was now the sole possessor of the twice-used atomic
bomb, and as late as 1947 Byrnes still believed that another
nation would need a minimum of seven years to master
atomic technology. Truman remembered Byrnes telling him
in early April 1945, "that in his belief the bomb might well
put us in a position to dictate our own terms at the end of the
war." After learning at Potsdam that the bomb had been
successfully tested, Byrnes had told Joseph E. Davies that
"the New Mexico situation had given us great power, and
that in the final analysis, it would control." In August 1945,
Byrnes had taken the position that international control of
atomic energy was premature and had told Assistant

Secretary of War John J. McCloy that he was "quite radically opposed to any approach to Stalin whatever" on sharing the bomb. At the London Conference he "wished to have the implied threat of the bomb in his pocket," and urged Henry Stimson on 4 September to aid his efforts to keep Truman from publicly mentioning the possibility of international control until after the London Conference. Stimson wrote in his diary that Byrnes's "mind is full of his problem with the coming meeting of the foreign ministers and he looks to having the presence of the bomb in his pocket, so to speak, as a great weapon."[5]

Byrnes had an equally formidable weapon in the economic power of the United States, because, alone among the Allies, America emerged from the war economically more powerful than when it entered. He was aware that all of the other members of the Council of Foreign Ministers needed American economic assistance for postwar reconstruction. Roosevelt had deliberately postponed discussion of a U.S. loan to Russia in order to gain bargaining power, and Truman had supported Congress's decision not "to use Lend-Lease money for rehabilitation purposes." Foreign Economic Administrator Leo Crowley's zealous interpretation of Truman's policy to begin restricting the flow of Lend-Lease supplies to Russia, although quickly countermanded by the president, made it clear to the Soviet government that the U.S. could use economic pressure to gain political concessions. The Truman administration also applied this pressure to the British and the French governments. Assistant Secretary of State Will Clayton told Byrnes on 18 August that he planned to open negotiations on an American loan to Great Britain while the meeting of the Council of Foreign Ministers was in progress. The unexpected termination of Lend-Lease on 21 August had placed the British in a particularly vulnerable position and now, as Prime Minister Attlee put it, "We weren't in a position to bargain." General de Gaulle had also made it clear to Byrnes during his 22 August visit to Washington that France needed American aid. Not surprisingly then, the secretary of state estimated that less than two weeks would be needed in London to decide the essential features of five peace treaties. With the bomb and the dollar "in his pocket," Byrnes anticipated little difficulty in securing the agreement of the other ministers to the kind of peace treaties the U.S. wanted.[6]

Byrnes's problem was his imprecise conception of the kind of treaties the U.S. wanted, because the only major decisions the American delegation made before arriving in London concerned the Italian treaty. He decided to advocate an easy peace for Italy and independence for the Italian colonies of Eritrea, Somaliland, and Libya. To prepare the colonies for independence, he had his aides prepare a proposal for a collective trusteeship under a governor appointed by the U.N. On the question of a border between Italy and Yugoslavia, the American delegation decided to advocate an ethnic line separating as many Italians as possible from as many Yugoslavs as possible. Byrnes wanted to invite Ethiopia, Yugoslavia, and Greece to present their views on the Italian treaty to the council, and then he expected the deputies to prepare a draft treaty by 1 November 1945 and Italy to present its views before the final draft was submitted to eligible U.N. signatories. With these few decisions made, the delegation disembarked to the music of American and British bands and "mild cheers" from a small group of spectators. The sight of wartorn London deeply impressed the American secretary of state, but he considered the devastation a "desirable reminder of the grave responsibility that was ours."[7]

Byrnes had met the other members of the Council of Foreign Ministers, but he did not show any interest in learning about them or the positions they might take. He looked upon them as Republicans, upon himself as a majority leader striving for consensus, and said about the Soviets in particular, "I know how to deal with the Russians. It's just like the U.S. Senate. You build a post office in their state and they'll build a post office in our state." One would be hard put to find similarities between any Republican and the Soviet representative on the council, Molotov. The foreign minister was the most experienced diplomat on the council, having held his position since 1939 when Stalin chose him to replace Maxim Litvinov. A short smiling man with rimless glasses and a grey moustache, Molotov stuttered badly and laughed soundlessly but had a remarkably close, though slavish, relationship with Stalin. Dulles, who had seen the best diplomats nations had to offer since the Hague Conference of 1907, maintained that Molotov— thorough, composed, deliberate, and tenacious—was the best of all of them. Like Byrnes, French Foreign Minister Georges Bidault, and Chinese Minister Dr. Wang Shih Chieh, Bevin was just beginning his diplomatic career. He had as much freedom to direct British foreign policy as Byrnes had, given the foreign minister's relationship with Prime Minister Attlee. Attlee believed in leaving foreign affairs in Bevin's hands and not interfering, or as he put it in an unflattering but telling analogy, "If you have a good dog, you don't bark yourself." Bevin was a short, stout former truck driver and labor leader with a temper that would be as much a liability in his new role as his ignorance of diplomacy. Bidault had met Byrnes in Washington during de Gaulle's visit and had had three conversations with him. Byrnes was impressed that the French foreign minister was a genuine war hero, who had been captured and imprisoned by the Nazis for over a year. American intelligence believed Bidault to be "Mr. X," the leader of all the French Underground before the Normandy landings, but the romantic aura surrounding him did not hide the fact that London was to be the first conference in which France was to participate as a great power since the war started. Wang, with a vague reputation for being stolid and shrewd, was as sensitive as Bidault to China's participation on an equal footing.[8]

The first session of the Council of Foreign Ministers opened with little fanfare on 11 September 1945 at 4:00 p.m. at Lancaster House. The five foreign ministers seated themselves around a great, green-covered round table with two advisers beside each. Bohlen and Dulles sat by Byrnes. Bevin welcomed them on behalf of his government and said that their armies had won the war and they must win the peace. After each minister responded to Bevin's remarks, they took up procedure as the first item of business. The ministers quickly agreed to Bevin's suggestions of a rotating chairmanship, of using a joint secretariat, to their deputies meeting each morning, and of their meeting each afternoon.

Bevin then raised the question that was to result in the most controversial decision of this session. He asked if the others agreed with his interpretation of the terms of reference of the council, namely, that all the members could attend the meetings and participate in the discussion but that only armistice signatories could vote on any given issue. Byrnes agreed with this interpretation but said the United States was willing to reconsider that decision and to allow all members to vote on every issue. Molotov responded that he was not empowered to revise Potsdam decisions. Then (from the American minutes of the proceedings) came the following exchange:

> Molotov inquired if Bevin suggested that all five representatives have the right to attend discussions if they wished to do so, but that decisions could be made only by the representatives concerned. If that were so, he agreed.
> Bevin said he wanted to know what the understanding was. Would all five attend the discussions, but if they had no interest, would not vote? If they were interested, they would vote.
> Byrnes said that so far as the U.S. was concerned, this was all right if it meant that they would not only be present but could participate in the discussions.
> Molotov said he had no objections.
> Bidault agreed to what Mr. Byrnes had said.
> This was agreed to.

The ramifications of this decision did not occur to any of the ministers until later, but what they had done was to broaden and to lengthen the treaty writing process. Whereas under the earlier understanding China could not discuss any of the European settlements and France was excluded from the Balkan and Finnish treaties, now all five nations could present their views on all issues. The decision also marked another step toward great power status for France and China, and toward minority status on the Council of Foreign Ministers for the USSR.[9]

This first session of the Council of Foreign Ministers also agreed, at Bevin's and Byrnes's insistence, to establish a Communiqué Committee composed of a press officer representing each council power. The American and British ministers wanted this committee to issue only the decisions reached at the end of each day's proceedings and not detail the discussions that went on. Byrnes and Bevin had in mind the precedent of publicized disagreements at the San Francisco Conference, but this decision would inadvertently create an equally bad press climate in London. Newsmen would find it so hard to get information of any kind that they would print a great many inaccurate rumors or, in Dulles's words, "backstairs gossip." Even the State Department would complain about not knowing what was going on. Assistant Secretary of State Dean Acheson, left in charge in Washington, wired the secretary of the American delegation, Theodore Achilles, on 11 September 1945, that "it would be helpful to recieve by cable full texts of all statements made by the Secretary to the press." Achilles had assumed that one of his duties would be to write a daily telegram reporting the day's proceedings to the State Department and accordingly drafted one following the first council session. Dunn and Dulles approved the text before Achilles took it to Byrnes who asked, "What's this?" Achilles answered, "This is our Delegation's telegram to the State Department telling what happened today." "Hell, I may tell the President sometime what happened," Byrnes responded, "but I'm never going to tell the State Department about it." Acheson persisted in requesting copies of official releases and draft proposals, but he received only copies of the council's press committee's communiqués just as the press corps did.[10]

The last item of business for the first plenary session of the Council of Foreign Ministers was the agenda. Bevin presented a list of twelve topics suggested by the members through prior communications, and the ministers quickly agreed to begin with the Italian treaty and the other topics decided at Potsdam. Molotov suggested, and the others agreed, that draft treaties for Rumania, Bulgaria, Hungary, and Finland be regarded as a single item on the agenda. Molotov also noted that Bevin had indicated earlier that Japan would be discussed but that it was not on the present list of possible subjects. The British foreign secretary replied that no nation had submitted a specific proposal about Japan and therefore none was included. Byrnes added that he understood from Potsdam discussions that no Far Eastern matters would be discussed and he was not prepared to discuss any. The ministers agreed to consider other items for the agenda later but to proceed for now with the Italian treaty. The British had prepared a draft on the political aspects of the Italian treaty, which the council agreed to discuss the next day.[11]

Procedural problems delayed discussion of the Italian treaty the next day because the American delegation submitted a memorandum suggesting that the views on Italian issues of Ethiopia, Yugoslavia, Greece, and Italy be heard by the council. To Byrnes's surprise Bevin insisted that if any government were heard the British Dominions and India should also be heard. Byrnes complained about the council's "serious difference of opinion over its organization and agenda" in these first meetings, but inasmuch as the differences were not serious and were easily resolved, the secretary's complaint was more of a reflection of his own unfulfilled expectations. Byrnes had made it clear to the other ministers that he wanted them to agree quickly on the principles of the Italian treaty, leaving the details to the deputies while the council adjourned, and not to meet again until the draft treaty was ready. In fact, at his suggestion the ministers when they convened their third session to discuss the British draft, used instead as the basis of their discussion "Suggested Directives to the Deputies" prepared by the U.S. delegation. The ministers quickly agreed on many of the principles he wanted to guide the deputies in writing the Italian treaty. These included minor rectifications of the French-Italian border, no changes on the Swiss-Italian and Austro-Italian frontiers, Italy renouncing all claims to Albania, the disposition of Zara and Dalmation Islands and Saseno, and a Bill of Rights for Italian citizens. At later meetings, the ministers also accepted the American suggestions on war crimes, restoration of Italian sovereignty, and Italian disarmament, with few amendments. These agreements were significant, and as Philip Mosely, who served on Dunn's staff, said, they "actually formed the basis of the work of the deputies when they finally began their labors in January 1946." But Byrnes was not satisfied because other

American suggested principles were not accepted. These included disposition of Italian colonies and the Dodecanese Islands, reparations, and the Yugoslav-Italian border. That he anticipated quick agreement on issues as complicated as these was indicative of his diplomatic naiveté. The secretary had deliberately decided to begin with the Italian treaty because he considered it the "simplest to draft." Now he learned that, as Joseph Davies wrote, "It bristles with difficulties."[12]

The first American proposal on which there was disagreement concerned demilitarizing the Dodecanese Islands and ceding them to Greece. Molotov insisted that the deputies study the issue longer because "the Soviet government attached particular importance to this area . . . because it was near the entrance to the Black Sea." Molotov agreed to Greece's claim for the islands but under persistent questioning from Byrnes and Bevin made it clear that he wanted to delay decision. The Soviet foreign minister said that "if he lived in North America he could decide the question without delay." Bevin responded that "it was difficult for him to understand why on Monday they could decide to cede islands to Yugoslavia and Albania but could not decide this matter. North America was about the same distance from both of them." Byrnes refused to "agree to the farce of transmitting the question to the deputies for study when there was nothing for them to study." The council agreed instead to the farce of deferring the Dodecanese issue from one meeting to the next until there was agreement.[13]

Byrnes took the precaution of explaining to Molotov the collective trusteeship proposal of the U.S. for the Italian colonies before the council discussed the issue. This private conversation was the first of several the two ministers had in London. Molotov agreed with the principle of a U.N. trusteeship but wanted individual nations as administrators, anticipating that Britain, the United States, and Russia would each take a colony. The Soviet Union wanted Tripolitania, but Byrnes argued that if each of the great powers took a colony to administer, the other nations "would regard the arrangement as a repetition of the division of spoils of war cloaked under a general trusteeship arrangement." The conversation ended, as would all the ones that followed, without agreement.[14]

Molotov repeated his arguments against the American trusteeship plan to the other ministers when the council took up the colonial issue. Byrnes fared little better with the French, because Bidault believed it "neither equitable nor wise" to take all of Italy's colonies from it, and was skeptical of the independence aspect of the American plan, "especially as these territories were adjacent to a part of the French Empire." Bevin maintained that he was "very much surprised" that Russia even advanced a claim to Tripolitania "in view of the vital interests of the British Government in the North African area." "The British claims in that area had been put forward on the same basis as had Russian claims in Eastern Europe," Bevin added, "namely security— a perfectly legitimate basis." Bevin also opposed leaving the colonies under Italian rule, as Bidault wanted. He reminded the ministers that Britain had made a public pledge to her allies, the Senussi tribesmen of the former Italian colony of Cyrenaica, that after the war they would not be returned to Italian rule. With the unqualified support of only the Chinese minister, Byrnes agreed to refer the colonial issue to the deputies.[15]

In a second private conversation Molotov told Byrnes that Stettinius had assured Ambassador Andrei Gromyko in San Francisco that the United States would support Russia's claim for a trusteeship. The foreign minister said that was why he had been surprised by the American opposition to the Soviet Union requesting administration of Tripolitania. Byrnes pleaded ignorance of the details of Stettinius's offer but was sure no specific territory had been mentioned.[16]

Bevin reported to his cabinet that "great difficulties" had arisen in the council over the issue of the Italian colonies. Fearing that "Russia might be anxious to establish herself on the African continent" and noting its "very strong negotiating position," Bevin planned to present "arguments of substance against encouraging, or allowing" Soviet expansion in Africa. The foreign secretary observed that the USSR "had been very successful in establishing position" in Europe and the Far East but that the U.S. seemed aware of the "trend of Russian interests."[17] Complicating British policy on the colonial issue was the fact, as Bevin pointed out, that Byrnes's plan for eventual Libyan independence was "an attractive one from the point of view of public opinion." Instead of opposing independence, Bevin advised that it was "wiser to play for time and avoid taking too definite a line on it for the moment." He would do this by suggesting the separation of Libya into Cyrenaica and Tripolitania, having the deputies study the practicability of Byrnes's plan, and insisting that the dominions present their views on the issue.[18]

Opposition to Bevin's strategy came from the Chiefs of Staff who favored securing a British position in Cyrenaica "even at the cost of giving Russia a free hand in a single neighboring territory such as Tripolitania." Under a collective trusteeship, it was argued, the USSR would "have a hand . . . in the affairs of every" colony.[19] The consensus reached, however, was that the collective trusteeship plan was preferable because "it would mean that the United States were committed to playing their part in the affairs of this part of the world and to taking a share in the responsibility for it." If the United States participated in the administration of the Italian colonies, it might even "bear a part of the cost." While agreeing that American involvement was "vital," the British cabinet also resolved "to keep any potentially hostile Power" out of the Mediterranean and especially to oppose "the entry of Russia, or a Russian base."[20]

In the Council of Foreign Ministers, the third point of contention with the Italian treaty was reparations. Byrnes advocated a lenient demand for reparations on Italy, limited to the assets of the Italian government and Italian nationals in each of the United Nations and to war machinery and equipment not needed by Italy for recovery. The Russian minister disagreed, and wanted Italy to pay less reparations than other Axis powers and to pay these in war factory and shipyard equipment. At Potsdam the Russians had suggested a total of $600 million in reparations but were willing now to reduce that figure and to have the total also divided among Greece, Yugoslavia, and Albania, with the Soviet Union's share being less than half the total. Bidault too wanted Italy to pay more in reparations than the United States wanted, being particularly concerned with restitution of, or compensation for, property stolen by Italy from the United Nations. Bevin insisted that after Italy paid for relief and debts, she would not have anything left for reparations. Molotov recorded his "extreme dissatisfaction" that agreement could not be reached on this issue, and suggested that there was no alternative but to send the issue to the deputies without guidance from the council. The others agreed.[21]

The last Italian issue causing disagreement in the council was the Yugoslav-Italian border and the city of Trieste. The foreign ministers heard the views of Yugoslavia, Italy, Australia, New Zealand, and South Africa before discussing the issue themselves. When the Council of Foreign Ministers began its discussion, there was only one major disagreement —sovereignty over Trieste which was predominately Italian but was surrounded by Slav dominated areas. The ministers agreed that the border should be based on ethnic principles and that Trieste should be a free port administered by an international commission. But Molotov supported Yugoslavia's claim to the city, basing his arguments on the nation's services to the Allied cause, Italy's ample number of ports, and Trieste's certain economic decline if it were detached from its Croat-Slovene dominated hinterland. The British and French supported the American plan to keep Trieste in Italian territory with Bevin maintaining that Trieste was the "only remaining potential cause of an irredentist movement." The council finally agreed to turn the border decision over to the deputies for detailed study and left the issue of Trieste unsettled.[22]

The Council of Foreign Ministers spent their first twelve meetings discussing the Italian treaty, but behind the scenes the Balkan treaties figured in a major way. The Soviet Union assumed the initiative in presenting draft treaties for Finland and the Balkan nations for the ministers to consider while they were still discussing the Italian treaty. When American Balkan advisers saw these drafts, they concluded that they "would eliminate American participation in the reconstruction of the Balkans and would guarantee to the

USSR an even more important role than her physical position and power would insure." These advisers decided "that urgent steps would have to be taken to impress the Secretary and his advisers with the reality of the Soviet 'trap' and the necessity of preventing acceptance of the Soviet proposals." Leslie Squires, secretary of the American Mission in Hungary, and Cavendish Cannon, political adviser to the U.S. delegation in London, presented this view to Byrnes.[23]

When Byrnes made his decision on the American response to the Soviet effort to perpetuate its control of the Balkans, he used as his guide the attitude suggested by the State Department for use at Potsdam. The State Department wanted Russia held responsible for holding free elections in the Balkans in accordance with the Yalta Declaration on Liberated Europe. Department observers believed that the Soviet Union would allow some democracy in Finland and possibly in Hungary but wanted puppet governments in Bulgaria and Rumania. In Rumania in particular, the Soviet Union controlled the Petru Groza government, which had been established as a result of a two-hour ultimatum given to the King of Rumania by Andrei Vishinsky. The State Department did not advocate U.S. intervention to introduce democracy in Bulgaria and Rumania, but did advise withholding diplomatic recognition and peace treaties in order to force Russian compliance. Both Truman and Byrnes had upheld these views at Potsdam and had added the necessity of admitting American newspapermen and radio correspondents to observe the proposed elections. Byrnes decided to continue this policy at London. He did not want to support either pro-Russian or pro-British governments in the Balkans, but, as Ben Cohen said, he was unclear as to how he could establish independent, free regimes. The secretary also decided to base the American position on lack of information about conditions in Rumania and Bulgaria and to couch his demand in the Yalta language of "broadly representative governments."[24]

Bohlen offered Byrnes the first opposition within the American delegation to this nonrecognition policy. In London Bohlen came to believe that the issue was explosive and urged Byrnes to move to a less provocative stance. Dulles joined Bohlen in opposition to Byrnes's policy, because he believed it constituted an attack upon the Petru Groza government in Rumania, which Russia would have to defend. Dulles told Byrnes that he doubted the "efficacy of nonrecognition in such a situation as Rumania. I said that it seemed like starting over again our policy of nonrecognition of the USSR—and on much the same grounds—which had proven a barren policy." Dulles asked Cohen to use his influence on Byrnes, but noted that if Cohen did, he did not change Byrnes's plans. The secretary apparently believed that the United States was in a position strong enough to force Soviet compliance.[25]

Byrnes initiated another private conversation with Molotov to discuss the Balkan treaties before the council considered them. The secretary told Molotov that the United States was "not interested in any way in seeing anything but governments friendly to the Soviet Union in adjacent countries." In reply, Molotov expressed his doubts, using the example of American and British opposition to the friendly Groza government. The foreign minister told Byrnes that if "Mexico had been at war with the United States and had invaded it, and for two years occupied a part of the United States, that the American Government would not tolerate in Mexico a government hostile to it." Byrnes agreed, saying that, "What he wished [to] plead for was some arrangement which would permit the Rumanian Government to be both friendly to the Soviet Union and at the same time representative of all democratic elements in the country." Byrnes had a Polish-type reorganization of Rumania in mind, but Molotov said that would be "too dangerous," adding that "no self-respecting government could tolerate the existence of a hostile government in a country which it had defeated." He urged Byrnes to wait for the already scheduled Rumanian elections, but the secretary wanted a representative government to sponsor the election. Molotov asked if the United States was asking for a reorganization of the Greek government before its elections because it was not representative. Byrnes replied no because there was freedom of press in Greece and the Americans were fully informed about what was happening there. Molotov's rejoinder was that "apparently in Greece the correspondents were happy, but the people were not; whereas in Rumania the people were happy but the correspondents were not." Molotov promised to remedy the press situation in Rumania, but Byrnes insisted on both access for the press and government reorganization. Molotov finally asked Byrnes not to hold up the writing of the Balkan treaties since the Soviet delegation had cooperated on the Italian treaty. The American diplomat agreed to continue working on the treaties if Molotov understood that the Americans would not sign them unless the governments were reorganized. Molotov said that if the United States made its position public, the Soviet Government would not regard this as a very friendly action.[26]

The Soviet minister initiated the next conversation with Byrnes about the Balkan treaties, after using the intervening time to hold up the Italian treaty on both the disposition of the Dodecanese and on a reparations settlement. Molotov was "forced" to tell Byrnes that if the United States did not sign the Rumanian and Bulgarian treaties, the Soviet Union would not sign the Italian treaty. Byrnes replied that he was sorry but that he had nothing to add to what he had already said since the U.S. Senate had to ratify these treaties and he had to assure them that these governments were representative. Molotov pointed out that the United States and Great Britain had imposed a government of their choice on Italy without the Soviet Union protesting, and that the British had done the same in Greece without the United States protesting. "The United States was helping Britain in every way in all sorts of dubious and unlovely affairs," Molotov lamented.[27]

On the same day as this conversation, the council deadlocked on another Italian issue, the Yugoslav-Italian border, and the United States delegation submitted directives for the deputies in writing the Balkan treaties. Maynard Barnes, American representative in Bulgaria, and Burton Berry, American representative in Rumania, had joined Squires and Cannon in London, and these four wrote the American directives. The directives specified that the United States would not negotiate a treaty with Rumania

and Bulgaria until they established representative governments that the United States could recognize. In opposition
to the Russian drafts the United States wanted international
control of the Danube, armaments limitation, reparations,
and equal economic access for all Allied nationals.[28]

The next day Byrnes sought out Molotov for still another
conversation and tried this time to make acquiescence to the
American position easier by offering, without much prior
planning, a radical departure in U.S. foreign policy: a
twenty-five year treaty with the other Big Three Powers to
assure the demilitarization of Germany. Byrnes said Stalin's
remark at Yalta that Germany had used Poland as a corridor
to attack Russia twice in twenty-five years had impressed
him, and so had Stalin's comment that if the United States
again withdrew from European affairs a recrudescence of
German aggression might become a fact. The secretary said
that if the Russians were interested, he would mention the
idea to Britain and France. Molotov could not give an answer
for his government "but personally he thought it was a very
interesting idea."[29]

When the Council of Foreign Ministers took up the treaties
for Finland, Rumania and Bulgaria, they disagreed only on
the American and British desire to impose arms limitations
and on an international regime for the Danube. Molotov
agreed to submit these disagreements for further study, but
not to all the deputies, only to the deputies of the armistice
signatory powers. In taking this stand, the Russian
representative sounded the first warning of the procedural
battle that would break up the London Conference. Molotov
said that "at their first meeting of the council, departing
somewhat from the terms of reference laid down at the Berlin
Conference, had agreed that all five members of the council
should participate in all discussions, whether or not they
were all directly concerned." He now believed that the "best
procedure" would be to let only the signatory deputies study
the treaty provisions, but Bevin and Byrnes refused on
grounds that this procedure would establish a precedent for
other ex-enemy states that they were not prepared to
accept.[30]

This disagreement set the stage for the first public
confrontation between Molotov and Byrnes on 21 September

1945. Molotov began by refuting the statement in the U.S. suggested directives that the Rumanian government was not representative. Using first the same arguments that he had used privately with Byrnes, Molotov added United States recognition of Spain and Argentina to that of Italy and Greece as evidence of American inconsistency. The issue, the Russian insisted, was that a different procedure was being required for American recognition of Rumania, and that the American explanation of this was that the Rumanian government was friendly toward the Soviet Union. Byrnes responded that the United States recognized the pro-Russian governments in Finland, Poland, and Hungary, and objected to the Rumanian government only because it was not representative.[31]

For Byrnes the day after this heated exchange, 22 September, was "the day that broke the back of the conference." He received a call from Molotov's secretary saying that the Russian delegation could not be present at the session scheduled for that morning but that Molotov wanted to meet with him at 11:30 a.m. Although Byrnes and his biographer, George Curry, recorded this conversation, there is no record of it in *Foreign Relations*, the National Archives, or in the Byrnes Papers. Byrnes said that Molotov wanted to discuss an Allied Control Council for Japan at this meeting, an admittedly "embarrassing situation" for Byrnes who knew that the British and Australians were interested in the same thing. The United States government had earlier rejected a Soviet request for a role in the occupation of Japan, and now Byrnes pleaded lack of preparation and promised to discuss Japan at a later time. The morning's difficulties had hardly begun before Bevin walked in. Molotov had invited the British foreign minister to come at noon but Bevin came early, unaware that Molotov wanted to talk with Byrnes first. The "embarrassing situation" worsened as Bevin withdrew to allow Molotov and Byrnes to finish their conversation. When Bevin returned, he learned with Byrnes that Molotov wanted to reorganize the Council of Foreign Ministers because he believed the present procedure allowing France and China to discuss the Finnish and Balkan treaties violated the Potsdam Protocol. The initial British and American response to this bombshell was that participation in discussion, but not voting on these treaties, had been approved at Potsdam. Molotov, however, disagreed and insisted upon a literal interpretation of the Protocol. Byrnes then suggested referring the issue to the heads of state, to which Molotov agreed, although he said Stalin had originally pointed out the procedural error.[32]

The Big Three foreign ministers agreed to continue with the points on the council agenda that did not involve these treaties while waiting for their superiors to confer. They called a council session for that afternoon and found Bidault furious that the morning's session had been cancelled without notifying him. The French delegation had arrived at the arranged time that morning to find the room empty and to learn that three of the foreign ministers were meeting privately. The Chinese delegation had apparently been informed of the cancellation because they had not shown up. Bidault angrily told the ministers that he wanted it understood that French rights must be respected. As chairman of this session, Molotov explained why he asked that the meeting be postponed, predictably not placating Bidault with his explanation. Byrnes later met privately with Bidault, who threatened to leave the conference if French rights to discuss European settlements were denied. The French foreign minister told Byrnes that he had dined with Molotov the evening before without the Russian mentioning procedure. Molotov did use the dinner to upbraid the French delegation for not supporting him and to say that the other delegations were uniting against him. Byrnes urged Bidault not to act hastily, but instead to wait and see what the Big Three heads of state worked out. Bidault reluctantly agreed.[33]

The secretary of state called Washington immediately after Molotov made his demand, only to find that the president was spending the weekend at Jefferson Island in Chesapeake Bay. Byrnes conferred instead with Admiral William Leahy, whom he told that Molotov was trying to break up the conference and asked that the "unusual step" of immediately drafting a telegram to Stalin over Truman's signature be taken. Byrnes wanted Truman to urge Stalin to direct Molotov not to leave London, and Leahy agreed and "urgently" requested Stalin not to allow Molotov to destroy the conference "because of the bad effect it would have on world peace." A few hours later Cohen communicated again with Leahy on behalf of Byrnes and transmitted this time the text of a longer telegram to be sent to Stalin by Truman. Byrnes insisted in this message that during discussions at Potsdam those present agreed that nonsignatory council members could be present and discuss but not vote. But the secretary agreed that under a literal interpretation of the Potsdam Protocol France and China did not have the right to discuss the Balkan treaties, unless, Byrnes added, they were invited to do so as Yugoslavia, Italy, and other nations had been. Byrnes wanted the unanimous decision at the council's first meeting to allow French-Chinese discussion to be considered an invitation, because denying them discussion rights now would "create a bad impression." Leahy sent this telegram and then secured Truman's approval of his actions. Clement Attlee also telegraphed Stalin and argued that the council had the right to establish its own procedure according to the Potsdam Protocol and had, therefore, acted correctly on 11 September. Attlee added the more telling argument that, if the council now rescinded a decision it had unanimously made, a dangerous precedent would be established. But as Molotov warned, Stalin agreed with the Russian delegation's position, saying the most important issue was that the council did not have "the right to waive particular points in the decisions of the Berlin Conference."[34]

Byrnes, now faced with the inability of the heads of state to solve the crisis, decided to act on his own. The secretary and his delegation took Molotov's objections at face value and tried to resolve the procedural conflict. Byrnes, Dulles, Cohen, Dunn, and Averell Harriman (who had recently joined the American delegation), prepared the initial American offer. The Americans advocated adjourning the present meeting and leaving the respective signatory deputies to draft the treaties. Following adjournment Byrnes wanted a second council session held in London on 15 November, which would be an international peace conference to consider the drafts prepared by the deputies.[35]

Bevin, informing his cabinet about the procedural dispute on 25 September, admitted that "the actual terms of the Protocol strictly interpreted lent some support to the Soviet view." He had told Byrnes that the Soviets were "strictly legally right, although morally wrong." Unlike Byrnes, Bevin already believed that the conflict over procedure was "only the outward manifestation of the fundamental disagreements" that had arisen over the territory which the Soviets saw as their "zone of influence." He also was concerned about the "increasing hostility and distrust between the United States and Soviet Delegations," because each "sought to strengthen its own position without regard" to the United Kingdom's point of view. Bevin wanted to make it clear to the Americans that it was "impossible for us to work with them if they constantly took actions in the international sphere, affecting our interests, without prior consultation with us." He had already told Molotov that the British "were being treated as inferiors" both by the Russians and the Americans.[36]

Convinced by Bevin that there was no hope of salvaging the conference, the cabinet agreed that the conference should not appear to break on the narrow issue of procedure but instead should be adjourned to give the governments time to discuss the best means of writing the peace treaties. Britain would then champion the participation of the small powers while seeking their support but avoiding the suspicion of establishing a Western bloc.[37]

Unaware of the British decision, Byrnes initiated a series of private meetings with Molotov and Bevin while the council continued to hold formal sessions to discuss nontreaty matters. In response to the secretary's proposal, Molotov continued to demand reversal of the 11 September decision and adherence to the Potsdam Protocol. So Byrnes next offered to accept the Soviet position if Molotov would agree to a peace conference. Instead, the Soviet minister presented his two colleagues with still another proposal, separate conferences to be convened only by the armistice signatories for the Italian, the Finnish, and all the Balkan treaties. Molotov pressured the Americans and British to accept his proposal by saying that he was not sure that the Soviet delegation would be ready to act on the Italian treaty in 1945, unless the United States agreed to an allied control council for Japan. The Soviet pressure appeared to influence

Cohen, because that evening he drew up a proposal accepting Molotov's procedure, dropping the conference idea, and adding only the stipulation that the treaties would not be considered final until others in the United Nations had been consulted, "preferably" at a conference.[38]

Dulles began to pressure Byrnes himself by telling the secretary that he could not guarantee Republican cooperation if he accepted the Russian procedure without a conference. Byrnes tried to find middle ground between Molotov and Dulles by insisting that only one conference be held but with participation in the conference limited to European members of the United Nations and non-European members who had made a significant military contribution to the war. Molotov had earlier registered his concern about exactly which nations would be invited to the conference and was generally agreeable to Byrnes's proposal. At the brink of agreement, Molotov chose to mention, for the first time since he introduced the procedural issue, the question of recognizing Rumania and Bulgaria. Molotov said that "without some solution to this question, the decision of the Council would have no meaning."[39]

Following this conversation, Harriman submitted a series of notes to the American delegation connecting for the first time the issues of recognition, Japan, and procedure. Harriman wrote that what Molotov had been after all along was to force the Americans and the British to recognize Rumania and Bulgaria. He was using the procedural issue as a device to strengthen his bargaining position and was using the Japanese issue to "divert attention from his unilateral actions in the Balkans to United States unilateral actions in the Pacific." Harriman wanted Byrnes to reassure the Russians at once about Japan because he believed that delay was "arousing unnecessarily their suspicions." "We can't get away with this brush-off," he warned, because the Soviets were "undoubtedly fearful that we are now ready to use Japan against them." Harriman advocated consulting the Soviet Union on occupation policy by "following the pattern of Balkan control commissions" where the supreme commander had the final word. To Harriman's dismay, Byrnes chose instead to postpone settlement of the Japanese issue. Harriman, whose offer to brief Byrnes before the London Conference had been refused, resented the secretary's "cavalier way with advisers" which he had complained about at Potsdam. "Jimmy Byrnes played his cards very close to his vest," Harriman recalled, "and he would seldom consult me." "It was not," Harriman said at another time, "a matter of personalities. Jimmy Byrnes just did not care to be confused by other people's judgments."[40]

On 29 September Molotov returned the procedural issue to the twenty-eighth meeting of the Council of Foreign Ministers by formally proposing a return to the Soviet interpretation of the Potsdam Protocol. Byrnes countered by presenting his conference proposal with the significant new addition of final approval of the treaties returning after the conference to those nations that were actually at war with the enemy state being considered. Molotov urged Byrnes to withdraw his proposal and let each group of armistice signatories summon their own conference, and when he refused, suggested that the council concern itself with the writing of a protocol to end their London session. Molotov startled his colleagues by insisting on separate protocols: "a protocol of three concerning the Balkan treaties, then the protocol of the four concerning the peace treaty with Italy, then a protocol of two concerning Finland, then a protocol of the five concerning all the remainder." Bevin considered this so ludicrous that he quipped, "This conference ought to move from here to a musical hall and forget about the decision adopted."[41]

Despite Bevin's flippancy, Byrnes was ready to compromise. Dulles recounted that early next morning the American delegates gathered in Byrnes's room before the council convened. Byrnes asked Dulles to come into the bedroom with him and told him privately that he thought he should accept Molotov's procedural demands and work for a conference later. The secretary wanted Dulles's support. Dulles, however, refused insisting that France and China would not only be publicly humiliated, but would also be alienated from the United States and Great Britain. Instead, Dulles recommended breaking off the conference rather than giving in to Molotov. Years later after Theodore Achilles read Dulles's account of this bedroom scene, he asked Mrs. Dulles about it. She recounted: "What Foster didn't say in that book was that he not only followed Secretary Byrnes into his bedroom to tell him that, but had followed him on into the bathroom, and told him, if he did not agree, he would telephone Senator Vandenberg who would denounce him on the floor of the Senate the next day." Dulles said Byrnes did not reply but rejoined the others and left for the council meeting at Lancaster House with Dulles "under the impression that Mr. Byrnes was going to disregard my view."[42]

At the council meeting the ministers agreed to separate protocols, but before Byrnes could act one way or the other, Molotov initiated what was to be the most dramatic scene of the conference. He said in reference to the 11 September decision that, "If anyone denounces the decision adopted by us in common, that decision ceases to be a decision. That is obvious." Bevin responded, "Someone takes part in a decision, then he denounces it and is free. That is the nearest thing to the Hitler theory I have ever heard." The Soviet foreign minister thundered, "Unless Mr. Bevin will withdraw his words, I shall leave the room" and started for the door. Harriman, who was present, observed that Molotov delayed his exit long enough to allow Bevin to apologize. Byrnes as chairman said that since everyone's nerves were on edge, he would adjourn the meeting until later that evening.[43]

During the interim Byrnes told Molotov that he had made a concession in accepting Molotov's procedure "and that all he was asking in return was that there be some provision made for the summoning of the conference," no matter what form. The Soviet diplomat said that what Byrnes wanted "was the appearance of an agreement when none existed" and frankly told Byrnes again that the procedural issue "was of secondary importance." A conference could easily be agreed on, Molotov said, if the United States would recognize Rumania and Bulgaria.[44]

Bevin asked Molotov and Byrnes to meet with him at his office because he wanted to discuss the inclusion of the 11 September decision in the protocol. Molotov did not want to mention the decision at all and further said he would not sign any one of the protocols in the presence of a minister whose nation was not an armistice signatory. Molotov even refused to discuss any but the general protocol in a full council meeting. He presented these views at the following council session and motivated Byrnes to suggest an alternative to omitting the 11 September decision altogether. Byrnes suggested stating in the general protocol that on 11 September France and China were invited to participate in all discussions, that they did so for sixteen meetings, and that on 27 September the Soviet representative introduced the idea that this violated the Potsdam Protocol. Molotov refused and declared that he would not sign any of the protocols or even a communiqué unless the council revoked the 11 September decision. Byrnes asked Molotov what the deputies were to do if there was to be no protocol or communiqué. Molotov replied that they had nothing to do and everyone should go home, but that he first wanted to introduce a statement explaining why he could not participate in the council. Bidault asked Molotov what was the purpose of his statement, and Molotov said he wanted it recorded in the protocol. "What protocol?" Byrnes asked.[45]

As the first session of the Council of Foreign Ministers was about to end in total disarray, the Chinese Foreign Minister Wang, who had seldom spoken during the conference, suggested, and the council agreed, to place the day of adjournment two days in the future so there would still be time to reach agreement. That evening Bevin sent Byrnes a "Very Personal to Mr. Byrnes" message, warning about the "very bad repercussions" of the conference breaking "on such a narrow point." Bevin told Byrnes he had reluctantly agreed not to discuss a Japanese control council "in order to keep common ground" with the United States and not to recognize Bulgaria and Rumania "in order to keep in step with the U.S.A." Bevin advocated not reaching a decision on the 11 September situation but agreeing to complete the treaty drafts according to Molotov's procedure. Byrnes disagreed.[46]

The next day the British foreign secretary met privately with Molotov, who characterized the procedural issue as a "misunderstanding" and "of trivial importance." Molotov repeated that the recognition of Bulgaria and Rumania was "the main cause of the difficulty," but added that if Britain and the United States were not ready to recognize these nations, Russia would wait. Bevin suggested that a commission independent of the representatives in those nations investigate the conditions there and privately report back to the council. His government, Bevin maintained, could accept governments in Rumania and Bulgaria that were friendly to the USSR, but not governments which were unfriendly to Great Britain. Turning to the issue of French participation in the council, Molotov observed that "sooner or later" France would have to be acknowledged as an equal power "but patience was required." On all the disputed subjects— procedure, recognition, and a peace conference—the Soviet minister maintained that "it was much better to wait. Nothing would happen in the meantime." Molotov did attempt a final trade of Russia in Tripolitania for Britain in Cyrenaica, observing that "a Russian trusteeship for ten years would do no harm." Bevin responded, "I wonder," and the conversation reached an unprofitable conclusion.[47]

The council met three more times, once until 2:55 a.m., and then on 2 October Byrnes moved from his position of abrogating the 11 September decision if a conference were called to refusing to rescind the decision at all. He said, "The invitation having been acted on, the world having been advised of it, now when Mr. Molotov proposes to withdraw it, I cannot agree to withdraw the invitation." Molotov responded, "You seem to have forgotten about the fact that you proposed to revoke the decision" if a conference were held, "a business-like approach." Byrnes, fearing the embarrassment of adjournment when he was acting as chairman the next day, privately asked Wang to suggest an end to the conference. Wang agreed and at 7:25 p.m. 2 October 1945 the first session of the Council of Foreign Ministers ended.[48]

The London meeting was the first conference in recent memory to end without the usual glowing reports of unity and optimism, much less without a protocol. The last communiqué given to the press read simply: "The Council of

Foreign Ministers met twice today, Mr. Molotov presiding in the morning and Dr. Wang in the afternoon. At the second meeting the Council decided to terminate its present session." These communiqués, labelled "gems of non-information" by *New York Times* reporter C. L. Sulzberger, had been the steady diet of the frustrated press corps covering the conference. The reporters registered their shock at the abrupt end of the conference and assumed the meeting was a failure, or in the words of one news story, "an abysmal fiasco." Byrnes worried on the plane home whether Americans would tolerate his ending the London Conference and feared blame for spoiling the peace. But in a 6 October radio speech to the American people Byrnes seized the initiative by openly describing the negotiations. He referred to the conference as exploratory in nature, "to find out on what points we were in agreement, on what points we differed, and on what points further study and data were required." He described the areas of agreement, the problems relating to recognition of Rumania and Bulgaria, and the concerns over procedure. Byrnes clearly implied that the Soviet Union was responsible for the breakup of the conference, but added he was determined to work toward compromise. Dulles, speaking on radio the next evening, supported Byrnes and urged the American people to do the same.[49]

Privately, Byrnes presented a far more negative view of what happened in London. He told Joseph Davies that the conference was much worse than he could have imagined. Byrnes said "that if he had told the Senate what Molotov had told him, they would have resented it and he himself was almost ashamed." Davies responded to Byrnes's version of the Balkan situation with an account of the October 1944, Churchill-Stalin agreement on control of the Balkans: Soviet 80 percent to British 20 percent influence in Rumania, Hungary, and Bulgaria; British 60 percent to Soviet 40 percent in Greece; and 50-50 percent in Yugoslavia. Byrnes replied that "he was sure Roosevelt had never been a party to any such arrangement. I told him Roosevelt had approved. His reply was heated."[50]

Byrnes had fastened onto the idea that the Soviets had violated the Yalta Declaration on Liberated Europe in the Balkans, and he was not willing to listen to Davies, Dulles, or

Bohlen to the contrary. The declaration had restated the Atlantic Charter principle of national self-determination and had promised the formation of provisional governments "broadly representative of all democratic elements in the population and pledged to the earliest possible establishment through free elections of governments responsive to the will of the people." The idealistic declaration had included no enforcement machinery, and, since the Red Army controlled the Balkans and the Soviet system had its own interpretation of "free elections," there was little reason for the Yalta participants to expect literal compliance. Roosevelt apparently needed the declaration for home consumption and had few illusions about its implementation. His attitude toward the Balkans appeared to be the same as his expressed sentiments on the elasticity of the Polish agreement at Yalta, which was "it's the best I can do . . . at this time." When the Soviets, two weeks after Yalta, had installed a puppet regime in Rumania, Byrnes had realistically reflected Roosevelt's attitude that "the Rumanian situation did not offer the best test case of our relations with the Soviets." But now that Byrnes needed an explanation for the failure of the London Conference, he insisted on a strict accounting of the Declaration on Liberated Europe. Attempting to negotiate the nonnegotiable was only one of Byrnes's mistakes on this issue. Although he was not responsible for encouraging the Soviets to sign an agreement they had no intention of fulfilling—a tactic that the United States was to use again and again in Cold War diplomacy—his self-serving use of lack of compliance further estranged the two nations. Finally, Byrnes did not understand the inconsistency between the Soviet desire to have friendly governments in the Balkans and the American desire to have free elections there. As the Soviets understood from seeing an anti-Communist government elected in Hungary, free elections in Rumania and Bulgaria would have undoubtedly produced anti-Russian coalitions. Given diplomatic historian William McNeil's choice between "ignorance or duplicity" as Byrnes's motivation, ignorance had to predominate, but Molotov could not be expected to believe that.[51]

Byrnes found others, however, who accepted his views. At a meeting of the secretaries of state, war, and navy, Byrnes told his colleagues, "The Russians were welching on all the agreements reached at Potsdam and at Yalta . . . it would not be wise for us to rely on their word today." Byrnes told Stettinius that "we were facing a new Russia, totally different than the Russia we dealt with a year ago." "Now that the War was over," Byrnes maintained, "they were taking an aggressive attitude and stand on political and territorial questions that was indefensible."[52] The secretary presented this same view to the cabinet, which led Secretary of Commerce Henry Wallace to comment that each point Byrnes made was "designed to show the Russians up in a bad light." Truman concluded that the government must not let the public know how the USSR "had tried our patience" because "we were going to find some way to get along with the Russians." Byrnes had, of course, already made the public aware of who was to blame for the failure of the London Conference in his radio address.

Byrnes remained convinced that "the Soviet Union was determined to dominate Europe." Perhaps this exaggerated response to the frustration of his high expectations for the London Conference was to be expected, because he went to London believing that the military and economic power of the United States would allow him quickly to decide the peace. For Great Britain, this expectation was realized, but Molotov totally ignored both the threat posed by the atomic bomb and possible denial of economic assistance. The very fact that Byrnes had a timetable in mind made him vulnerable to Soviet diplomacy, and so did his desire to present a harmonious front to the world. His greatest handicaps were his inexperience and his lack of preparation, and both of these were accented by his dominance of American foreign policy at this critical time. He alone, without consultation with the president or with the State Department, made the decision to break off the London meetings when that policy was thwarted by the Soviet Union. In London he faced a formidable mass of complexities—concrete issues involving the national interests of many nations, with long-range ramifications. His ignorance of the issues, his simplistic solutions, and his impatience with negotiation made him an easy target for Molotov.[53]

Molotov, not Byrnes, dominated the London Conference. Dulles said Molotov demonstrated "an adroitness which has seldom been equalled in diplomacy. Mr. Molotov has sized up with consummate skill possibilities through which, by artful exploitation, he might advance his ends;" and Byrnes himself wrote that "I had no experience that prepared me for negotiation with Mr. Molotov." Dulles observed that Molotov used a different approach for each of the other foreign ministers. He tried to take advantage of Byrnes's habit of speaking "off the cuff" by constantly drawing him out and asking Byrnes to clarify and explain, hoping for misstatements. Molotov capitalized on Bevin's quickness to anger by treating him as a banderillero treats a bull by arousing him and then hoping his repentance would bring concessions. Dulles thought Molotov wanted to force Bidault to walk out of the conference and tried to motivate him with petty slights and insults. Since Chinese Foreign Minister Wang could not be roused to anger, Molotov ignored him to make it clear that he considered China unimportant. Byrnes thought Molotov must be descended from Job, because "he has unlimited patience as well as a fine mind and tremendous energy. Any exhibition of impatience or bad temper by others gives him amusement."[54]

Molotov truly appeared to view the London talks as exploratory, unlike Byrnes who decided they were exploratory once they failed. Although the Soviets seemed to have definite postwar goals in mind—Yugoslav control of Trieste, Mediterranean ports, reparations, and control of Eastern Europe—they needed to know American policy. Molotov quickly learned that the United States and Great Britain wanted Trieste to remain with Italy, opposed Russian expansion into the Mediterranean, wanted to limit Italian and German reparations, and, worst of all to the Soviets, wanted a role in the Balkans while denying Russia a role in Japan. Adam Ulam, historian of the Soviet Union, maintains that Stalin was "near panic" when the United States refused the USSR a share in the occupation of Japan, because Stalin accepted this as evidence that the Americans intended to throw their atomic weight around. However, the Americans, Ulam argues, did not realize this and continued to overestimate Soviet postwar strength.[55]

Historians disagree as to whether Byrnes's refusal to discuss a control council for Japan or his refusal to recognize Rumania and Bulgaria motivated Molotov to introduce the procedural issue and then to abort the conference.[56] Both issues were undoubtedly important to Molotov as was the difficulty over Trieste, Tripolitania, and reparations. Molotov was also upset with Bidault's failure to support Soviet policy in the Balkans and came to fear French support for the American and British positions. Since Byrnes offered to negotiate all of the issues raised except Japan, a control council that was probably the explanation for Molotov's obdurance, and chief among Byrnes's mistakes in London.

From the Soviet perspective, Molotov's introduction of the procedural mistake was brilliant. The issue slowed down the writing of the treaties, which interfered with Byrnes's timetable. It pressured the United States both to recognize Rumania and Bulgaria and to establish a Japanese control council, publicly exposed Allied disunity to the dismay of the other Allies, and limited treaty writing to more controllable numbers. Best of all, with the procedural issue Molotov was on legally correct ground. Although the Potsdam participants had agreed verbally that France, with no mention of China, could discuss the peace treaties of nations to which it was not an armistice signatory, their written statement had failed to reflect their understanding. The Potsdam Protocol—conveniently for the Soviets—omitted all reference to French and Chinese discussion privileges and specified only that each treaty should be drafted by the nations that signed the armistice, with France to be considered a signatory in the case of Italy. Even though the foreign ministers again in London agreed that their rules of procedure would allow French and Chinese discussion of all treaties, Molotov could accurately claim that their agreement violated the specific terms of the Potsdam Protocol.

The most interesting question about the London Conference was why Byrnes did not attempt to use his atomic-dollar diplomacy. The military and economic power of the United States must have been omnipresent, but neither subject was ever broached directly. The scientist Vannevar Bush had pointed out to Truman in September that atomic power, the "gun on our hips," might be difficult to use in diplomacy because "there is no powder in the gun, for it could not be drawn, and this is certainly known." Whether the Russians agreed, their response had been to turn the subject into a continuing joke. Molotov had asked Byrnes in a social setting if he had an atomic bomb in his hip pocket. Byrnes had responded, "If you don't cut out all of this stalling and let us get down to work, I am going to pull an atomic bomb out of my hip pocket and let you have it." Later at another party Molotov had toasted, "Here's to the atom bomb—we've got it!" only to be abruptly shouldered from the room by another Russian. In a later toast Molotov said, "Of course we all have to pay great attention to what Mr. Byrnes says, because the United States are the only people who are making the atomic bomb." Whether legitimately or not, the Soviets were telling Byrnes that atomic diplomacy would not work against them.[57]

Clearly, Byrnes wanted a compromise, even, in Molotov's words, "the appearance of an agreement when none existed." Byrnes was willing to accept Molotov's procedure if he were given the face-saving device of a peace conference, an even more narrowly conceived peace conference than envisioned at Potsdam. Byrnes was also willing to accept a face-saving Polish-solution to the Rumanian and Bulgarian situations. Only on Japan did Byrnes refuse to yield. Molotov then, not Byrnes, largely decided the fate of the first meeting of the Council of Foreign Ministers. The Soviet foreign minister would not accept Byrnes's appearance of an agreement. By holding out for more, the Soviet Union could test the determination of the United States and gain time to consolidate its Eastern European sphere. As Philip Mosely observed, the Soviet Union was "quite content with the impasse;" and Averell Harriman added that by the time another meeting of the foreign ministers was arranged, the United States would be "faced with a number of entrenched Soviet positions and *faits accomplis*." The Soviet view was shortsighted, if eventually successful. The long-range result of the London Conference was a hardening of the American attitude against the USSR, which would eventually evolve into the cold war—an outcome that would benefit neither the Soviet Union nor the United States.[58]

CHAPTER THREE

THE MOSCOW CONFERENCE OF FOREIGN MINISTERS
15–27 December 1945

Despite James Byrnes's frustrating London experience and his subsequent condemnation of the Soviet Union, he "resolved . . . that the deadlock had to be broken; peace was too important to be lost by default." Byrnes had assumed at the first meeting of the Council of Foreign Ministers that the sheer military and economic power of the United States would motivate compliance with American demands. Now that he knew better, he began to search for a way to reopen negotiations, although the continued division within the Truman administration over the Soviet Union complicated his efforts. One group of Washington policy makers believed the USSR had unlimited expansionist goals and that the worst American policy would be one involving concessions. A second group believed that security considerations motivated Soviet actions and that continued negotiations would prove successful eventually. This second group, however, warned against American insistence on Russian withdrawal from Eastern Europe while denying them a role in administering Japan and Italian colonies. Despite their anti-Soviet rhetoric, neither Byrnes nor Truman had yet sided completely with one group or the other. Neither man was doctrinaire; both were pragmatists.[1]

Predictably, Byrnes pursued a moderate course by initiating a series of moves that he could defend to both camps in the administration. On 10 October the secretary announced that he had invited the nations that had defeated Japan to participate in a Far Eastern Advisory Commission. This gesture was ostensibly conciliatory, but he intended to serve as chairman of the commission, which would be housed in Washington and would not have the power to affect the status of General Douglas MacArthur, supreme allied commander in Japan. On the same day Byrnes asked Mark Ethridge, publisher of the *Louisville Courier-Journal,* to head a commission to Rumania and Bulgaria to report on conditions there. In London the secretary had based his nonrecognition policy in part on lack of information; now he could claim to be gathering objective data while knowing in advance what that data would be.[2]

On 12 October Byrnes instructed Harriman in Moscow to deliver a conciliatory message to Stalin from the president. The message assured the Russians that the American nonrecognition policy was not "motivated by an unfriendly attitude towards the Soviet Union" and urged acceptance of Byrnes's peace conference procedural compromise. Although Stalin was vacationing at his country home in Sochi in the Caucasus area of the Black Sea, he placed a plane at Harriman's disposal in order to see him quickly. During their 24 October conversation, Stalin suggested that a new conference of the Council of Foreign Ministers decide which nations should be invited before deciding whether a peace conference should be held. Harriman responded that he was sure the president would approve another meeting of the Council of Foreign Ministers, but only after they settled the peace conference issue. Stalin insisted the next day on simultaneously settling the Japanese and the procedural questions, although he generally approved the peace conference idea. Since Harriman was not authorized to deal with the Japanese issue, he dropped the idea of calling another conference of the foreign ministers, but Byrnes could now report that he had assumed the initiative in reopening negotiations with the Soviet Union.[3]

On 24 October reporters asked the secretary if the Soviet request for a reconstruction loan had been pigeonholed. "That is not true," Byrnes replied, but he had in fact "had it placed in the 'Forgotten file.'" On 31 October Byrnes delivered an address directed at Moscow to the *New York*

Herald-Tribune Forum of Foreign Affairs in which he reiterated his desire to have governments friendly to the Russians in the Balkans.[4]

Finally, the secretary reluctantly adopted a new strategy on international control of atomic energy. Truman had assumed the initiative in advocating international control in his 3 October message to Congress without consulting him. In response, on 3 November, Byrnes hastily asked Vannevar Bush, Director of the Office of Scientific Research and Development, to formulate a plan for the United States to present to her atomic partners, British and Canadian Prime Ministers Clement Attlee and Mackenzie King, during their 15 November Washington visit. Bush advocated inviting the Soviet Union to join with the Americans, British, and Canadians in giving the United Nations control of atomic energy with inspection safeguards. Truman, Attlee, and King quickly approved Bush's plan as rephrased by the State Department, and Byrnes planned to invite Russian partici- pation at the first meeting of the U.N. General Assembly in January 1946. Byrnes was again in the middle by offering the Soviet Union an atomic role, but so gradually that the American atomic monopoly would continue for some time.[5]

Despite Byrnes's efforts to keep diplomacy moving, the deputies of the Council of Foreign Ministers, left behind in London, had experienced "a completely blank month" without even the pretense of a meeting. James Dunn wrote to Byrnes: "I do not believe it is dignified for our Government to have me stay on here indefinitely." Byrnes then suddenly thought of a rationale he could use to promote another conference of the foreign ministers. He recalled that he was alone in his office on Thanksgiving Day when he remem- bered the Yalta Agreement, unaffected by the Potsdam creation of the Council of Foreign Ministers, that established regular meetings between the Big Three foreign ministers. Byrnes considered this a legitimate pretext for him to meet with Molotov and Bevin without offending the French and Chinese. The Big Three ministers could discuss the issues that disrupted the Council of Foreign Ministers and perhaps agree to resume the council meetings. The only distinction between the meeting that Byrnes planned now to propose and the council meetings would be the absence of France and China. The same issues would be discussed.[6]

The next day Byrnes wired Molotov that since the ministers had met in San Francisco during the U.N. Conference, at Potsdam during the heads of state meeting, and at London during the Council of Foreign Ministers meeting, "I suggested the December meeting be held in Moscow." He believed Molotov to be responsible for Russian obstinacy at London but "in Moscow where I would have a chance to talk to Stalin, we might remove the barriers to the peace treaties." Not only did he not realize that Stalin controled Soviet diplomacy, he also did not bother to inquire if Stalin would be in Moscow in December, much less if Stalin were willing to see him. Harriman reported that Molotov "was obviously much pleased" with the suggested meeting, and asked, "Do you wish me to attempt to find out if Stalin will be in Moscow at that time?"[7]

Byrnes next wired Bevin, saying, "I suggest" about the proposed meeting but flatly adding that "as the Secretaries have met at San Francisco and London, the December meeting [will] be held in Moscow." He learned that the British resented the American initiative when the American ambassador to the United Kingdom, John G. Winant, cabled: "Situation serious, unilateral action deeply resented by both Bevin and Cabinet. Bevin refuses to talk tonight or to attend conference [in] Moscow." The British foreign secretary reacted partly in response to having learned first of the proposed Moscow meeting from his ambassador in Moscow, before Byrnes's telegram arrived, and partly out of ire at not being consulted before the Soviets. Bevin had complained to Harriman during the London Conference that American unilateral actions had repeatedly embarrassed the British. "They were ready to support American policies provided they had a chance to thrash out questions before we took decisions," Harriman observed, but "again this was a question of Byrnes going ahead without consultation."[8]

Winant finally arranged a teletype conversation the next day between the two ministers. Byrnes explained to "Ernie" that he had not informed Bevin of his proposal earlier because he thought it proper to ascertain first if Molotov was willing to act as host. In fact, his telegram to Bevin was sent before Molotov had actually decided to issue an invitation. The British diplomat told "Mr. Byrnes" that he and Attlee believed that having another conference "without adequate preparation would only lead to another failure." Bevin doubted the wisdom of meeting without first using ordinary diplomatic channels because "there is no indication that Stalin has changed his mind" on any of the London issues. Bevin also warned Byrnes that his schedule involved the handicap of working with a deadline in mind, because the ministers would have to leave Moscow by Christmas to attend the January meeting of the United Nations. Bevin said the Russians would "stall till the last moment and then try and force us to come to some agreement before we go so as to avoid another failure." Finally, Bevin insisted that, although he did not want to "gang up" against the Soviet Union, "in view of the commitments I made to you when in London I think it is only right and proper that I should have now from the United States Government a clear statement as to their policy."[9]

Winant told Byrnes later that Bevin was "desperately anxious to talk" with Byrnes before a Moscow conference and suggested that Byrnes offer to stop in London on his way to Moscow. Byrnes was not willing to do that because he feared the Soviet reaction to American-British negotiations, but he did send the British a proposed agenda for Moscow and a statement of the American position on each item. He also assured Bevin that their governments should work in "closest cooperation" but that "it is not necessary or desirable that we should reach agreement on every detail before discussions with the Soviet Union." Bevin still refused to agree to the conference and suggested instead that the foreign ministers meet in London during the U.N. meeting. Byrnes argued that a Moscow meeting would have the advantage of obtaining Stalin's views and of presenting the atomic energy proposal to the Russians before the U.N. meeting. The secretary also expected Molotov as host to be "more pliable" and finally asked how they could refuse to go now that Molotov had agreed. To this last argument, Lord Halifax, the British ambassador to Washington, replied,

"You've got us in a bit of a hole." Byrnes, however, continued to insist that he intended to go to Moscow with or without Bevin. His obstinacy forced the British foreign minister to reply that "in deference to your strong views" he would go. After all this Joseph Davies told Byrnes that he was sorry Bevin had agreed to go because he was a red rag to the Soviet bull, and "Jim said he felt that way himself and would not have been disappointed if he had not gone."[10]

Byrnes's difficulties in securing British cooperation made him aware that he was about to repeat what many considered his London mistakes. Again, there would be no time to work out agreements through diplomatic channels before the ministers met, no time to think through the American position, and no time to anticipate changes in the Soviet and British positions. Again, he and a small group of advisers would decide American policy, bypassing the State Department, Congress, and the president, who was vacationing in Florida. Byrnes characteristically defended himself against the charge that the London Conference had failed due to insufficient preparation by maintaining that "it was always intended that the technical work on the treaties should be prepared by the Deputies and they never got started on their work because of conflicts which in no way were caused by lack of preparation." Even Molotov had told Harriman that the principal mistake at London was inadequate preparation, but Byrnes again maintained before Moscow that "I was not unmindful that no meeting should be held until there was greater assurance of progress toward agreement on the outstanding questions. But I felt that at this critical time continued drift and delay would be exceedingly unwise." Robert Murphy, Byrnes's political adviser on Germany, noted: "This is not conventional diplomacy. But Byrnes was not a professional diplomat, and he was in a hurry." Charles Bohlen, who was not consulted about the conference, also complained that the meeting was hastily improvised and maintained that Byrnes "ran much of the foreign policy from within his head."[11]

Complicating Byrnes's European improvisations was the introduction of charges against American foreign policy in China by Ambassador Patrick J. Hurley. In a dramatic and unexpected resignation statement released to the press, Hurley maintained that the United States was supporting "Communism and imperialism" in Asia. His efforts to harmonize conflicting groups in China, Hurley asserted, had been frustrated by "professional foreign service men" who "sided with the Chinese Communist armed party and the imperialist bloc of nations whose policy it was to keep China divided against herself." Hurley's allegations generated a Senate Foreign Relations Committee investigation in December 1945 at which first Hurley, and then Byrnes, were called to testify. On 7 December Byrnes defended American Foreign Service officers in China and announced a hastily contrived China policy, which involved replacing Hurley with former Chief of Staff George Marshall, continuing to aid the Chinese in disarming the Japanese, and avoiding involvement in the emerging Chinese civil war. The controversy over Hurley's charges and Byrnes's response caused many senators to question the secretary's conduct of American foreign policy just as he was about to leave for the Moscow Conference.[12]

Adding to Byrnes's difficulties with the Senate was his handling of the issue of international control of atomic energy. First, he had failed to consult the Foreign Relations Committee until minutes before Truman, Attlee, and King publicly announced their agreement. The committee chairman, Tom Connally, and the ranking Republican member, Arthur Vandenberg, angrily refused to participate in the picturetaking session and left after Connally told Byrnes that the administration's authority did not extend to sharing atomic energy information without consulting Congress. Vandenberg proceeded to make a pointed speech in the Senate in which he maintained that it was in the Congress "where a basic and unavoidable share of the responsibility for these fateful decisions inevitably resides and where it is going to stay." Byrnes's advisers, without consulting or informing the Senate, nonetheless went on to change significantly the Truman-Attlee-King agreement by eliminating the requirement of completing one stage before implementing the next in the proposal to be presented to the Soviet Union. When the secretary read this version to a group of senators that included Connally and Vandenberg, who had been invited to his office on 10 December for a briefing on the Moscow Conference, he was "insulted" that they believed he was going to reveal secret, scientific information to the Russians without adequate safeguards. Since Byrnes had his bags packed and was leaving immediately, he failed to convince the senators, and they took their doubts about his intentions to the president.[13]

Truman was having his own problems as a result of his ignorance of Byrnes's plans. In the midst of the frantic arrangements for the Moscow meeting, Truman had said in a press conference that no further Big Three meetings were planned because American policy now was to have the U.N. handle peace settlements. Byrnes told Bevin, the press, and Truman that what Truman meant was that no further Big Three heads of state meetings were planned and that the peace conference idea was still American policy. "You may be asked about these again," Byrnes wrote the president, "and if you can't avoid answering, at least you'll know what I said." Although Truman assured the angry senators that Byrnes was authorized only to secure Soviet agreement to U.N.'s control of atomic energy and that any agreement reached at Moscow would be subject to Senate approval, Truman himself was skeptical about Byrnes. On 8 December the president had told Joseph Davies that "Byrnes was acting too much on his own and was not keeping him advised." Truman characterized Byrnes as a "conniver" and wanted Davies to talk to him about what he planned to do in Moscow. Davies tried to "reassure the President. But it couldn't be done. He had been poisoned and his mind was 'sot'—Jim is through."[14]

After Molotov and Bevin agreed to meet with Byrnes in Moscow, Byrnes had even less time to prepare than he did before London. The ministers announced their 15 December meeting on 7 December, and Byrnes planned to leave on 12 December. He had a new policy that he planned to implement at Moscow, which was based on his belief that the Japanese issue, not the Balkans, had stymied the London Conference. He had reached this conclusion after Stalin appeared more interested in discussing Japan with Harriman in October than the recognition of the Balkan nations. Byrnes said that at London he had thought Rumania and Bulgaria were the crucial issues, but "now, we suddenly realized we had been wrong. The remarkable performance that had led to the breakdown of the London Conference had been stimulated by the Russians' belief that they were not being consulted adequately by our officials in Japan."

Byrnes's new policy was quid pro quo negotiation. He told Bevin he was now ready to offer the Soviet Union an Allied Council for Japan in addition to the Far Eastern Commission. In exchange he planned to press for a broadening of the Rumanian and Bulgarian governments "to include some responsible leaders of the principal peasant parties with a promise of free elections as soon as foreign troops are withdrawn." On the procedural issue within the Council of Foreign Ministers, he now believed that Stalin accepted his peace conference proposal, although questions about the number of conferences to be held and the nations to be invited remained to be settled. Byrnes also told Bevin that he intended to push for an independent Korean government or at least a U.N. trusteeship for Korea. He also wanted China discussed so he could explain the limited purpose of the American military mission in Northern China and get a statement from the Russians on their own intentions in China and Manchuria. He intended, in addition, to work for the withdrawal of all Allied troops from Iran. In return, he planned to offer the Soviet Union a share in the control of atomic energy.[15]

This time Byrnes took the initiative in forming an agenda: control of atomic energy, procedure in the Council of Foreign Ministers, Japan, Korea, China, Iran, and recognition of Rumania and Bulgaria. Molotov accepted these items tentatively, but wanted to add evacuation of American forces from China and British forces from Greece, and to move the atomic energy proposal from first to last place on the agenda. Bevin objected to discussing issues involving China and France in their absence and suggested specifically that Byrnes remove the procedural issue from the agenda because he feared the United States and Great Britain would be "maneuvered into giving away" the position adopted in

London. Although this preliminary exchange of views pointed to differences certain to surface in Moscow, the secretary contented himself with the rationalization that these talks should be exploratory and that no fixed agenda or procedure was necessary.[16]

Byrnes left Washington early the morning of 12 December with an even smaller group than he had taken to London. Benjamin Cohen, Bohlen, and Colonel Hugh Kelly, military aide to the secretary, again accompanied him, while James B. Conant, president of Harvard University and chairman of the National Research Council, had replaced the ailing Vannevar Bush the day before as atomic energy adviser. This time Byrnes bypassed an ocean voyage for air travel directly to Paris to pick up H. Freeman Matthews, director of the Office of European Affairs, and John Carter Vincent, director of the Office of Far Eastern Affairs. Byrnes did not want to meet with French officials because they were not happy about their exclusion from the Moscow Conference, especially since they first learned of the meeting, due to poor timing on his part, from the press. To avoid an embarrassing encounter, when Paris airport administrators grounded the American plane due to poor visibility, he took a smaller plane on to Berlin rather than spend the night in Paris.[17]

The next day the large American plane picked up Byrnes and his party, and they left for Moscow only to get lost in a heavy snowstorm inside Russia. Bohlen served as translator for the American pilot and Soviet navigator as they flew very low looking for familiar Moscow landmarks. Bohlen assured the secretary that they were in no danger because there were no mountains here, and he replied, "I could accept your assurance if only you could tell me where 'here' is." With only enough fuel for a return trip to the nearest usuable airport in Berlin, the pilot finally sighted a Moscow airport and safely landed. Although the American delegation arrived late and at the wrong airport in a full blizzard, a second team of Allied officials were there to greet them. George Kennan, the American chargé d'affaires in Moscow, said someone hastily put up two iron posts with American and Soviet flags, and Byrnes, with only a light coat and no overshoes, stood between them in deep snow and made a brief speech. Then

Kennan drove the exhausted Americans to Spasso House, the American embassy, for hot soup and drinks.[18]

The Moscow Conference began at 5:00 p.m. the next day, 15 December, at Spridinovka Palace with Molotov as chairman. After agreeing to meet daily at 4:00 p.m., the ministers took up the question of the agenda. Molotov immediately resumed his London tactic of placing Bevin on the defensive by insisting that not only withdrawal of British forces from Greece but also British occupation policy in Indonesia be placed on the agenda. Byrnes solved this problem by securing agreement to informal discussion of controversial issues that a minister did not want placed on the formal agenda suggested by Byrnes earlier. Bevin then embarrassed himself by objecting to Molotov's request to move control of atomic energy from first to last place on the agenda, only to learn that Byrnes did not object. The ministers adjourned at 9:00 p.m. for a "vodka break."

Kennan observed that Bevin looked disgusted with everything and appeared convinced that Byrnes was unconcerned about American-British relations. Kennan thought Molotov was aware of the division between his colleagues and planned to take advantage of it. Kennan said that Molotov "had the look of a passionate poker player who knows that he has a royal flush and is about to call the last of his opponents. He was the only one who was clearly enjoying every minute of the proceedings." Kennan also observed that Byrnes "plays his negotiations by ear, going into them with no clear or fixed plan, with no definite set objectives or limitations. He relies entirely upon his own agility and presence of mind and hopes to take advantage of tactical openings." Harriman had counseled Byrnes to ascertain the Soviet position on Japan before the conference opened, but Byrnes chose to present his own papers on Japan and council procedure. He did not show the papers to Harriman in advance, and Harriman complained that they "took no account of my discussions with Stalin at Garga." "It was typical of the way Byrnes did his business," Harriman observed. Dr. Conant was surprised to learn that the American delegation had almost no staff papers to use for briefing or guidance.[19]

The next day the British foreign secretary told Byrnes alone that he found Soviet policy "disturbing" because "the Russians were attempting to undermine the British position in the Middle East." Bevin thought, "The world seemed to be drifting into the position of 'three Monroes.' Just as a British admiral, when he saw an island, instinctively wanted to grab it, so the Soviet Government if they saw a piece of land wanted to acquire it." The two men agreed to talk with Molotov separately and frankly about "how uneasy Soviet intentions made us."[20]

Molotov made the British and American ministers considerably more uneasy when they began discussing the issue of procedure for the Council of Foreign Ministers. Byrnes had resubmitted his London proposal accepting the Soviet position on preparing the first drafts of the treaties and then referring the drafts to a peace conference, but adding in deference to Stalin's comments to Harriman that the final drafts be prepared by the armistice signatories. Byrnes considered this last point a significant concession and was "disappointed" when Molotov responded with a proposal limiting peace conference consideration of the drafts to those nations that had actually waged war against that specific enemy. Byrnes realized that "this meant that there really would be a separate conference for each treaty" and told Molotov that they "were farther apart on this issue than he had expected." Molotov pointed out that there was now agreement on a conference and that after World War I different nations had participated in the drafting of different peace treaties at one conference.[21]

Continuing to press for broader participation in the peace conference, Byrnes presented a list of twenty-one nations, which "actively waged war with substantial military forces" and which should "be privileged" to attend the peace conference and to have their views heard. In contrast, Molotov's plan allowed twelve nations to attend. Bevin, supporting the American proposal, told Molotov that it had the "head and tail of the Soviet proposal" and that its middle, the conference, "would give satisfaction to a wide circle of states." Molotov considered the American list of nations too extensive and objected in particular to India because it was not an independent nation. He said that he could not agree to invite India unless the three Baltic Republics—Latvia, Estonia, and Lithuania—were invited. Byrnes immediately agreed to drop India if Molotov would agree to the rest of his list without adding the Baltic nations, although Byrnes later wrote that, "Mr. Bevin, of course, could not agree to exclude India." Bevin countered by agreeing to accept the Baltic republics if India were retained.[22]

Since the ministers could not agree on a list of nations, Byrnes decided to take up the issue with Stalin when he went with Bohlen and Harriman to the Kremlin 19 December after Stalin's return from his Caucasian retreat. Not only did Byrnes believe that Stalin would be more amenable than Molotov in negotiations, he also considered the Soviet leader to be "a very likeable person." Kennan saw Stalin differently and said, "An unforewarned visitor would never have guessed what depths of calculation, ambition, love of power, jealousy, cruelty, and sly vindictiveness lurked beneath this unpretentious facade." In arguing for the American list of nations, Byrnes explicitly told Stalin, "They would not have a vote or any final say in the treaties but merely be present and make their views known." Nonetheless, Stalin improved on Molotov's efforts to add to Soviet representation at the conference by favorably comparing the participation of the Baltic nations in the war with that of Norway, Holland, and Belgium, which were on the American list. Stalin offered not to object to these three or India if the Baltic republics were included, adding that since this action would give Britain and Russia six votes each, he would also consider the possibility of the United States having six votes. Despite this formidable response, Byrnes later wrote that he left Stalin under the impression that "he would not want to reverse Molotov's decision that night but might do so later."[23]

During the session the next afternoon Molotov briefly left the conference table to take a telephone call from Stalin and returned to tell Byrnes that he accepted the American list of nations. Byrnes immediately wired French Foreign Minister Bidault and Chinese Foreign Minister Wang Shih-Chieh of the breakthrough, but not Washington, although he did communicate with Truman the same day on the subject. The

Big Three ministers reached final agreement on the procedural issue on 21 December and accepted "in principle" two new American proposals: holding the peace conference in Paris not London, as had been suggested all along, and convening not later than 1 May 1946. The ministers also agreed to inform France and China of their agreement, not knowing that Byrnes had already done so. Byrnes even suggested informing the other members of the Council of Foreign Ministers "in such a manner as not to allow the whole agreement between the three governments to be held up in the event of objections on the part of France or China." The Chinese immediately responded favorably to the procedural settlement, but the French postponed consideration pending the next cabinet meeting, which was delayed by Bidault's Christmas wedding. The French minister, however, assured the Americans that de Gaulle "will give vent to some recriminations but that in the end he will 'go along' with us." Byrnes then notified President Truman of the agreement, and on Christmas Day, 1945, released news of the peace conference to the press, but omitted the decision to hold the meeting in Paris because the French had not yet been notified of the change of site. Byrnes referred to the announcement of the conference as "a Christmas gift" to "help restore 'peace on earth.'"[24]

Byrnes secured much the same caliber of agreement on Rumania and Bulgaria. In their first private conversation in Moscow, he presented Molotov with a copy of Mark Ethridge's report on conditions in the Balkans and again offended Bevin by not giving him a copy, although British officials in Rumania and Bulgaria had opened their files to Ethridge. Byrnes assured Molotov that Ethridge was "absolutely independent," but had a "sympathetic attitude towards the Soviet Union." He said that he had intended to publish the report, but had decided, instead, to bring it to Moscow because Ethridge, while not recommending U.S. recognition, did offer suggestions that would make recognition possible. He concluded that he hoped a way for the United States to recognize these nations could be found so the Americans could "give the peoples of these countries some economic help which they sorely needed." The Soviet foreign minister predictably refused to credit Ethridge with objectivity, noting that the journalist had to be aware of Byrnes's opposition to recognition, but he agreed to consider the report. Byrnes next proposed that Rumania and Bulgaria be reorganized to include representatives of all political parties and that these enlarged governments then sponsor free elections using a secret ballot.[25]

When Byrnes brought up his proposals for discussion in an informal session with Bevin and Molotov on 22 December, Molotov declared that the American suggestions were unacceptable because general elections with secret ballots had just been held in Bulgaria and that the people had participated "to an unusual degree." In Rumania, he continued, the complaints by the king against the government had been the result of the encouragement from the American and British representatives there and had caused a delay in elections. He maintained that the presence of the Red Army had not influenced the elections held in Austria, Hungary, Finland, and Bulgaria, and would not in Rumania. He refused outright to participate in any action that would overturn the results of the Bulgarian election, but agreed to cooperate in broadening the Rumanian government "on the condition" that the ministers would agree to conclude a treaty of peace with Rumania.[26]

Not satisfied with this response, Byrnes decided to go over Molotov's head to Stalin once again and returned to the Kremlin on the snowy night of 23 December. He told Stalin that "he had had a difficult time with Molotov on this subject," and Stalin smiled and said that "this was unexpected news." Byrnes again couched his desire to settle the Balkan issue in terms of placing the United States "in a position to render them [the Balkans] essential economic assistance." Urging Stalin to suggest a plan that would give representation to all the political parties in Rumania and Bulgaria, Byrnes continued to insist "that surely it would be possible to find persons who were both representative of these parties and at the same time friendly to the Soviet Union." Stalin responded that inasmuch as "the Soviet Union was already being accused of interference," he could only suggest that the Big Three advise, not pressure,

Bulgaria "to include some members of the loyal opposition in the new Government," but added that "there could be no question of the reorganization of the Government." Stalin approved Molotov's idea of doing more in the case of Rumania, and "in a pinch" he would suggest that the Rumanian government be reorganized to include "loyal persons" from the National Peasant and Liberal parties. He particularly refused, however, to broaden the Rumanian Ministry of Interior, as Byrnes had wanted, because that would "stick a boot in the face of the Rumanians." Neither Harriman nor Bohlen, who were present, considered Stalin's token concessions of value, but Byrnes, according to Harriman "leaped at it." "In a matter of minutes" Stalin and Byrnes agreed that a commission composed of Andrei Vishinsky, Harriman, and Archibald Clark Kerr, British ambassador in Moscow, be sent to Rumania to arrange for the inclusion of additional ministers and that the Soviet government advise Bulgaria to expand its new government. When Stalin asked Byrnes to discuss this accord with Bevin, the secretary joked "that although they were supposed to have a bloc with England, he had even neglected to inform Mr. Bevin soon enough about the proposed meeting in Moscow." Stalin replied "that this was obviously only a cloak to hide the reality of the bloc."[27]

Bevin, who doubted the practicality of Byrnes's "uncompromising attitude" toward recognition of Rumania and Bulgaria, readily accepted the Balkan settlement. Even with British approval, the three foreign ministers spent considerable time hammering out language on which they could agree. Byrnes was concerned that the ministers added be "truly representative of their parties" and that they be placed "in important positions," while Molotov wanted to exclude specific Rumanian leaders and include only those considered "loyal" to the present Rumanian government. The secretary finally agreed, against the advice of almost all the American delegation, not to put up for membership in the Rumanian government specific Rumanians who, the other Americans thought, had every right to be there. Kennan, in particular, had contempt for Byrnes's efforts to salvage "some fig leaves of democratic procedure to hide the nakedness of Stalinist dictatorship in the respective East European countries," and maintained that it was "absurd" to think that adding one or two non-Communists to the Rumanian and Bulgarian cabinets would change the governments there. Molotov also wanted a strong statement of the American and British intention to recognize these nations once their governments were altered, but the Americans and British reserved the right to judge the effectiveness of the changes made. The ministers reached substantial agreement on language for the Rumanian accord but came to the day of adjournment without a Bulgarian statement.[28]

Byrnes believed he fared better on the Far Eastern issues, especially on a Far Eastern Commission and an Allied Council for Japan. The Soviet Union agreed with little objection that the eleven-power commission would meet in Washington and formulate Japanese policy for the four-power (USSR, U.S., China, and Great Britain) Allied Council, sitting in Tokyo to advise General MacArthur. MacArthur was not obligated to accept the advice of the council if the "exigencies of the situation" did not permit, and he alone decided if they did or did not. Later in the conference the Soviets showed as afterdinner entertainment for the British and American delegates what Conant characterized as an "incredible film" showing the Red Army singlehandedly winning the war against the Japanese. The Americans later wondered if the movie was an "intentional insult" and considered ways of protesting, one suggestion being to write their objections and throw the paper in a wastebasket, knowing that someone in the Kremlin would be sure to read it. The Soviet film might have been in response to Byrnes's actions the night before when he kept several thousands, including leading Soviet officials, waiting close to a half-hour for him to arrive at a special performance of the ballet, *Zoluhka*, at the Bolshoi.[29]

The Russians also accepted the secretary's proposal for a unified Korean administration as a first step toward establishing a joint USSR-U.S. trusteeship there, but Molotov proved more difficult on the question of American troops in Northern China. Byrnes submitted a memorandum the first day of the conference to explain that "American Marines are in North China for the purpose of assisting the Chinese Government in the demobilization and deportation of Japanese troops." The secretary also said that Chinese "revolutionists"—so-called since Stalin had said "at Potsdam that they were not Communists"—were between the Japanese and Chinese President Chiang Kai-shek's Nationalist troops. If the Marines could prevent the Japanese from surrendering to the revolutionists, they would help prevent civil war in China. Molotov responded that "he did not see how it could be tolerated that Japanese forces were still in being," and said that Chiang had "exaggerated the strength of the communist forces" because it "was a well known Chinese practice" to let others do the fighting for them. He said that "eight years of war should have been long enough for Chiang Kai-shek to learn how to handle Japanese, particularly after the latter had capitulated," but he reaffirmed his government's support for the Nationalists.[30]

Molotov later submitted a proposal calling for the simultaneous withdrawal of both Russian and American troops from China. Byrnes refused to agree and insisted that the disarming of Japanese soldiers "was a complicated question and might take some time." He did, however, bring up the subject with Stalin in an effort to reassure him about American intentions. Stalin warned Byrnes that if "we desired to help Chiang Kai-shek we sould not give him help in such a manner as to destroy his authority with the Chinese people." Stalin did not press further; he expressed instead his hope that General George Marshall's mission to China as President Truman's representative would succeed in avoiding civil war.[31]

Byrnes had a great deal more difficulty with his proposal to set a date for the withdrawal of Allied troops from Iran. He raised the issue at the request of the government of Iran because the United States was a signatory with the Soviets and British to the Declaration of Iran, which, signed at the Teheran Conference, promised respect for Iran's independence and territorial integrity. Iran wanted the declaration upheld because of a separatist uprising in the northern province of Azerbaijan, which had led the Iranian government to attempt to send troops into that area. Soviet authorities refused to allow the troop movements, and Iran now feared Soviet support for the insurgents or a Soviet attempt to incorporate the province. At first Molotov refused even to place the issue on the agenda unless removal of British troops from Greece and Indonesia was also added, but the ministers finally agreed to discuss all three issues informally. Byrnes and Bevin decided privately to "cut the ground" from under the Soviet government's pretense of defending democracy in Persia, which "offended American sensibilities," by urging the Iranians "to make early concessions to the demands formulated by the Azerbaijanians." But when Byrnes discussed this issue first with Stalin, Stalin maintained that "the Iranian Government was hostile to the USSR" and that he must defend the Soviet Baku oil fields located close to their common border. The secretary of state later called this "the weakest excuse I ever heard him make." He told Stalin that he feared Iran would raise this question at the first session of the United Nations and embarrass the Big Three, but Stalin replied that Byrnes "could rest assured that the Soviet Union had no designs territorial or otherwise against Iran."[32]

The British foreign secretary fared little better with Stalin; the Soviet leader told him "frankly and honestly" that the Soviet government did not plan an early withdrawal. Bevin then suggested that the Three Powers establish a tripartite commission "to advise and assist" the Iranians in introducing provincial government into their system and to facilitate troop withdrawal. Stalin agreed to discuss the British proposal, but when Byrnes later pressed Stalin by saying that if the issue were not settled, the United States would support Iran before the United Nations, Stalin responded that "they were not afraid" because "no one had any need to blush" if this question came up in the U.N. Stalin later asked Bevin what Byrnes's position was on the tripartite commission and was told that Byrnes had not committed himself. The next day Molotov told Byrnes privately that he considered the British plan "in general acceptable," and the secretary responded that he did not particularly like the proposal but if it could be adopted as "a possible first step in the direction of a solution" he would accept it.[33]

Byrnes assumed from this conversation, despite his own lukewarm response, that Molotov accepted the British solution. But when the three foreign ministers discussed the issue together for the first time the next to the last day of the conference, they did so after a heated exchange on the Bulgarian issue. Molotov tried unsuccessfully to leave the language involving troop withdrawal as vague as possible and used for comparison the U.S. draft on troop withdrawal from China. Molotov argued that "in Iran just as in China no impossible demands should be put forward," but Byrnes insisted that there was "no relation" between the two situations, and Molotov asked to postpone the issue. When Iran came up the last day of the conference, Molotov said that since nothing had come of the Iranian discussions, they should be dropped. Byrnes quickly agreed and said that "he did not wish to jeopardize" the good work that the conference had accomplished, but at the end of the meeting Bevin repeated his concern that the Iranian issue had not been settled and asked, "What is my next step?" Molotov inscrutably replied, "You know that well."[34]

Byrnes thought that he had reason to be pleased with the Russian response to his atomic energy proposition, because he had been advised not to expect Soviet cooperation. In remarkably similar telegrams from Harriman to Byrnes on 27 November and from Clark Kerr to Byrnes by way of Bevin on 3 December, the two ambassadors in Moscow had described the "new siege mentality" that the atomic bomb had produced in the Soviet government. Both had begun by describing Soviet history as a search for "something like security for their country, their system and their own bodies." Through all the years of revolution, intervention, civil war, ostracism, purges, and finally the German invasion, the Soviets had "trembled for the safety of their country and their system as they trembled for their own."

> Then came the turn of the tide and with it first the hope and then a growing belief that the immense tension of national security was at last within their reach. As the Red Army moved westwards belief became confidence and the final defeat of

> Germany made confidence conviction. . . . Then plump came
> the Atomic Bomb. At a blow the balance which had now seemed
> set and steady was rudely shaken. Russia was balked by the
> west when everything seemed to be within her grasp.

Kerr thought that after the first shock wore off the Kremlin
had believed the West would share the bomb with them, "but
as time went on and no move came from the West,
disappointment turned into irritation and, when the bomb
seemed to them to become an instrument of policy, into
spleen." Harriman believed that "this attitude partially
explains Molotov's aggressiveness in London;" and, given
"the prickliness of which they are capable," Kerr advised the
British and Americans to discuss U.N. control of atomic
energy with Molotov before the General Assembly meeting.[35]

In fact, Byrnes's first problem with the atomic issue came
from the British on the second day of the conference. He had
supplied Bevin with an advance copy of the American
proposal and had agreed to delay submitting it to the Soviets
in order to give Bevin time to communicate with London.
Bevin said his initial reaction was that the proposed atomic
energy commission ought to report to the Security Council,
not to the General Assembly, and that the deleted paragraph
about not proceeding to the next stage until the prior one was
successfully completed should be restored to the proposal.
Byrnes replied that if the Security Council were involved, the
Soviet Union could use its veto privilege, but he agreed to
consider Bevin's suggestions. The next day he proceeded to
present the U.S. proposal to the Soviet Union without either
informing Bevin or adopting the British changes. Kennan
said the British delegation believed that Byrnes had given
his word to delay presentation, making Bevin, who saw the
secretary's action as "bad faith," furious. Two days later
Byrnes amended the original American draft on atomic
energy to include the separate stages paragraph.[36]

When the three foreign ministers finally discussed the
subject on 22 December, Conant reported that "to my utter
amazement and contrary to all predictions" Molotov
accepted the American proposals and suggested only that
the proposed U.N. Commission be put under the jurisdiction

of the Security Council instead of the General Assembly. Byrnes accepted the suggestion that the commission report to the Security Council, but still wanted the General Assembly to approve the policy suggested by the commission so as to avoid a Russian veto. Molotov argued against General Assembly control, but eventually agreed to language implying Security Council dominance; and he also objected to the addition of the separate stages paragraph but finally accepted it. Byrnes later wrote, "As a result the proposal that we had expected would provoke extensive discussion was agreed to with less debate than any other subject on the agenda."[37]

Stalin hosted the foreign ministers at a Christmas Eve banquet the evening they reached agreement on the atomic energy issue. During the dinner several toasts went awry, following the precedent set by Bevin at a luncheon the day before by saying in response to a toast by Harriman: "And let's hope we don't all get sacked when we get home." Byrnes's remark, "whom war hath joined together, let not peace put asunder," was received with a notable lack of appreciation. This was followed by Molotov's bomb-in-pocket routine, who "rather floored" Dr. Conant by asking him during a reception: "do you have one in your pocket?" He further added that, since everyone had had enough to drink to allow the exploring of secrets, he would toast Conant, "who, perhaps, had a bit of the atomic bomb in his pocket." Conant said Stalin, "apparently in anger, although it may have been a prearranged scene," said, "This is too serious a matter to joke about. . . . I raise my glass to the American scientists and what they have accomplished. We must now work together to see that this great invention is used for peaceful ends." Bohlen believed that Stalin's comment, which was made without consultation with Molotov and which had humiliated him, indicated a change from the Kremlin's earlier public stance of atomic indifference.[38]

The Moscow Conference of the foreign ministers lasted eleven days with seven formal and seven informal sessions, with Stalin meeting twice each with Byrnes and Bevin, and with Byrnes meeting twice privately with Molotov and once with Bevin. The conference came to an end on schedule on 26

December when the ministers met formally for the last time at 11:00 p.m. to sign a protocol. Byrnes was concerned that there had been no agreement on Bulgaria and Iran, but preferred adjournment rather than to allow "heated arguments" to destroy the decisions that had been made. Byrnes and Bevin signed the English language texts of the protocol only to learn that the Russian language texts were not ready for Molotov's signature. When the Russian copy of the protocol was brought to the Soviet diplomat, he examined it and said "with a broad smile" that his people "by mistake" had included the Russian version of the Bulgarian draft, rejected earlier by the British and Americans. Molotov said that "he hoped that such good work would not be wasted and that the documents would be signed as they were, including the sections on Bulgaria." Byrnes and Bevin refused, and Molotov asked if they would accept the first half of the American proposal and the second half of the Russian. Byrnes again refused, saying that since Molotov had come half way, he might as well accept all of the American proposal. "To my amazement," Byrnes said, "he did." Bevin hopefully inquired if "Mr. Molotov wished similarly to reconsider the Iran question?" Molotov refused, and the ministers finally signed the amended protocol at 3:30 a.m., 27 December. The American delegation left Moscow four hours later, exhausted from the Russian schedule of working at night and sleeping during the day, but, as the secretary said, "with a greater hope as a result of the Moscow Conference."[39]

Press coverage of the Moscow Conference communique reflected Byrnes's optimism. President Truman stated that he was in "complete accord" with his secretary of state; Undersecretary Acheson referred to Byrnes as "St. Nickolas"; Joseph Davies congratulated Byrnes on a job "magnificently done." But unlike the aftermath of the London Conference when Byrnes feared blame and received instead approval, this time the expected commendations quickly turned to charges of high handedness and appeasement. The secretary's troubles began with poor timing (his third for this conference) of the simultaneous release of the communiqué in Washington, London, and Moscow, which resulted in Truman's discovering its contents, not from the secretary of state, but from the press. Since Byrnes had continued his London policy of independence from both the president and the State Department, Acheson learned of the planned simultaneous release from a radio news report and wired Moscow for the text of the communiqué. When Harriman had offered to help draft the customary daily summary to Washington, the secretary had told him: "The President has given me complete authority. I'm not going to send any daily reports. I don't trust the White House. It leaks. And I don't want any of this coming out in the papers until I get home." Bohlen had received much the same reply when he asked Byrnes why he was not sending regular reports to the president. Byrnes "sharply" told the former State Department liaison with the president that he knew when it was and wasn't necessary to report to the White House. Actually the secretary kept Washington better informed during his Moscow negotiations than he did at London, but Acheson believed the Moscow communications to be "few, terse" and "inadequate" despite his telling the press that "Mr. Byrnes has been very helpful indeed in keeping us informed as to the progress of the Conference."[40]

The undersecretary was in the unenviable position of being caught between the president and the secretary of state, a position which "required that I never talk with either about the other, that I should keep both as fully informed as possible about problems and developments. Sometimes the pincers pressed pretty hard." Acheson noted that "the President fretted at the silence" from Moscow and, after the communiqué confusion, decided to mediate Byrnes's request that arrangements be made for a radio address to the nation the night of his return. "This was not in accordance with etiquette, nor was it wise in view of the President's state of mind." Acheson believed. "Both required that he report first to the President, get straightened away there, and then make his speech with the President's blessings." Acheson arranged for the secretary to speak on radio the day after his return and then informed the "thoroughly incensed" president that he was sure Byrnes planned to report to Truman directly from the plane. The undersecretary then met Byrnes at the airport and gently told him that Truman was upset, later writing that the secretary "was disbelieving, impatient, and irritated that Mr. Truman had sailed down the Potomac on the *Williamsburg* leaving word for him to follow."[41]

Byrnes later wrote that he had called Truman for an appointment as soon as he arrived back in the United States and an hour later received this pleasant message: "Happy to hear of your safe arrival. Suggest you come down today or tomorrow to report on your mission." Truman's version was that Byrnes called him to see if his broadcast had been arranged and that Truman's response was that "you had best come down here posthaste and make your report to the President before you do anything else." Byrnes described his private meeting with Truman as "cordial," saying he explained the communiqué mixup had occurred because of State Department delay in translating the coded message. Truman said he told Byrnes that he didn't like the way in which he "had been left in the dark about the Moscow Conference." "As President," Truman said, "I intended to know what progress we were making and what we were doing in foreign negotiations." Both Truman and Byrnes gave their versions of the *Williamsburg* scene to Acheson who said that "both impressions were quite possibly entirely genuine." Truman had a habit of exaggerating his bile, Acheson said, while in reality he was not a harsh or sarcastic person. Byrnes, on the other hand, would not take as personal criticism Truman's telling him he wanted to be better informed.[42]

Byrnes left his *Williamsburg* conference with the president to make his radio report to the nation on 30 December, and his speech was a political accomplishment. He first did obeisance to Truman and then he directly responded to press criticisms of the risks involved in his brand of unconventional diplomacy. Byrnes said, "In this modern world where events move with lightning speed there is not time to wait for agreements to be reached by the slow exchange of diplomatic communication." Next, the secretary, just accused of not adequately informing the administration of his negotiations, described in detail the settlements reached in Moscow. Byrnes presented each settlement as a compromise, not as an

ideal solution, in effect appealing first to those in the Truman
administration who wanted a settlement with the Soviet
Union and then to those who feared compromise as
appeasement. Byrnes concluded by stressing the Moscow
achievement of "better understanding" between the three
powers. Following his speech, the secretary returned to the
presidential yacht anchored off Quantico for New Year's Eve
dinner and an evening of singing old Navy songs. Byrnes
described the evening as "fun," and no one else present
commented on any strain between the president and his
secretary of state.[43]

Regardless of whether presidential hyperbole or secre-
tarial imperviousness was the accurate explanation for
Byrnes's post-Moscow encounter with Truman, the Moscow
Conference did mark a turning point in the president's
attitude toward the Soviet Union. Truman said that he
studied the Moscow communiqué after he saw Byrnes and "it
became abundantly clear to me that the successes of the
Moscow Conference were unreal." The president concluded
that Byrnes "had taken it upon himself to move the foreign
policy of the United States in a direction to which I had not,
and would not, agree. Moreover, he had undertaken this on
his own initiative without consulting or informing the
president." Truman said that in order to make his objections
"perfectly clear" to the secretary, he sat down and wrote
Byrnes a letter in longhand which he read to him at their
next conference on 5 January. Byrnes said that he never
heard of this letter until it appeared in 1952 in William
Hillman's biography of Truman, *Mr. President.* The president wrote in his letter that he did "not intend to turn over the
complete authority of the President nor to forego the
President's prerogatives to make the final decisions" and
that he expected to "be kept fully informed on what is taking
place." Truman told Byrnes that he had just read the
Ethridge report "on those two police states" and that "I am
not going to agree to the recognition of those governments
unless they are radically changed." The president also said:

> I think we ought to protest with all the vigor of which we are
> capable against the Russian program in Iran. There isn't a
> doubt in my mind that Russia intends an invasion of Turkey

and the seizure of the Black Sea Straits to the Mediterranean. Unless Russia is faced with an iron fist and strong language war is in the making .... I do not think we should play compromise any longer.

Truman concluded his account of this scene by saying, "Byrnes accepted my decision. He did not ask to be relieved or express a desire to quit." In contrast, Byrnes said, "Had this occurred, with my deep conviction that there must be complete accord between the President and his Secretary of State, I would have resigned immediately."[44]

The secretary did not resign immediately, but, since the president no longer intended to allow him to decide American foreign policy, Byrnes did have to measure what he considered the accomplishments of Moscow against what Truman wanted. The president told Byrnes:

> We should refuse to recognize Rumania and Bulgaria until they comply with our requirements; we should let our position on Iran be known in no uncertain terms ... and we should maintain complete control of Japan and the Pacific. We should rehabilitate China and create a strong central government there. We should do the same for Korea.
>
> Then we should insist on the return of our ships from Russia and force a settlement of the Lend-Lease debt of Russia.
>
> I'm tired of babying the Soviets.

Truman now considered anything less than these proposals appeasement, but the president's attitude after Moscow was analogous to Byrnes's before London. The president, now that he was suspicious of his secretary of state and interested in running his own foreign policy, was not thinking in terms of negotiation; he was thinking in the context of atomic-dollar ultimatums. The secretary had already learned that the Russians, in Joseph Davies's words, "will not scare," and at the Moscow Conference Byrnes had successfully used his new foreign policy tactic of quid pro quo negotiation.[45]

He traded the Russians token concessions in Japan for token concessions in the Balkans, and American troops stayed in China while Soviet troops remained in Iran. The Soviet Union agreed to a powerless peace conference and the United States agreed to a limited Soviet atomic role. These agreements were not made possible by Byrnes's clumsy threat to publish the Ethridge Report, or by his naive promise to render economic assistance to the Balkans, or by his transparent efforts to avoid the appearance of an American-British bloc, or by his grand strategy of going straight to Stalin. They were made possible by Soviet willingness to accept them. Byrnes would have settled for any of the compromises by the end of the London meeting of the Council of Foreign Ministers, but Molotov was not willing then; at Moscow he was.[46]

What changed Soviet policy is open to speculation. The Moscow agreements were as realistic a compromise for Russia as they were for America, which is not to say that either side gained more than the "appearance of agreement where none existed." Kennan had accurately said about Byrnes at Moscow:

> In the present conference his weakness in dealing with the Russians is that his main purpose is to achieve some sort of an agreement, he doesn't much care what. The realities behind this agreement, since they concern only such people as Koreans, Rumanians, and Iranians, about whom he knows nothing, do not concern him. He wants an agreement for its political effect at home.

Kennan, however, erroneously concluded, "The Russians know this. They will see that for this superficial success he pays a heavy price in the things that are real." The Moscow settlement did not involve the United States paying "a heavy price"; the settlement was equally superficial for both sides. Byrnes's main Moscow accomplishment was the resumption of diplomacy and the possibility of that diplomacy continuing through the Council of Foreign Ministers.

CHAPTER FOUR

THE PARIS CONFERENCE OF THE COUNCIL OF FOREIGN MINISTERS
25 April–16 May 1946

At the beginning of 1946 the American public resolved the ongoing debate in the Truman administration about whether national security interests or ideological expansion was behind postwar Soviet policy. At the end of the war with Japan, an American Institute of Public Opinion poll had revealed that 54 percent of a national sample believed the USSR could be trusted to cooperate with the United States. By the end of the London Conference of the Council of Foreign Ministers only 44 percent had faith in Soviet-American cooperation, and by February 1946 the figure was 35 percent. A mid-March survey revealed that 71 percent of those polled disapproved of the policy that Russia was following in world affairs, and 60 percent believed that the United States was "too soft in its policy toward Russia." As previously stated, neither Byrnes nor Truman was doctrinaire in his approach to foreign policy, but both men were politically sensitive. Because of Byrnes's peripatetic schedule as secretary of state, the president was the first to learn of changing public opinion and its ramification for the 1946 congressional elections. This political factor, added to his doubts about his secretary of state and the pressure already within his administration, influenced his decision to direct American foreign policy and to harden the American attitude toward the Soviet Union. Byrnes was a quick learner and during the early months of 1946, after he mended his fences with the president, he turned his attention to Congress and to the American public.[1]

During the January 1946 meeting of the U.N. in London, the secretary became aware that his bipartisan foreign policy was in danger of disintegration. Both Vandenberg and Dulles were members of the American delegation, and the issue that concerned them most was the American proposal for the international control of atomic energy. Even before the release of the Moscow communiqué Vandenberg wrote that he would be home sooner than anyone expected "if at London I collide with a Truman-Byrnes appeasement policy which I cannot stomach." He described the Moscow agreement on atomic energy as "one more typical American 'give away' on this subject." When Truman and Acheson reassured him that adequate controls would accompany each stage in establishing international control, Vandenberg concluded that "the circumstances *now* probably *demand* that I go" to London to make sure that controls were written into the United Nations agreement. As soon as Byrnes learned that the Republican members of the American delegation were working to prevent acceptance of the Moscow proposal, he announced, with Truman's approval, the creation of a Secretary of State's Committee to suggest security measures to protect American interests after the establishment of a U.N. Atomic Energy Commission. Byrnes also decided to go to London, although he had returned from Moscow only a little over a week before. After Vandenberg and Dulles consulted with the secretary in London, they toasted themselves over forcing Byrnes to strengthen the American position. "Thank heavens that Jimmy Byrnes hates disagreements," Vandenberg said, "because I don't know where I would be if he decided to continue this fight."[2]

The U.N. unanimously agreed to create an Atomic Energy Commission but then became involved in a bitter dispute between the Soviet Union and Great Britain over troops in Iran and Greece. Byrnes returned to Washington without engaging in the debate, and Vandenberg and Dulles returned later to criticize him for leaving after being impressed with Ernest Bevin's impassioned stand against the Soviet representative, Andrei Vishinsky. *New York Times* correspondent James Reston believed that Republicans favored "a bolder" and "much more forthright" policy of leadership in world affairs than the administration was now following. They were motivated, he remarked, by political concern over the coming elections and the public's attitude toward appeasement. On 27 February Vandenberg threw down a bipartisan gauntlet to the Truman Administration by speaking in the Senate to the question, "What is Russia up to now?" In calling for a new American foreign policy, Vandenberg urged the United States to speak as plainly and to sustain its ideals and goals as vigorously as the Soviet Union did. "There is a line beyond which compromise cannot go," he said, "but how can we expect our alien friends to know where that line is unless we reestablish the habit of saying only what we mean and meaning every word we say?" Vandenberg praised Bevin as "sturdy," Bidault as "able," and even Vishinsky as "brilliant," but he did not mention Byrnes. He received a standing ovation for his comments and eventual credit for motivating a more forceful American foreign policy, but he knew when he rose that Byrnes was scheduled to speak the next day.[3]

Byrnes's 28 February speech to the Overseas Press Club in New York was the first statement of the Truman administration's new foreign policy that began emerging after the Moscow Conference. As early as 21 January the president in his first State of the Union message had declared that the "great and dominant objective" of United States foreign policy was "to build and preserve a just peace," but he warned that when difficulties arose among the Allies the United States did not propose to remove them "by sacrificing its ideals or vital interests," because America's ultimate security required more than "a process of consultation and compromise." Then on 9 February Joseph Stalin, in a rare public speech in Moscow, had asserted that a peaceful international order was impossible because of the incompatibility of capitalism and communism. Stalin had told his audience that the Soviet Union must strengthen her economy with more five-year plans so that "our country [will] be insured against any eventuality." These remarks were interpreted both as being an effort to spur Russian acceptance of more economic deprivations and as evidence of a new Soviet hard-line foreign policy. Most Americans and many within the Truman administration chose the latter interpretation, and during these first months of 1946 there was ample evidence to support this analysis and further motivate a firm American response.[4]

Averell Harriman had reported that the commission on Rumania failed in its efforts to make the Groza Government more representative, and Vishinsky had announced that the Soviet effort to broaden the Bulgarian government had been unsuccessful because of the drastic demands of the opposition parties. The American people had also learned for the first time of the Yalta agreement to cede South Sakhalin and the Kurile Islands to the Soviet Union, and on 16 February the Canadian government had announced the arrest of twenty-two atomic spies working for the USSR, further hardening the American attitude toward the Soviet Union. On 20 February the president had told Admiral Leahy that he intended immediately to enforce a stronger position against the Communists.[5]

On 22 February George Kennan's remarkable telegram assessing Soviet motivation had arrived from Moscow. The American Chargé had repeatedly criticized America's Soviet policy and had been ignored by the State Department, but this 8000 word telegram had come at a crucial transitional period in diplomatic planning, and its influence has been difficult to exaggerate. Kennan had written that the first premise of the Soviet outlook was that of "'capitalist encirclement' with which in the long run there can be no permanent peaceful coexistence." Kennan pictured Marxist dogma as all important in Soviet affairs: "In this dogma, with its basic altruism of purpose, they found justification for their instinctive fear of outside world, for the dictatorship without which they did not know how to rule, for cruelties they did not dare not to inflict, for sacrifices they felt bound to demand." Kennan concluded that

> we have here a political force committed fanatically to the belief that with the United States there can be no permanent modus vivendi, that it is desirable and necessary that the international harmony of our society to disrupted, our traditional way of life be destroyed, the international authority of our state be broken, if Soviet power is to be secure.

Kennan's telegram had provided the intellectual justification of the foreign policy the administration was ready to announce.[6]

Byrnes, in his 28 February speech, approved in advance by Truman, said bluntly that "All around us there is suspicion and distrust, which in turn breeds suspicion and distrust." The United States as a member of the U.N. covenanted not to use force except in defense of the charter, but "we have a responsibility to use our influence to see that other powers live up to their covenant. And that responsibility we also intend to meet. . . . We must make it clear in advance that we do intend to act to prevent aggression, making it clear at the same time that we will not use force for any other purpose." In order to fulfill American responsibility, Byrnes said that "we must be able and ready to provide armed contingents that may be required on short notice." More specifically, he said, "We have openly, gladly, wholeheartedly welcomed our Soviet Ally as a great power, second to none in the family of the United Nations. Only an inexcusable tragedy of errors could cause serious conflict between us in the future." He then listed the errors that would be inexcusable: use of force contrary to the charter, holding troops in sovereign states without their approval, prolonging the making of the peace, seizing enemy properties before a reparations settlement, and conducting "a war of nerves to achieve strategic ends." The secretary of state had mended his fences.[7]

If there was any doubt left that the United States had a new foreign policy, it was soon dispelled by two successive events: Churchill's iron curtain speech and the Iranian crisis in the United Nations. In mid-February Byrnes visited Churchill in Florida and heard from him an outline of the speech he planned to give in Fulton, Missouri, at the president's request. Later Byrnes and Leahy read the final copy of Churchill's speech and gave a resumé of it to Truman, who anticipated "that the Soviets would charge the British and Americans were 'ganging up' on them" and this way he "could truthfully say he had not read the speech prior to its delivery." Truman, according to Churchill, changed his mind on the train to Fulton and read the speech and said that "it was admirable and would do nothing but good though it would make a stir." After the presidential introduction of "I know he will have something constructive to say," the former British prime minister said that although the Russians did not want war, they did want "the fruits of war and the indefinite expansion of their powers and doctrines. From what I have seen of our Russian friends . . . I am convinced that there is nothing for which they have less respect than for military weakness." Churchill ended with a call for an American-British alliance, a "fraternal association of the English speaking peoples," to resist Soviet advances around the world. Stalin condemned Churchill's proposed alliance as "racist" and warned him and his British and American friends against beginning a war with the Soviet Union, because "they will be beaten as they were beaten twenty-six years ago."[8]

The American secretary of state chose to ignore Stalin's warning and decided to demonstrate dramatically his new foreign policy to his appeasement critics on the Iranian issue. At the January U.N. meeting in London the Security Council had returned the issue to Soviet-Iranian negotiation when the Soviet Union had promised to withdraw their troops by 2 March 1946. When Russia reneged on this public pledge, Byrnes made public a note he sent to Moscow on 5 March demanding Soviet withdrawal and initiated, or perhaps manufactured, a week of incredible tension in the United States. On 6 March the American vice-consul in Azerbaijan wired Washington that "exceptionally heavy Soviet troop movements" toward Teheran, Iraq, and Turkey were in progress. When Byrnes learned this, he slammed one fist into the other and said, "Now we'll give it to them with both barrels." On 8 March he demanded an explanation of the troops movements from Molotov, who had not yet replied to his earlier demand for troop withdrawal. Molotov, again, did not respond and on 12 March Byrnes told the American press that Russian tanks were moving toward Teheran. The Soviet press denied this report, and James Reston later wrote that the State Department had exaggerated the importance of the troop movements.[9]

When the Security Council convened in New York on 25 March, George V. Allen, U.S. ambassador to Iran, brought

Byrnes a copy of the resolution the Iranian ambassador would introduce to urge U.N. sanctions against the Soviet Union. When Byrnes asked Allen if he had written the statement, he denied it but did see in it an American hand. The secretary responded that everyone was entitled to a lawyer. Since the U.N. January meeting, Moscow and Teheran had been negotiating a settlement to their problems, and the Russians had objected to resubmitting the issue to the Security Council and had again publicly promised to withdraw their troops within five to six weeks. The Iranian government then rebuked its ambassador in the United States and instructed him to withdraw the issue from the U.N. The Iranian ambassador refused and, with Byrnes's personal and public support, added the issue to the U.N. agenda. In response, on 27 March the Soviet ambassador to the U.N., Andrei Gromyko, angrily walked out of the chamber. On 4 April the Soviet Union and Iran announced a formal agreement on troop withdrawal in early May and Iranian sovereignty over Azerbaijan. From this agreement Russia received oil concessions from Iran, the Iranian government regained control of Azerbaijan and promptly executed the separatist leaders, and James Byrnes received praise from the president, the Republicans, and the American public.[10]

While Washington formulated a new foreign policy toward the Soviet Union, the deputies of the Council of Foreign Ministers met in London as agreed at the Moscow Conference. James Dunn continued to represent the United States; Ronald Campbell represented Great Britain; Fedor Gusev served as the Soviet Deputy, and Maurice Couve de Murville represented France. The four deputies first met at Lancaster House on 18 January using the 4-3-2 formula of all four deputies drafting the Italian treaty; only the American, British and Soviet deputies drafting the Balkan treaties; and the British and Soviet deputies drafting the Finnish treaty. Dunn and his staff continued the positions established by the secretary at the London council meeting but developed a negotiating strategy to bolster their stand. Jacques Reinstein, Dunn's financial expert, informed the State Department that he planned to disagree deliberately with the

British because "I think it would be healthy to have a little rowing between the two of us with the Soviets as observers." Reinstein started to warn the British about his tactic but decided not to because "this will enable us to argue with them in a more genuine fashion." Byrnes suggested the tactic of putting a ceiling on armed forces in the Italian treaty, as the Soviets wanted, provided they accepted a ceiling in the Balkan treaties. The secretary also wanted Dunn to concentrate on Italian inability to pay reparations as a response to Soviet insistence on Italian obligation to pay. Byrnes said that the U.S. was "not (repeat not) prepared to make a substantial concession on this point even at the cost of failure to reach agreement with the Soviets on the treaty."[11]

The deputies began with the Italian treaty and agreed at their second meeting to establish a Commission of Experts to visit the disputed Italian-Yugoslav border area and recommend a boundary which "should be in the main the ethnic line leaving a minimum under alien rule," as the ministers had agreed at the London Conference. The deputies took a month to agree on precise instructions for the commission, because the Soviet deputy wanted the words "in the main" eliminated so the Italian majority inside Trieste could be overlooked in favor of the Yugoslav majority surrounding the city. A flu epidemic infecting Gusev and then the other three deputies further delayed the proceedings. Dunn complained to Byrnes on 19 February about "the drift of the discussions" and warned that he saw "little chance of keeping the 1 May deadline" for the peace conference. On 27 February Dunn wrote H. Freeman Matthews that the deputies had not resolved any of the important Italian issues or even started discussing the Balkan treaties.[12]

Dunn described the work of the deputies as "shadow boxing," saying, "We have spent literally days of consecutive sessions talking about the same subject in the same form, restating our same positions without making any advance whatever toward arriving at a real development of the subject at hand." Progress at these meetings, Dunn wrote, "really comes down to the fundamental fact of whether the Soviet Government really wants at the present time, from the point of view of policy, even to provide for the conclusion of treaties with Italy or the Balkan States." Dunn was convinced that the Soviets did not support the American goal of early treaties to provide political and economic stability but to maintain "puppet stooge governments" and Red Army forces in the Balkans. "It may be, however, that they are deliberately postponing all agreements until the eleventh hour anticipating that our wish to hold the conference will force us to accept compromises at the last possible moment so it can be held." He urged the department to formulate contingency plans for the possibility that the deputies would not agree on draft treaties by 1 May. He favored American insistence on going ahead with the peace conference:

> I do think that we have to begin somewhere, sometime to carry out a policy of dealing with questions of importance to us in Europe on the basis of our own policy without waiting to be dragged around by the hair by some other nation and winding up by stultifying our own actions and finding that we are only carrying out the dictates of someone else's policy.

On 5 March Byrnes informed Dunn that he planned to call a meeting of the Council of Foreign Ministers on 15 April in order to speed up the preparation of the treaties and be ready for the peace conference 1 May.[13]

Byrnes made his decision to call a meeting of the Council of Foreign Ministers in the midst of the Iranian crisis and contingent this time on prior British approval. Bevin immediately objected to the meeting of foreign ministers until the Iranian issue was settled, and the secretary replied that he was "much disturbed" by Bevin's reaction but agreed to wait. Byrnes and Bevin agreed to insist in the interim on meeting the 1 May deadline. The secretary wired Dunn to "suggest to Couve de Murville advisability of French Government inquiring within next ten days through diplomatic channels rearrangements for conference, and thus making clear that French Government is also proceeding with intention to hold conference on schedule." The French obligingly complied, and Dunn, judging from Gusev's reaction, informed Byrnes of the likely Soviet response. Gusev held that the peace conference was not a peace conference but "a conference for the purpose of considering draft peace treaties," and "if no drafts were ready, a new situation had arisen which was not contemplated by the Moscow agreement."[14]

Byrnes also suggested to Dunn that work on the Balkan treaties be simultaneously carried on with the Italian treaty discussions, not only to speed up the proceedings but also "to have on record at this stage some indication of our willingness to consider Balkan treaties." Dunn replied that the Russian attitude toward the Rumanian draft "differs markedly" from the Italian because they now gave "the impression of being prepared to push ahead." But Dunn warned that the deputies would be unlikely to reach agreement on a Rumanian treaty that did not contain provisions confirming the special Russian position there. Since the Americans and British were not willing to do this, these meetings were again stymied. When a *New York Times* reporter asked a deputy if the crisis of world affairs affected their work, he replied, "Oh, no. We are living peacefully in our beautiful ivory tower. Nothing affects us and we hear only faint murmurs from the outside world. We see the same old familiar faces and talk about the same old familiar things day after day." The American delegation sent the State Department lyrics to the tune of "As Time Goes By": "A country can be an enemy. And still be an ally. This no one can deny. The issues are all still the same. As Time goes by. Arguments on minutes. Are never out of date. Shuffling with one's paper. While the other fellows wait. Repeating the same position. The progress isn't great. This no one can deny. As time goes by."[15] On 4 April, the day that the Soviet-Iranian agreement was announced, Byrnes wired London, Moscow, and Paris to suggest a 25 April meeting of the Council of Foreign Ministers and quickly secured consent. Altogether the deputies held thirty-nine meetings on the Italian draft, fifteen on the Balkans, prepared for their ministers a report on the treaty articles on which they agreed or nearly agreed, and wrote a statement of each nation's position on the unagreed articles. Dunn also prepared for Byrnes a summary of what he believed the Soviet attitude would be at the Paris meeting of the Council of Foreign Ministers. Dunn was

certain that the USSR would make the necessary concessions to allow the treaties to be concluded only if it could gain
specific advantages from the treaties. He also noted the
importance to the USSR of the effect the treaties would have
on Soviet relations with ex-enemy states and with the allied
nations. He said that Soviet treaty gains could come only
from the Italian treaty because the only acceptable Balkan
treaties would be the ones that confirmed the Soviet position
there. He thought that the Russians had given up hope for
Tripolitania, although they might still insist on a trusteeship
in order to gain bargaining power. The Soviet hopes for bases
in the Dodecanese, Dunn said, were still viable, but he did not
believe they would break off negotiations if they were
thwarted. He did not believe Moscow would accept an Italian
treaty that did not give it a share of the Italian navy,
substantial reparations, and an agreement on the Yugoslav-
Italian border acceptable to Yugoslavia.[16]

Armed with Dunn's realistic analysis, Byrnes was better
prepared for the Paris session of the Council of Foreign
Ministers than he had been for the London and Moscow
meetings. He sought to strengthen the American position by
deliberately creating a carrot-and-stick negotiating climate.
C. L. Sulzberger wrote in the *New York Times* on 17 April
that "all sorts of clearly 'planted' and 'inspired' stories have
been emanating from Washington" indicating that the
United States would pursue a "tough" policy in Paris. The
facets of the "tough" policy included American insistence
that Italy keep Trieste, that Greece get the Dodecanese, and
that no great power get colonies. In the midst of this press
campaign, Byrnes invited the Soviet government to begin
negotiating with the U.S. in May for a $1 billion loan from
the Export-Import Bank. Sulzberger commented that the
loan was the "bait" peeping from behind Byrnes's "smoke-
screen of tough talk." Other news stories stated that Byrnes
intended to stay in Paris as long as necessary in order to
avoid a time limit trap, because he and Bevin now agreed
that the 1 May peace conference was out of the realm of
possibilities. The press also believed that the secretary was
ready to risk failure of the Paris Conference rather than meet
Russian demands, and several news stories mentioned the

possibility of negotiating unilateral treaties if collaboration in peacemaking failed.[17]

As proof of the secretary's intentions, the press noted that Arthur Vandenberg, now a symbol of the tough policy toward Russia, and Senator Tom Connally, chairman of the Senate Foreign Affairs Committee, would accompany Byrnes to Paris. Byrnes had invited Vandenberg to Paris after the senator had complained that he would "take no further part in these State Department adventures" unless he was "'in' when and where decisions *were* really made." Harold Stassen had recently joked to Vandenberg that when the secretary of state goes "conferencing," Republicans want to be in on the take off, not just the crash landings. In response Byrnes promised Vandenberg that he would make no decisions in Paris without the senator's concurrence, and Vandenberg exulted to Dulles "Perhaps I *can* keep a bit of the good old iron in his backbone as you did at London."[18]

Joseph and Stewart Alsop reported another straw in the wind, a suggestion from Acheson and Will Clayton to Byrnes that he abandon his treaty-by-treaty negotiations in Paris and press for a general European settlement. The two diplomats wanted a regional U.N. Security Council to execute the settlement and an economic reconstruction organization financed by the United States, with the goal of both being to maintain European unity. Finally, the secretary decided to propose formally the twenty-five year German disarmament treaty and not to press the Soviet Union to include France in all the council discussions, as Bevin wanted to do because the meeting was being held in Paris.[19]

Byrnes made one other significant decision before flying to Paris: he decided to resign as secretary of state. He wrote later that a routine medical checkup on 12 April had revealed "additional myocardial damage," and his physician had recommended that he "avoid excessive mental and physical strain." The secretary said that he had decided then to write a letter of resignation and on 16 April delivered it personally to the president. He explained to Truman that he had dated his resignation 1 July in order to finish the Paris negotiations and to give the president time to choose a successor.

Acheson confirmed a part of Byrnes's version of his resignation. He too had decided to resign before Byrnes left for the Paris Conference because he feared more conflicts between Truman and Byrnes and did not want to be caught in the middle again. Byrnes, on receiving Acheson's letter of resignation, thought it a good idea if he too, for reasons of health, did the same thing. Byrnes then, according to Acheson, filed his own letter with the president but did not complicate matters by filing Acheson's. Truman remembered only that throughout 1946 "it was understood between him and me that he would quit whenever I could designate his successor," and he had, therefore, made immediate efforts to secure George Marshall as Byrnes's replacement.[20]

The Paris Conference of the Council of Foreign Ministers began at 5:00 p.m., 25 April 1946, at Luxembourg Palace, built 250 years earlier by Henry IV for his consort. Each delegation arrived separately and walked solemnly up the long red carpeted staircase lined with members of the Garde Republicaine saluting with drawn sabers. The delegates gathered around a replica of the large, round, green-covered table in the Grand Salle, with Vandenberg, Connally, and Bohlen seated with Byrnes. French Foreign Minister Georges Bidault, the youngest of the four ministers, opened the meeting and immediately won from Molotov what Byrnes called a "striking withdrawal" from the Soviet position: agreement that all four powers would discuss all five treaties. The problem that had been used to break up the London Conference was solved ostensibly because the Soviet Union did not want to hinder the efforts of the French Communist party in the upcoming elections. Since the foreign ministers did not agree on an agenda before arriving in Paris, their first heated, two-hour long disagreement came immediately after Bidault insisted that German issues be discussed and when Bevin refused to do so formally without the other interested Allied nations present. Byrnes was willing to discuss Germany informally but only if the Austrian treaty was also added to the agenda. Saying he was unprepared, Molotov flatly refused to discuss Austria, but again supported France, this time in its desire to discuss Germany. A unanimous agreement being impossible, the ministers agreed to begin with the Italian treaty issues and, then at Bidault's invitation, adjourned for champagne. The council went until its fourth meeting without an agenda because Bidault persistently called for a discussion of Germany. Finally, the ministers agreed to discuss the five peace treaties first and then Germany, with Byrnes reluctantly dropping the question of Austria.[21]

During the Italian treaty discussions, Molotov continued the Soviet demand for $300 million in reparations based on Italy's obligation to pay for damages caused, and Byrnes and Bevin continued to refuse, stressing Italy's inability to pay. Bidault, assuming the role of mediator between East and West which he would play throughout the conference, agreed with Molotov that Italy must pay reparations, but agreed with Byrnes and Bevin that Italy's capacity to pay must be considered. Bidault also continued his persistent advocacy of French interests by refusing to accept a list of countries due reparations that did not include France. When the ministers agreed to instruct the deputies to examine the extent of Italy's capacity to pay the claims made, first Bevin and then Byrnes insisted that British and American reparation claims be considered along with the French and the Soviet—a strategy, Vandenberg observed, which "will probably laugh the Soviet claim out of the conference." Actually, Molotov's strategy was not laughable because he told the council that "no decision on a treaty with Italy could be reached without a clear reply on the reparations question."[22]

The council fared little better in discussing disposition of Italian colonies, because each of the Big Four powers continued to suggest a different solution. The U.S. delegation still wanted a U.N. trusteeship with an appointed administrator, and the French still wanted Italy as trustee of her former colonies. In an attempt to harmonize the Soviet and French positions, Molotov suggested a collective trusteeship for each colony with an Allied power and Italy serving as joint trustees, e.g., the USSR and Italy administering Tripolitania. Bevin still preferred that Italy be stripped of her colonies, Libya (including both Tripolitania and Cyrenaica) be given immediate independence, and Ethiopian and

British claims to Eritrea and Italian Somaliland be considered. Although each minister argued his position at length, the impasse continued, and the council agreed to defer discussion until later. Molotov also forced a deferment of the Dodecanese issue, although he agreed with the others that these islands should be taken from Italy and ceded to Greece, but "under what conditions" remained to be settled. Bevin frankly asked Molotov if the Dodecanese were "a bargaining point," and Molotov replied that "that was a point worthy of attention."[23]

On the Italian-Yugoslav border issue, the Commission of Experts reported that after five weeks of investigation they could not reach a unanimous recommendation, but they had accumulated a wealth of information which the American expert, Philip Mosely, hoped would at least limit the controversy about what the facts were. Instead, Molotov used the commission's report as a rationale for hearing again the views of the Italian and Yugoslav governments on the information collected, admitting that the Soviets would be in a difficult position unless the council heard the views of Yugoslavia. Although Byrnes and Bevin objected at first to the delay involved, the council heard representatives from Italy and Yugoslavia on 3 May. Vandenberg correctly predicted that when the ministers discussed border solutions there would be "fireworks," because each of the four powers advocated a different line to separate Italy and Yugoslavia. After each minister unsuccessfully attempted to convince the others of the validity of his boundary, Byrnes suggested, since the British and French lines were largely in between the American and Soviet lines, that a compromise be reached approximating a combination of the British-French lines. Molotov refused and insisted on first deciding the disposition of Trieste. The other three ministers refused to cede Trieste to Yugoslavia as Molotov wanted, so Byrnes suggested a new approach, a plebiscite in the disputed area between the American and Soviet lines. Earlier Vandenberg had suggested to Byrnes to let the people of the area decide and "Byrnes leaped at the idea; but all our experts immediately said that a plebiscite would be fatal because well organized Communist minorities would control the plebiscite with a reign of terror."

Molotov was interested in a vote if the area could be enlarged, but both Bevin and Bidault opposed a plebiscite.[24]

As early as 28 April Byrnes decided to resort to a private meeting with Molotov in order to break the conference deadlock. He invited Molotov, his deputy minister Andrei Vishinsky, and his translator Vladimir Pavlov, Benjamin Cohen, and Charles Bohlen to dinner at his suite in the Meurice Hotel, former headquarters for German General Dietrich von Choltitz during the occupation of Paris. Molotov used the occasion to charge that American "actions were not those of a friend and that his government was the victim of an 'anti-Soviet campaign'" in which both the Iranian case and the Security Council were being used. Byrnes reminded Molotov that he had warned him in Moscow that he would support Iran in the United Nations, but Molotov went on to denounce Churchill's iron curtain speech. His tirade elicited a lecture from the mild-mannered, soft-spoken Cohen on Churchill's courage without which, he said, they would not be here now.[25]

Byrnes then said that Americans were confused about whether the aim of the Soviet Union was "to search for security or expansionism." To "effectively take care of the question of security," Byrnes again suggested a revolutionary departure from traditional American foreign policy, a twenty-five year treaty between the Allies to guarantee German disarmament. The idea of such a treaty had originated with James Reston who had convinced Senator Vandenberg of its efficacy before the war had ended. Vandenberg had first proposed the treaty in a 10 January 1945 speech; and Byrnes, before becoming secretary of state, asked Truman on 11 June 1945 to request the views of the State Department on a treaty "somewhat along the lines suggested by Senator Vandenberg." At the London Conference Byrnes had first mentioned the treaty possibility to Molotov who appeared interested and said that he would ascertain the response of Moscow. Hearing nothing more from Molotov, Byrnes next had raised the treaty question with Stalin at the end of the Moscow Conference and had believed Stalin was interested. Now, however, Molotov objected to the treaty on the grounds that it appeared to postpone disarmament when the Allies had already agreed to immediate disarmament.[26]

Although Byrnes was confused and discouraged by Molotov's response, he reintroduced the treaty with changes to meet Molotov's objections to the full council the next day. He told the council that its slow progress was due to a lack of confidence in each other. To change this, he said, the U.S. proposal would "guarantee that this time the United States was not going to leave Europe after the war." Vandenberg wrote that Molotov was "maddeningly obdurate, and refused even to understand the proposition." Molotov also refused to discuss the treaty until the council investigated present efforts to disarm Germany, especially the occupied British zone. Vandenberg told Vishinsky afterward that "life was simpler for me when I was an isolationist. Another couple of days of this and I'll be more isolationist than ever." Bevin, agreeing that the Russians had "badly received" the American proposal, registered his own surprise that Byrnes had announced the treaty because it had been communicated to Great Britain in "strictest confidence."[27]

Bidault suggested to Byrnes the next move to break the council's deadlock—small informal meetings. Byrnes approved, and so did the other ministers when Bidault suggested the change to them, but the first informal meeting exacerbated the existing tension instead of relieving it. Molotov began by stating the "direct connection" that the failure of the United States and Great Britain to fulfill their promise to recognize the Bulgarian government had on the peace treaties. He maintained that some of the experts working on reparations had received instructions not to reach a settlement, and Bevin retorted that Great Britain was growing accustomed to "similar unfounded accusations." In the midst of rising tempers, Bidault suggested a reparations compromise using Italian current production as the source but waiting until Italy no longer needed American and British relief; but Bevin and Byrnes objected on grounds that Italy needed first to repay British and American loans. Molotov replied that he was aware that American loans were being granted to Allied countries, but Italy was a defeated nation, and added flatly that "no decision on the peace treaty could be made unless the reparations question was settled." Byrnes responded that if that were the situation, "there would be no treaty." Vandenberg later said Byrnes first cleared this answer with him and Connally and that after making it, "Molotov immediately denied that he had said *what he did say*. In other words, when his bluff was called, he instantly backed water."[28]

The deterioration of diplomacy continued when Byrnes later in the meeting suggested using captured Italian warships as reparations, pointing out that this had been done to compensate Brazil. Molotov said that "it only remained to compare the losses suffered by the Soviet Union and Brazil and then everything would be clear." Bevin wanted to discuss the Dodecanese but said he was sure the Soviets would not allow it. Molotov did refuse to discuss the Dodecanese and the "selfish" British proposal for Italian colonies and maintained that "England wishes to keep all the Italian colonies for herself." Bevin responded that that "was a strange statement for a representative of a country which by its own admission covered one-seventh of the earth's surface." Molotov retorted that "this area had been acquired legally," to which Bevin replied it was also secured "through the medium of secret treaties and that perhaps England had made a mistake not to conclude similar arrangements during the war." The meeting ended with that exchange. Byrnes and Truman engaged in a teletype conversation that evening, which was the secretary's sixty-seventh birthday. The president approved Byrnes's stand, saying, "Do everything you can to continue but in the final analysis do whatever you think is right and tell them to go to hell if you have to." Truman suggested the tactic of a recess for the ministers "to consult with their governments if Molotov refuses to work with you under existing conditions."[29]

On 5 May Molotov invited Byrnes to dinner and suggested a "trade" by which Yugoslavia would be favored in the Italian border settlement in exchange for its renunciation of all its claims for reparations, with Greece doing the same in exchange for the Dodecanese. When Byrnes immediately refused, Molotov and Vishinsky made what Byrnes believed to be "obvious propaganda charges" that the U.S. was engaged in a policy of "'imperialist expansion'" with references to its bases in Iceland, troops in North China, and its desire to obtain bases in Turkey, Egypt, Iran, and elsewhere. Byrnes vigorously pointed out the "complete absurdity of these charges" and left. Interestingly, Byrnes then had Connally ask Vandenberg if he thought Trieste could be traded as Molotov suggested. Vandenberg said no. A member of the Russian delegation complained to Bohlen that since the Americans were supposed to be the world's greatest traders, they should trade on Trieste. Bohlen replied, "perhaps a little pompously," that the United States would never trade with the fate of human beings. The next morning Molotov repeated his offer to the other ministers in a second informal meeting and, when Bevin refused, reiterated his charges of imperialism. Molotov said, "It is sufficient to say that England has troops and military bases in Greece, Denmark, Egypt, Iraq, Indonesia, and elsewhere." Bevin responded that "he hoped now that Mr. Molotov had gotten that off his chest, he felt better," and another meeting was adjourned.[30]

The ministers decided at this juncture, as they had earlier decided during the impasse in London, to take up the Balkan treaties. But, as with the Italian draft, agreement was still impossible on the same issues that they had been unable to settle in London. These included a commission on the Danube, equality of economic opportunity clauses, and troop withdrawals. Bevin and Byrnes introduced a new controversial subject by suggesting that Russian reparations demands on Hungary be lowered. The Soviet and British delegations, however, did reach agreement on the Finnish treaty.[31]

Deadlocked then on both the Italian and Balkan treaties, the Council of Foreign Ministers, not too optimistically, turned to the convocation of the peace conference. Byrnes suggested that the deputies prepare a statement of matters on which there was agreement and matters on which there was still disagreement to submit to the peace conference on 15 June. Molotov agreed that a report from the deputies on the status of the draft treaties would be helpful, but insisted that according to the Moscow agreement the draft treaties must be prepared before a conference was convoked. Bevin argued that the word used in the Moscow agreement was "completed," not "agreed on." Bidault, "not entirely disillusioned" by their lack of progress, suggested that the council continue to resolve its outstanding disagreements, then adjourn to let the deputies work toward an accord, and reconvene around 15 June with the prior commitment to set a date for the peace conference. The other ministers were in general agreement with this plan, but Byrnes wanted to set a date for the peace conference immediately, preferably 1 or 15 July. Molotov agreed to either date, but stipulated that the draft treaties must be completed first. Bevin said that "they had to face it, that if any one of them didn't agree on a treaty, the Peace Conference would never be held." And still another session ended on a dismal note.[32]

The logjam began to break that evening, 10 May 1946, when the Soviet delegation announced that they would now accept the French colonial plan for an Italian trusteeship. Bevin immediately agreed to Tripolitania being under Italian control but wanted Cyrenaica, where most of the Senussi tribesmen lived, under a British trusteeship. Byrnes was willing to accept the French plan if a ten-year time limit was invoked. Bidault ended this moment of concord by refusing to accept a temporary Italian trusteeship but soon afterwards accepted the Soviet demand for $100 million in reparations from Italy's current production given a two-year moratorium. Byrnes also agreed to the $100 million figure provided it was drawn from capital war-making machinery, Italian assets in the Balkans, surplus naval vessels, and two Italian merchant vessels. Molotov was dubious about the value of the capital equipment and Italy's foreign assets and refused outright to accept naval vessels as reparations. Vandenberg optimistically wrote in his diary following this reparations exchange that "this is obviously the easiest point at which to make some concessions to Molotov." Bevin, reflecting Vandenberg's confidence, reported to Attlee that the deadlock might be broken.[33]

Byrnes told Vandenberg before the next meeting that "it was time to bring things to a head" and informed the other ministers that he was "more optimistic in view of the progress that had been made in the last twenty-four hours." It was Molotov, however, who again moved the council toward agreement, although in Vandenberg's view Byrnes "held Molotov's feet to the 'fire' in an attempt to do so." Molotov said that agreement was necessary only on "fundamental questions" before a peace conference could be called and maintained that there were no fundamental questions left unsettled in the Balkan treaties. Molotov wanted a settlement on Italian reparations and Trieste before fixing a conference date and bluntly pointed out that "the Soviet Government had made a big concession concerning the Italian colonies" and "that he hoped that this concession was correctly understood." Apparently it was not, because Byrnes presented a new colonial solution: a one-year period in which the Big Four powers would administer Italy's colonies and try to agree on a permanent arrangement, and if they failed, turn the issue over to the United Nations. Bidault said he believed this "appeared to reverse the trend toward solution," and Molotov called the American plan "a disappointment." But when discussion turned to the Yugoslav-Italian frontier, Byrnes announced his acceptance of the French line and so did Bevin.[34]

Despite these obvious advances, Byrnes decided to call Washington that night and arrange transportation home. He also showed Vandenberg a motion for adjournment that he planned to use the next day, 14 May, "after a conclusive and final demonstration that we are deadlocked for the time being." Accordingly, Byrnes proposed, as Bidault had earlier, that after discussing Germany, the council adjourn until 15 June and that they now schedule the peace conference for 1 or 15 July. The ministers agreed to discuss Germany and after doing so Byrnes suggested that special deputies be appointed to begin preparation of draft treaties for Germany and Austria. Though Molotov refused saying "May God help us to complete the work on the treaties which are now before us," he did agree to the American request to revise the Italian armistice terms so that the Italian government could function independently. The ministers finally decided to end their present meeting, to leave the deputies working in Paris, and to reconvene 15 June without setting a prior date for the peace conference.[35]

Bevin and Bidault disagreed with the manner in which Byrnes ended the conference. The British wanted to establish Trieste, not the peace conference, as the cause of the deadlock, and Bidault was irritated with the "cavalier way" Byrnes had suggested that Germany could be settled in one session. The cordial relations between Bevin and Bidault, established out of shared anger, resulted in Bevin's reporting to the cabinet that "we can have anything we wished of France. If we wanted an alliance tomorrow, we could have it."[36]

The second session of the Council of Foreign Ministers ended after nineteen days on 16 May, with Vandenberg complaining that "it took two sessions today to make the disagreement plain and to fix the responsibility." Byrnes returned to Washington 19 May and spent two hours with President Truman discussing the conference. He had supplied the president with an immediate summary of each meeting in Paris and had communicated directly with him by phone and teletype. In a radio report to the American people the next evening, Byrnes stressed first the bipartisan nature of United States foreign policy and then the firmness of the American position. "We must not try to impose our will on others," he said, "but we must make sure that others do not get the impression they can impose their will on us." He characterized the progress made in Paris as "disappointingly small" and, in frankly detailing the disagreements over the Italian treaty, even stated that the Soviet representative would have traded a favorable settlement on reparations, colonies, and the Dodecanese for a Yugoslav-controlled Trieste. Agreement on the Balkan treaties, Byrnes said, was blocked by Soviet "refusal to permit the countries of Eastern Europe to open their gates to the commerce of all nations." Byrnes flatly stated for the first time publicly that if the Council of Foreign Ministers would not call a peace conference for the coming summer the United States would ask the U.N. to assume responsibility for the peace treaties. He also warned the Soviet Union that "the quest for security may lead to less rather than more security in the world," but ended on a more conciliatory and optimistic note: "Our problems are serious, but I am not discouraged."[37]

Vandenberg supported Byrnes before the Senate, to the press, and in his private correspondence. The senator had been primarily concerned in Paris that the United States should "demonstrate that the 'appeasement' days are over," and quite soon became convinced that "Byrnes gives every evidence of 'no more appeasement.'" At one point, bored with the negotiations, facing an election in Michigan, and wanting to participate in important Senate hearings, he had considered leaving Paris early "as I am sure Byrnes will make no major surrenders." After the Paris Conference Vandenberg said Byrnes "did a magnificent courageous and constructive job" and paid him a high compliment: "Paris was Munich in reverse." Though he had characterized Byrnes's diplomacy as "able" and "distinguished," in Paris he seems to have worried about Byrnes improvisations. He wrote, "Our delegation has ceased even to be 'briefed' on the day's work. Byrnes runs it catch-as-catch-can." He considered this "exceedingly dangerous," and said, "He makes too many moves on the impulse of the moment. He gives me the feeling that he improvises as he goes along."[38]

In contrast, both Vandenberg and Connally came to admire Molotov's negotiating skill. Vandenberg reluctantly wrote, "I confess that I admire the way Molotov argues tenaciously for his positions." Connally characterized Molotov as "cordial and friendly," but when it came to a final showdown on an issue, he didn't give an inch more than he believed necessary. "Certainly, he is one of the ablest diplomats I have ever known." A high French official, whose views were known to Vandenberg, also commented favorably on Molotov, and maintained that "the only concessions in the Conference were made by Molotov." The Frenchman believed Byrnes went to Paris "determined not to make the slightest actual concession," giving the "impression of a clever politician determined not to give an inch but anxious to convince the public that he was trying to reach an agreement despite Russian stubbornness." He noted that "Neither Byrnes nor Bevin tried to find out how far the Russians would go toward compromise but spent their time trying to put the onus for the deadlock on the Russians. Byrnes seemed more interested in convincing the Russians that the sucker season was ended, and that henceforth the Americans would be tough."[39]

Neither Vandenberg's complimentary "no appeasement" appraisal of the Paris negotiations nor the French official's uncomplimentary intransigent analysis exactly fitted the facts. True, Molotov, as even Vandenberg saw, "was in a 'trading mood.' He constantly referred—day after day—to the fact that he had made a 'big concession' (namely Tripolitania) and what was he going to get in return. He asked that question a hundred times." Byrnes, in an early Paris conversation with Bidault, also mentioned that "American opinion was no longer disposed to make concessions on important questions." Byrnes told Bidault that "he had been subjected to considerable criticism for 'appeasing' Russia and yielding too much. This period, however, had passed." Byrnes said "he had been very much impressed with the way opinion had rallied behind" his tough stand on Iran. But as Senator William Fulbright had said earlier in 1945, "To be tough or soft toward a nation is not a policy."[40]

Byrnes's proven talent to harmonize conflicting positions did not go unused in Paris, but the political necessity of juggling Truman's and the American public's demands under the watchdog eyes of Vandenberg and the press, tested him as the Congress and the Office of War Mobilization had not. His new tough foreign policy of necessity had a quid pro quo base, but Molotov was first to make significant concessions on Tripolitania, the French colonial plan, the Dodecanese, and Italian reparations. Apparently unnoticed by Vandenberg and the French official, Byrnes quickly moved to an amended French colonial plan, to the Soviet reparations demand, and to the French line as a Yugoslav-Italian border. The Paris Conference of the Council of Foreign Ministers paradoxically was both the most successful and the must unsuccessful meeting the ministers had held since the end of the war. With concessions by Molotov and Byrnes, the diplomats successfully moved closer to negotiating treaties they all could accept.[41]

But with the increasingly hostile American attitude toward the Soviet Union and with the Soviets reciprocating with shrill propagandistic rhetoric, the foreign ministers created a tense, suspicious climate which was not conducive to diplomacy. Perhaps most unfortunate of all, the United States and the Soviet Union emerged from the Paris talks publicly pitted against each other. Earlier, Moscow had saved its sharpest attacks for the British, but beginning in 1946 the United States became a preeminent capitalist enemy. Even in his 20 May broadcast, Byrnes described the negotiations in terms of the Soviet position and the American position. Vandenberg wrote, "Except for the Soviets, the rest of us could have *agreed* on *everything* in six days." These assessments overlooked the fact that the British and the French had positions on many issues that were in conflict with the United States and in agreement with the Soviet Union, but the assessments were indicative of the emerging polarization of the Russians and the Americans. In Paris Byrnes's new approach to foreign policy forced him to operate on two levels, public intransigence and private diplomacy. How long he could walk this international tightrope remained to be seen.[42]

CHAPTER FIVE

THE PARIS CONFERENCE OF THE COUNCIL OF FOREIGN MINISTERS SECOND SESSION
15 June–12 July 1946

During the Paris recess of the Council of Foreign Ministers, Joseph Davies wrote that "Relations between Russia, Britain, and the United States are at their lowest ebb." Molotov, replying in kind to Byrnes's report to the nation on the council's lack of progress, had presented each issue from the Soviet perspective as the secretary had done from the American. "The so-called 'peace offensive' proclaimed in certain American circles boils down in some cases simply to a desire to impose the will of two governments upon the government of a third state," Molotov said. He characterized Byrnes's proposal to turn peacemaking over to the United Nations as contrary to the Potsdam and the Moscow agreements and accused him of using "methods of pressure, threats and intimidation." The new American ambassador to the Soviet Union, Walter Bedell Smith, talked to Molotov about his comments on the Paris Conference and advised Byrnes that the Soviet diplomat "did not intend to withdraw or compromise." Smith concluded, "I judge that the honeymoon is over." Bevin agreed with Byrnes that "we must devise an alternative method" to writing the peace treaties if the Council of Foreign Ministers deadlocked again, "as we cannot afford to be bound any more by a procedure that has failed." The foreign secretary warned Byrnes that "in our choice of methods we are up against a very difficult decision which may have incalculable consequences." The "showdown" which Bevin preferred was calling the peace conference without Russian cooperation because this "might be more expedient and easier to justify" than consulting the United Nations, "many of whom took no part in the fighting." The British and Americans also exchanged views on the feasibility of bilateral peace treaties but did not agree on a common solution.[1]

Byrnes left for Paris on 14 June on the presidential plane, the *Sacred Cow.* Truman underscored the importance of the second session of the Paris Conference, which the *New York Times* referred to as "the last call to the Conference table," by seeing off the American delegation at the airport. Vandenberg and Connally again accompanied the secretary, although Vandenberg suggested during the recess that the senator's presence might not be required this time. Byrnes insisted, and Vandenberg agreed to return when "it became obvious that my absence at this recessed meeting would be misinterpreted."[2]

Vandenberg described the atmosphere at the opening session of the Council of Foreign Ministers on 15 June as "tense." The tension derived in part from intelligence received by Byrnes that the Soviet Union had approved Yugoslavia's seizing control of Trieste if the council did not reach a favorable settlement at this conference. The presumed Soviet plan was for Yugoslavia to enter Trieste after "'spontaneous' demonstrations resulting in prearranged riots" in Italy and Greece had supplied the "pretext." Smith in Moscow confirmed that the Soviets seemed "to be engaged at least in old-fashioned eastern European maneuver of show of force" because "Russia is very sensitive to what it considers to be western underestimation of its strength." The American ambassador to France, Jefferson Caffery, added that French officials were pessimistic about the success of the council because "the Russians were giving the impression of being more intransigent than at the last meeting, although this may be part of devious Russian maneuver designed to soften up opposition for bargaining purposes."[3]

At the first council meeting Molotov appeared to set the stage for Yugoslav action when he described the political situation in Italy as "extremely acute," given Italian dissatisfaction with their recent election abolishing the monarchy. He ominously mentioned the "direct threat of civil war" in Italy and wanted the council to add an examination of the political situation in Italy to its agenda by inviting the Italian government to present its views on those questions. The British and the American delegations assumed that these were delaying tactics, and Bevin, leading the resistance, declared that it would be a "great mistake" for the council to consult with "a belligerent country" when the council had yet "to consult with the Allied nations who fought against Italy." The ministers, nevertheless, agreed to proceed with their previous agenda of the five treaties and German questions after Molotov had gained the addition of the Italian political situation by agreeing himself to discuss Austria. The council did not invite Italy to present its views, but Bidault called the settlement of "the question of the agenda in record time" a "favorable augury for future work."[4]

Ambassador Smith suggested an alternative interpretation of Soviet strategy at the Paris Conference a few days later. He believed that the Russians were "quite as anxious as we are to avoid a complete breakup" of the Council of Foreign Ministers and that they might need time "to make the changes of position which with them are the essential preliminary to any compromise." He suggested that the Soviet Union planned "to pose as defender of Italian sovereignty and independence against the imperialistic designs of British and United States" by stressing the "Italian contribution to the victory over Germany" and that "this trend, given time to develop, may preface a less rigid attitude on Trieste."[5]

Molotov proved Smith correct when he continued to recommend that Italy present its views on different questions before the council and to take a more lenient attitude toward Italy on treaty issues. When the ministers discussed the disposition of Italian property in Allied states, for example, Molotov suggested that only one-third of this property be held for payment of claims against Italy and that the remaining two-thirds be returned to it. This left Bevin in the awkward position of insisting that all Italian property in

Great Britain was needed to liquidate claims and debts. Molotov was free to observe that "Mr. Bevin was always pleased when he saw that he was likely to obtain something." Again, when the council discussed the length of the period during which Italy would be subjected to the economic provisions of the treaty, Molotov suggested only one year, but Great Britain wanted two years and the United States three. Molotov successfully compromised at eighteen months and pointed out that "all delegations were anxious to ease Italy's situation." Even on the subject of reparations, he managed to champion Italy by maintaining that the amount Britain would receive from Italian property in England and in damage claims within Italy would equal the Soviet claims for $100 million. He suggested that "it would be well if Great Britain did not regard Italy as its colony" and that Italy's "tremendous expenses in maintaining the British army of occupation" be reduced so that Italy could pay "the Soviet moderate claims."[6]

This maneuvering, accompanied by restatement of positions, continued for the first five days of meetings. Then on 20 June, again at Bidault's suggestion, the ministers met informally. The French provisional president and foreign minister wanted the meeting to be "really informal" with only the four ministers and two interpreters present, but when Byrnes insisted that Vandenberg and Connally attend, each of the other ministers came accompanied by two advisers and an interpreter. Bevin and Bidault wanted the discussions "kept secret and confined to those present," but again Byrnes said that "he could not undertake any commitment in regard to the U.S. Press not to answer questions concerning the position of the U.S. at these meetings."[7]

During the discussion of the Italian colonies, Byrnes returned to the original American proposal of a U.N. trusteeship with a neutral administrator, but as a concession to the French, with no certainty of independence at the end of ten years. Both Molotov and Bevin preferred the last American proposal, namely that Italy renounce sovereignty to the Four Powers, which would have a year to reach agreement on a permanent solution, but if they failed to do so, would refer the question to the U.N. When Bidault reluctantly concurred, Byrnes reintroduced that proposal, and the resulting agreement to consider a temporary solution to the colonial problem became the conference's first success. Molotov wanted an advisory commission representing the Four Powers to administer the colonies during the year's interim, but Bevin refused to allow any change in the present British and French military occupation until the council reached a permanent decision. The British delegation did approve a commission in the colonies to study the problem during the year and to report its recommendations to the ministers. Although Bevin believed that he was "taking a risk" in binding Britain to an eventual U.N. decision, given the unlikelihood of council agreement, he considered the risk preferable to a diplomatic breakdown. A few days later Vishinsky told Cohen "that he was not very much concerned about the colonial question now," and on 3 July Molotov agreed to both a temporary plan and to continued British and French administration. The Soviet foreign minister added that he made "concessions in this matter in the hope" that the council would reciprocate on the question of reparations to the Soviet Union.[8]

The council frustrated Molotov's hope for a reparations settlement for several more weeks. Byrnes had informed his deputy during the conference recess that the department "feels that no more concessions to Soviet viewpoint on reparations should be made," and he continued his earlier stance of agreeing to the $100 million figure only if the money came from the sources he specified and not from Italian current production. Bevin's return to the original British stand that Great Powers should not receive reparations from Italy led to a long discussion between the Soviet and British delegates as to whether Italy would suffer more by having Britain seize her foreign assets permanently or by paying the Soviet Union for damages caused by making deliveries from current production for only six years. Molotov finally suggested that "Italy be asked which claims would be easier to fulfill." Byrnes interrupted to ask "whether he could insert a few words in the private conversation between Mr. Molotov and Mr. Bevin" and brought the discussion back to the proposal of the United States. Molotov insisted that the reparations sources advocated by Byrnes totaled only half the amount the Soviet Union demanded and that the difference would have to come from current production. Byrnes offered to make up the difference with Italian warships that the United States had captured, but Molotov characterized these ships as war booty that the Potsdam Conference declared could not be used as reparations.[9]

Byrnes eventually tied settlement of reparations to the Trieste issue and told Molotov that "if we could settle Trieste, the other questions would not be too difficult." This decision had come out of a two-hour session which the American delegation had held on 21 June. According to Vandenberg, they were attempting "to figure out the irreducible minimum of concessions (not of 'principle,' but *within* 'principle') which would be possible if Molotov would show any disposition to bargain." Although Byrnes did not reveal it to Molotov for four more days, the delegation had decided that they would accept "deferred reparations" from current Italian production if the USSR would supply Italy with raw materials from which finished goods could be made.[10]

The council began its discussion of Trieste and the Yugoslav-Italian border in an informal session, with Bidault pointing out "that they were confronted with two choices: either to repeat the old positions, or to make an attempt to find some new solution." The ministers chose to repeat their old positions, but when they finished, Bidault "put forward without enthusiasm" the recommendation that an international regime under the U.N. be created for a designated part of the disputed area including Trieste for a certain period of time. The Frenchman added that "this was not a preferred solution but we should think of the consequences of a failure to agree on this question." The ministers unenthusiastically agreed to discuss the idea; and Bidault, asking that its origin be kept secret, said, "not a word to the Queen Mother," but he added that "if this idea found favor they would not deny its origin, but if it was not to be accepted it was best to say nothing about it."[11]

That evening Molotov dined with Byrnes and made what the secretary said was apparently a final effort to obtain

Trieste for Yugoslavia. Byrnes ended their conversation by saying that since the United States could not agree to transfer Trieste to Yugoslavia, and apparently the Soviet government could not agree that it should remain with Italy, they should consider Bidault's proposal and turn the issue over to the peace conference or look for another alternative. The American delegation had already decided at their earlier strategy meeting to accept an international solution for Trieste, and it was soon advised by the American ambassador to France that "the French had several indirect indications that, in the final analysis, the Soviets might agree to some form of internationalization."[12]

On 24 June Molotov came to Byrnes's suite at the Hotel Meurice to say that he might accept U.N. participation "if in advance" he had reason to believe that such a decision would "facilitate the solution of other questions." After receiving Byrnes's assurances, Molotov suggested declaring the Trieste area an autonomous district under Yugoslav sovereignty but with an international statute. Byrnes told Molotov that his proposal differed considerably from the French but he would consider it. The next afternoon Byrnes met privately again with Molotov for another round of what Byrnes called "position sounding." He began by saying that the United States could not accept the transfer of Trieste to Yugoslav control "either openly or in disguised form," and Molotov responded that he would accept "extreme measures provided they could reach agreement on other questions." "If they could settle Trieste," Byrnes told Molotov for the third time, "the United States Delegation was prepared to modify its views on reparations." Byrnes then offered to agree that deliveries from Italian current production could make up the difference in reparations on the condition that the USSR provided Italy with raw materials. Molotov next asked that if agreement were reached on the treaties, would the United States then sign all five, including the one with Bulgaria. When Byrnes replied that he saw no difficulty in doing that, Molotov said he was "prepared to take another extreme step" and proposed dual Italian and Yugoslav sovereignty over the Trieste area with one Italian governor and one Yugoslav governor. Byrnes dismissed this idea as "impracticable"— not really a settlement but a constant source of conflict"—

and pressured Molotov by returning to his former stand in favor of the French line as the Italian-Yugoslav border. Molotov went ahead and presented his dual sovereignty plan to the other ministers and added the threat that Yugoslavia might refuse to sign a treaty that did not give her Trieste. When the other ministers remained unconvinced and refused to agree on any of the other alternatives, Bevin complained that "the procedure of this conference was not to decide anything." Molotov replied that "Bevin should not underestimate his services in helping to produce that result."[13]

As at all the other conferences of the Council of Foreign Ministers, once an impasse had been soundly established the ministers took up the Balkan treaties. They repeated their arguments on the Danube and on equal economic opportunity in Eastern Europe, with Bevin increasing the tension of the meeting by remarking that "he could not help having certain suspicions as to what lay behind the Soviet attitude." Then in the middle of a three and a half hour long meeting, Molotov thanked Bevin for agreeing to a Soviet proposal to dispose of Rumanian assets in allied nations, and Bevin replied that "he had been trying to set an example to Mr. Molotov in the hope that the latter would come up to it some day." This, apparently, was the day, because the meeting ended with what Vandenberg described as a breathless round of agreements. The ministers completed the Hungarian treaty, decided the size of the Bulgarian navy (one ship), settled the Franco-Italian border, and agreed to a Rumanian renunciation of claims provision, which was sponsored by the French but used the language of the American proposal. Byrnes said that this "indicated the existence of a French-American bloc," and Molotov responded that "the bloc was being joined by the Soviet Union" because he accepted the proposal.[14]

As a joke, Byrnes suggested that "they make it a good afternoon and settle the question of the Dodecanese." Slowly puffing his cigarette and smiling, Molotov surprised the ministers by saying that he had no objection. Bevin in disbelief asked him if he agreed that Greece should receive the islands, and he said that he did. Byrnes asked for a minute or two to recover. Vandenberg wrote in his diary that evening, "Everybody is speculating tonight as to what it means. Have we won our point? Has Molotov decided, at long last, that we do mean what we say? Is he now prepared to go along? Or is he building up what he will call Russia's cumulative 'surrenders' (on relatively minor issues) in order to make the world think it is our fault if the Council breaks down over final disagreements on the major issues?"[15]

The Council of Foreign Ministers made no more progress until 29 June when Bidault attempted again to resolve the intricate problem of Trieste. He suggested that Italy and Yugoslavia participate with the Four Powers under the U.N. in the administration of the free territory of Trieste and that Italy and Yugoslavia share in naming the governor of the area. Bidault said that if they failed to agree on a governor, the Four Powers could do so. Molotov agreed to consider this new proposal but clearly intended to gain more for Yugoslavia than what was offered. The bargaining tactic that the Russian diplomat began to use—as Byrnes was using reparations to gain a Trieste settlement—was a postponement of the peace conference for which Byrnes had continued to campaign. Byrnes again found himself in a time bind, because the U.N. session was scheduled for 1 September 1946. He feared that the peace conference would not have enough time to complete its work if it met later than 20 July, and he continued to press hard for it, in spite of Molotov's insistence that the Moscow declaration provided for the treaty drafts to be finished before the conference convened. Byrnes said that the Moscow agreements "appeared to be sacred" only when in reference to the treaties, but not when it came to convening the peace conference on 1 May, nor when they provided that France should not participate in the drafting of Balkan treaties. Molotov had agreed to submit to the peace conference unsettled matters like Italian reparations to Yugoslavia and Greece and Bulgarian reparations to Yugoslavia and Greece, and this did not violate the Moscow agreements, so Byrnes therefore asked why could not other unsettled issues such as reparations to the Soviet Union and Trieste also be settled by the peace conference? The answer, obviously, was that the Soviet Union did not want them to.[16]

The second session of the Paris Council of Foreign Ministers reached a negotiating standoff at this juncture. Molotov could delay the peace conference, and Byrnes could postpone a reparations settlement. Trieste became the expendable issue and was the first of these three issues to be settled. Vishinsky sought out Ben Cohen again on 30 June to see if the Americans would accept the Soviet line as the Yugoslav-Italian border if Trieste were internationalized. Cohen replied negatively and insisted on the French line, so Vishinsky turned to reparations. He said the Soviet delegation was disappointed that Byrnes had not mentioned Italian current production in the regular council meetings, because the reparations issue was the problem concerning the Soviets most. At the next council meeting Molotov agreed to the French proposal on Trieste but attempted to get a border in between the Soviet and French lines. Bevin announced that now "they had the bull by the horns;" but Byrnes immediately noticed that the new Soviet line "cut the port off from its shipyards, it severed the city from its water supply, and placed its power transformers in Yugoslavia." Bidault then announced that "he had become accustomed to sacrificing himself in attempts to arrive at compromises" and that at the "risk of irritating everybody" he would "make an improvised proposal." Bidault suggested that Yugoslavia get everything east of the French line and the bulk of the territory west of the line be incorporated into the Trieste territory. After a period of silence, Molotov asked that "the Council accept, without amendment, the proposal made by Mr. Bidault." As Vandenberg later wrote, "He took Byrnes and Bevin by complete surprise;" and the two Western ministers asked first for a recess and later asked that discussion be postponed for a day.[17]

The American delegation speculated that Bidault had "cooked up this 'compromise' in advance agreement" with Molotov when the two had met privately the day before, but Bidault denied collusion. Byrnes and Cohen used the intervening time to convince Vandenberg that the Trieste proposal, with changes, was viable. After four hours of discussion Vandenberg agreed and personally typed the amendments Byrnes would suggest first to Molotov and then to the council. The secretary told Molotov that both the Yugoslavs and Italians had let it be known that they opposed internationalization, so he wanted the ministers to accept the French line as the border and let the peace conference decide what area, if any, on the Italian side should be internationalized. Molotov responded that "he did not know what Mr. Byrnes wanted" because he had accepted the French line and the international plan at Byrnes's suggestion and with the understanding that then "all other questions could be settled in twenty-four hours." The Russian diplomat opposed sending the issue to the conference on grounds that it "would cause great friction and set big powers off against little powers." Nonetheless, Byrnes presented his proposal to the full council, and they agreed to it. The decision of the Council of Foreign Ministers on Trieste was to establish a free territory with a democratic government under the supervision of the U.N. The Security Council, after consulting with Italy and Yugoslavia, would appoint a governor for the area. The other details of the permanent statute would await recommendations from the peace conference.[18]

The Trieste compromise left the council facing the problems of reparations and a date for the peace conference, and Molotov immediately made the setting of a conference date dependent on a reparations settlement. Byrnes argued, in a tactic worthy of Molotov, that the peace conference was next on the agenda, followed by Germany, and that a date should be set before they discussed the reparations issue. Molotov then began to suggest dates much later than the one Byrnes wanted and used the September U.N. meeting as his rationale. Byrnes said that when this question of the date was settled, he would agree to add the question of reparations to the agenda ahead of all other issues. Molotov then argued that the treaty drafts would not be prepared until the reparations question was decided, so a date could not be set. Bidault suggested settling both issues simultaneously or agreeing to discuss both at the next meeting, but Byrnes, joined by Bevin, insisted on a conference date first. Bidault said that he "could not work miracles everyday," and the meeting adjourned. Vandenberg wrote afterwards, "If the

Ruskies think *I* am 'tough' I wonder what they thought of Byrnes tonight."[19]

When the council convened the next day—"another important Fourth of July," as Vandenberg said—Bidault suggested that they adjourn their formal session for an informal meeting in his office with only the ministers and their interpreters attending. The French foreign minister wanted a settlement on both issues, 29 July for the conference date, and $100 million in reparations for the Soviet Union. Byrnes immediately argued that this would give "the appearance of being forced into an agreement in order to secure a peace conference." He said that he could not "bring any new approach to the reparations problem if it was to be discussed under threat of a refusal to call a peace conference." Molotov said that "there was no question of any threat," that he only "expected reciprocity of treatment." Byrnes insisted that Bidault's proposal "would be interpreted as a deal," and Bevin added that he "could not defend his position in Parliament if he went out of this room with the implications that he had bought a peace conference for $100,000,000 from the Soviet Union." Molotov cleverly said that "this exchange of views left him with the impression that there was no basic objection to the Soviet claims and that if he were correct in this he would not object to taking up, first, at the regular session the date of the peace conference and then reparations, with the expectation that both would be settled today." Byrnes replied that he "was most happy" to hear this and that he "was prepared to stay in session until the reparations question was settled." The ministers reconvened in formal session, and, as Byrnes said, "in five minutes" decided on 29 July as the date for the peace conference. The American secretary of state had bought himself a peace conference.[20]

Byrnes immediately submitted a new reparations proposal that he had with him all along. He proposed acceptance of the $100 million figure with Italian current production made from the Soviet raw materials making up the difference in value derived from factory and tool equipment, Italian assets in the USSR, the Balkans and the Soviet Zone of Germany, and two Italian merchant vessels. The American plan also specified a three-year moratorium on payment and a six-year limit on fulfilling the reparation demand. There followed a six-hour debate that convinced Vandenberg that Byrnes had not bought the peace conference in the secret session. Molotov accepted the American proposal as a basis for discussion but wanted no moratorium, replacement of Italian assets in the USSR, Hungary, and in the Soviet Zone in Germany with Italian assets in Finland, and removal of the two ships as reparations. Molotov also objected to the Soviet Union's supplying Italy with raw materials. Bevin unsuccessfully suggested a two-year moratorium and an eight-year delivery period, and Byrnes a two-year moratorium and a six-year delivery period. Exasperated, the British foreign secretary shouted, "Whenever one tried to satisfy the Soviets it was found to be impossible." Byrnes told Molotov that supply of raw materials was the most important issue to him and "if Mr. Molotov would agree to that, then the question of the moratorium was not important." Finally Molotov did, and the ministers settled on a two-year moratorium and a delivery period of seven years. The Council of Foreign Ministers had settled their last outstanding issue, but, before they could relax or adjourn, Molotov created another. He told the ministers that China could not cosponsor the peace conference with them and that the council needed to agree on rules of procedure for the conference to follow.[21]

Byrnes later wrote, "We expected that the invitations would be issued the next day, but we grossly underestimated the resourceful stubbornness of Mr. Molotov." Molotov refused to allow invitations to the peace conference to be sent until the council established rules for the conference, and he used the exclusion of China from sponsorship of the conference as a bargaining point. Byrnes found himself in a weak position because he had lost his leverage against Molotov with the settlement of the reparations issue. Perhaps because of this, the ministers returned to the bitter wrangling of the first Paris session. Bohlen believed that Molotov had made a serious mistake in not securing agreement to procedural rules to protect Russia's minority position at the conference before agreeing to a conference date and that instructions had come from Moscow to remedy this situation. The American interpreter noticed that Vishinsky enjoyed Molotov's discomfiture as he struggled to secure agreement to a procedure which the other ministers believed they had the right only to suggest to the conference, not to dictate.[22]

Rather brazenly, Molotov couched his desire to impose rules in terms of preventing the conference from becoming a "rubber stamp." Vandenberg said Molotov's "utterly transparent performance" had everyone except the Soviet delegation laughing out loud. Byrnes said that there would be no danger of having the "rubber stamp theory" attributed to the Council of Foreign Ministers if they said nothing about the organization of the conference and its rules of procedure. Molotov managed to hold up the issuance of the invitations for four days after the council had publicly announced the date of the conference, placing them, Bevin said, "in a state of humiliation." Bohlen wrote that after a dinner break during which the British foreign minister had a few drinks, Bevin returned to the meeting angry. When Molotov began attacking Great Britain, Bevin rose with his hands in fists and started toward Molotov, saying, "'I've had enough of this, I 'ave,'" and Bohlen said later, "for one glorious moment it looked as if the Foreign Minister of Great Britain and the Foreign Minister of the Soviet Union were about to come to blows." Vandenberg reported that Molotov remained undisturbed by the furor he was causing and paid no attention to the speeches being made at him. When Byrnes angrily reminded Molotov of their reparations conference agreement and said, "'I've kept my word, you should keep yours,' the place was breathless" but Molotov did not even "ruffle."[23]

Molotov was particularly anxious to have the peace conference divided into five separate conferences, one for each treaty with only the nations at war with that specific enemy nation participating as he had postulated at the London and Moscow Conferences. He also wanted two separate economic commissions established at the peace conference, one for the Italian treaty and one for the other treaties; and he wanted both the commission recommendations to the full conference and the conference recommendations to the Council of Foreign Ministers to be determined by two-thirds majority votes. At Moscow the ministers had agreed that the Soviet Union would have three votes (USSR, Byelorussia, and the Ukraine), and, with twenty-one nations attending the conference, eight votes could block a recommendation. With three votes to start with, and with Poland, Yugoslavia and Czechoslavakia attending, Byrnes believed Molotov thought he could easily get two more. Byrnes attempted to establish a bargaining stance of refusing to discuss procedure until the invitations had been sent, but he failed because he also insisted that the procedural decisions of the council be presented to the conference as recommendations only. Bevin complained that "the peace of the world seemed to be held up on a point of procedure nearly every day the Council met."[24]

While continuing to hold up the issuance of the invitations, Molotov tried to secure council agreement to support at the conference a few basic procedural principles that they would only recommend. Byrnes and Bevin refused and insisted on their right to consider any proposals on procedure put forward at the conference. Finally on 8 July at another of Bidault's suggested informal meetings with only ministers and interpreters present, Molotov offered a series of compromises in order to secure adherence to his position. He agreed that the invitations could be issued in the name of the council with no specific mention one way or the other of China as sponsor of the conference. The conference would have a general commission to coordinate the work of five political commissions (one for each treaty), one legal commission, one drafting commission, one military commission, and two economic commissions. Molotov suggested that France be allowed to participate in all five of the political commissions, and he was willing to require only the political commissions to vote under the two-thirds rule. Bidault suggested allowing political commission reports not receiving a two-thirds vote to be presented to the full conference at which a two-thirds vote would be required to refer the recommendation to the council, and Molotov agreed. In answer to Bevin's question of whether he would be expected to support each of these recommendations before the peace conference, Molotov replied that they were wasting their time discussing them unless they supported them. Bevin said that "unless the Soviet views were accepted Mr. Molotov regarded the discussion as a waste of time." After three and a half hours the ministers adjourned to allow Bidault time to draw up a clean draft of the suggestions to which they all agreed.[25]

Byrnes returned to the American delegation, shook his head, complaining that "it wasn't possible to hurdle Molotov's continuing demands that the invitations should be tied to the rules, and the Big Powers likewise." Vandenberg thought Byrnes saw "that his Peace Conference was about to disappear in thin smoke up the chimney;" but a half hour later Byrnes returned to the "secret session," and "about eleven o'clock he returned—all smiles." Vandenberg wrote "The miracle had happened—(as it so often does if we just cling long enough to our ideals when dealing with our Soviet friends). No one seemed to be able to explain what occurred. In fact, there was some difference of opinion between Byrnes and Bohlen . . . as to just what *had* occurred . . . ." What had apparently happened was the same thing that had occurred before at London and at Moscow when the Soviet effort to get the conference divided into five conferences had failed. They simply postponed the discussion until they met again in another arena—this time it would be at the peace conference itself. For the present, the ministers agreed to send out the invitations the next morning, 9 July, excluding China from sponsorship of the conference but allowing China's presence at the meeting and a share in the chairmanship of the plenary sessions. The council decision also involved "rules of procedure which have been recommended for its consideration." The rules embodied Molotov's plan of organization for the conference with the additional promise that commission minority reports would go to the full conference, for consideration along with two-thirds majority reports. In agreeing, the secretary said that "he wished it clearly understood that when the conference convened the United States was entirely free to accept or reject on its merits any amendment or new proposals concerning rules of procedures which might be offered."

Molotov concurred, saying that "it was up to the head of each Delegation to decide its view on any new suggestion or amendment to its rules of procedures"; but the council agreement on independent action on rules was the issue that Molotov would return to oppose at the peace conference.[26]

The Council of Foreign Ministers still had two items left on its agenda, Germany and Austria, and the ministers chose to begin what was to be their last five acrimonious meetings with a discussion of Germany. From the end of the war until early in 1946 American officials had considered French objections to treating occupied Germany as an economic unit and French demands for separating the Rhineland and Ruhr as the primary stumbling blocks to a unified Allied policy on Germany. With the accelerating American suspicions of Soviet postwar intentions, however, United States occupation leaders, Robert Murphy in particular, began to see the advantages for Russian zonal entrenchment, given French recalcitrance. The Allied failure to implement the Potsdam agreement on economic unity had left the United States supporting its food-deficient zone to the cost of two hundred million dollars a year instead of receiving food imports from the Soviet zone as anticipated. In addition, the Potsdam reparations agreement involved the United States, Britain, and France supplying the USSR with ten percent of the capital equipment that was "unnecessary for the German peace economy." To halt the dismantling of industrial plants and to pressure the Russians and the French to comply with the Potsdam agreement on a unified economy, General Lucius Clay, military governor for the United States zone, suspended reparations shipments on 3 May 1946. Determined to force a German settlement, Byrnes wanted a response from the Russians and the French on his offer of a twenty-five year German disarmament treaty and work to begin on a German peace treaty.[27]

Molotov opened the discussion on Germany with the first of what Bidault called "a number of soliloquies" by offering a rebuttal of Byrnes's disarmament proposal. Molotov read from a prepared text that was published in the press the next day, and which Clay thought was "for propaganda purposes in France to aid French Communists." Molotov first argued that the length of the treaty period was too short; it should be forty years. He saw the measures prescribed to disarm Germany as "restricted and utterly inadequate," and argued that the proposed treaty "evades the question of liquidating the remnants of German fascism" and "envisages the possibility of terminating the Allied occupation of German territory." Molotov, finally, complained that "Mr. Byrnes' draft also fully ignores the necessity to secure reparations deliveries."[28]

Byrnes immediately supplied Molotov with a point by point response which agreed first to a forty-year period and then noted that the language prescribing disarmament measures was taken from that agreed to by Generals Zhukov, Eisenhower, Montgomery, and DeLattre de Tassigny. Byrnes added, "I know of no better qualified men to draft a demilitarization program." The treaty did not attempt to deal with political questions, Byrnes continued, and said nothing about terminating occupation. He later wrote that Molotov's remarks convinced him that "he had no idea of discussing the treaty in a serious manner but was simply looking for excuses for delay. And my patience was exhausted." He told Molotov that "when the United States is willing to make a drastic departure from its policies of the past and offers this treaty in order to help insure the security of Europe we resent having that offer met with irrelevant arguments on reparations and minor difficulties of the occupation." He suggested that the council appoint special deputies to begin work on the German treaty to see if agreement could be reached on the issues that concerned Molotov.[29]

Bidault and Bevin agreed to the appointment of special deputies, and then each made his own statement on Germany. As Bidault had stated earlier, France wanted the Rhineland separated from Germany and administered by France, the Saar annexed by France, and the Ruhr placed under international control. Bidault believed that Germany must lose forever "its centralizing and militaristic Prussian character" and that the American draft treaty would be "the crown of the edifice" to accomplish disarmament and demilitarization. Foreign Secretary Bevin said: "There are three possible approaches to the peace of Europe: A balance of power between states of equal strength; Domination by

one power or two blocs of power; United control by the Four
Powers with the cooperation of their allies." Bevin was
"determined to prevent a division of Europe" and believed
the American treaty could be used as a means toward that
end.[30]

Ignoring the comments of the British and French, Molotov
read from a second prepared statement, released to the press
before the meeting and publicly advocating, for the first time
by any Ally, German reconstruction under lenient auspices.
Molotov maintained that "it has of late become fashionable
to talk about the dismemberment of Germany" but that the
"Soviet Government has always held that the spirit of
revenge is a poor counsellor in such affairs." He concluded
that "it would be incorrect to adopt the course of Germany's
annihilation as a state or that of its agrarianization,
including the annihilation of its main industrial centers." He
suggested completely disarming Germany militarily and
economically, placing the Ruhr under Four Power control,
establishing a definite reparations program, and establishing a single German government. Once these conditions had
been met, a German peace treaty could be written. In the
meantime, he refused Byrnes's suggestion of special deputies
and wanted instead another session of the Council of
Foreign Ministers on Germany. He did want the immediate
appointment of two commissions, one to investigate disarmament progress and the other to draw up a plan to liquidate
Germany's military industries.[31]

Byrnes considered Molotov's "performance" the opening
round of "a battle for the minds of the German people." He
declared, "The fact was our policy toward Germany had not
been satisfactorily clarified," and the evening after Molotov's speech met with General Clay and Robert Murphy to
formulate a response. Clay had proposed the merger of the
British and American zones of occupation in Germany to
Byrnes during the first session of the Paris Council of
Foreign Ministers. The secretary now concluded that "the
time had arrived to move forward in the consolidation of the
zones to the fullest extent possible."[32]

The next day Byrnes both opened and closed the council
sessions by reading from two statements prepared the
evening before by the American delegation. He stated first

that "the American Government never sought to impose a peace of vengeance upon Germany" and that the United States "regards the economic revival of Germany as essential to the economic revival of Europe." He concluded by calling upon the Four Powers to instruct the German Control Council to establish "the Central German Administrative Agencies necessary to secure economic unity in Germany" but warned that "we cannot continue to administer Germany in four air tight compartments." He then told the others that until Germany was organized as an economic whole, "the United States will join with any other occupying government or governments in Germany for the treatment of our respective zones as an economic unit." Bidault did not respond to his invitation, and Molotov postponed his observations. Bevin, to whom Byrnes had earlier and privately suggested zonal cooperation, had opposed a "clear division between Eastern and Western Germany" until it was "clear that we must abandon hope of Russian cooperation." Now, seeing Molotov's attitude on Germany as "intransigent," Bevin supported the American proposal. The council ended its first revealing discussion of Germany by agreeing to hold a special session on German questions sometime after the peace conference.[33]

The last agenda item of the Council of Foreign Ministers was the Austrian treaty. Both the United States and Great Britain had submitted draft treaties for Austria, and Byrnes proposed that the ministers refer these to the deputies with instructions that they begin work on a treaty to submit to the council. With the same naiveté (or ignorance) that led Byrnes to urge Stalin to make recognition of the Balkans possible so that the United States could aid postwar reconstruction, Byrnes now urged Molotov to hasten an Austrian treaty because "it will enable the Soviet Government to withdraw her soldiers." Molotov responded with a proposal that would make the drafting of an Austrian treaty dependent upon the council's providing, first for the denazification of Austria, and then for the immediate evacuation of "437,000 foreign nationals, so-called displaced persons" from Austria. These included Russian and Ukrainian White Guards, the followers of Soviet Lieutenant General Andrei Andreivich Vlasov, who was chairman of the German-sponsored Committee for the Liberation of the Peoples of Russia. Byrnes told Molotov that "when a man says he does not want to return to his home for political reasons, if he is afraid to return to his home, we must consider the position of the United States, which was developed by peoples from all over the world, many of them political refugees." Although Bevin joined Byrnes in arguing against making the solution of the displaced persons problem a condition for writing an Austrian treaty, Bevin admitted later that he did not find himself in "a good position to counter" Molotov's allegations. The *London Times* referred to the last day's discussion as the "most ragged and the worst," and Vandenberg called it "a total loss," noting that the last time the council adjourned there had been "many pleasing speeches." This time Bevin curtly ended the second session of the Paris Conference of the Council of Foreign Ministers on 12 July, by saying, "We shall meet at the peace conference."[34]

Without Byrnes's knowledge, Benjamin Cohen had suggested to President Truman that he advise Byrnes to stay in Europe and rest until the peace conference convened on 29 July. Cohen told the president that Byrnes "has been working under considerable nervous tension and while he seems quite well, the strain on him has been great." Truman responded by suggesting that Byrnes vacation in Switzerland, but the secretary decided "much could be done in two weeks at home" and returned to National Airport to be greeted by the president and Admiral Leahy. On 15 July, for the fourth time, Byrnes reported by radio to the American people, somberly remarking that "after every great war the victors find the making of the peace difficult and disappointing" and candidly confessing "that prior to our meeting in April I had little hope we would ever reach agreement. After our April meeting I had less hope." On a more optimistic note, however, he declared that the prospect for peace treaties with five countries was now bright. In describing the compromises on Trieste, reparations, and colonies, he freely admitted that "the drafts of treaties agreed upon are not the best which human wit would devise. But they are the best which human wit could get the four principal Allies to agree upon." He did not mention the Balkan treaties, but he did detail the lack of progress on the German and Austrian treaties and emphasized his initiative in combining zones of occupation. He added, "We will either secure economic cooperation between the zones or place the responsibility for the violation of the Potsdam Agreement." Byrnes was most enthusiastic about the council's agreement to hold a peace conference, and for the first time he voiced the unrealistic expectation that the treaties would be signed by the delegates before the peace conference adjourned.[35]

The next day Vandenberg defended the results of the Paris Conference of the Council of Foreign Ministers and Byrnes before the United States Senate. He complimented Byrnes on his "splendid performance" and characterized the conference as the council's "most successful effort." Vandenberg had learned that "what may be desired is limited by what can be attainable" and that "the measure of failure is not the presence of compromise." Vandenberg equaled and perhaps surpassed Byrnes's candor in describing the Paris negotiations when he reported on the "appalling disagreement" on German questions in the council. He said that the German discussion "disclosed the true depth of cleavage between the great powers upon this subject. Here the differences were not only acute; they were often acrimonious." But despite these "disappointments" the senator believed the world was closer to peace now that America's "dearest dream," the peace conference, was soon to convene. Tom Connally repeated to the Senate on 19 July much of what Byrnes and Vandenberg had said. Connally believed that the Council of Foreign Ministers "had travelled a hard road" but that it had reached an "outstanding" decision in calling the peace conference. He considered the German and Austrian discussions "not without value" because they contributed to "better understanding."[36]

During the Paris negotiations French Foreign Minister Georges Bidault, paraphrasing Talleyrand, had declared, "Our aim must be an equality of dissatisfaction." The Council of Foreign Ministers achieved this goal with its settlement of the Trieste, reparations, colonial, and peace conference issues. Each of the foreign ministers moved considerably away from his original position to allow compromises to be made. The success of the second session of the Paris Conference was due in large measure to Byrnes's diplomacy. Many of his contemporaries mentioned that he was a quick learner, and by midsummer of 1946 Byrnes had begun to learn the art of diplomacy. More importantly, Byrnes had learned from an expert, Molotov himself. Many of the negotiating techniques which Secretary Byrnes had successfully used in Paris against the Soviet delegation, Molotov had earlier successfully used against him. Just as Molotov had earlier used Byrnes's desire to have a peace conference as a lever to secure American compliance to Soviet domination over the Balkans, so had Byrnes used the desire of the Russian minister to secure reparations from Italy to get a Soviet agreement to the internationalization of Trieste. Byrnes had not only established the connection between solving the Trieste problem to reparations, he had also forced Molotov to make concession after concession on the Yugoslav-Italian border before finally accepting the internationalization scheme which Byrnes approved. Once the ministers agreed about Trieste, Byrnes continued to withhold a reparations agreement until a peace conference date was established. He again used a favorite Molotov tactic, the agenda, to rationalize his actions. Because the peace conference came next on the council's agenda, he could insist on a conference date before reparations despite having assured Molotov that once Trieste was settled he would agree on all other issues. This was one of the few times in all the sessions of the Council of Foreign Ministers when Byrnes clearly held the initiative. The establishment of definite negotiating limits to which the entire American delegation agreed made Byrnes's success possible. His suggestion that the Soviet Union supply Italy with raw materials allowed him to gain both Italian and Vandenberg's support for his reparations settlement. Byrnes placated Vandenberg by doing instinctively what Acheson later learned: consult patiently in advance with the senator in order to get his agreement to almost anything.[37]

Byrnes also had had the time by the summer of 1946 to become familiar with the issues involved in the peace treaties. When Molotov argued that as an ally Yugoslavia deserved a favorable Trieste settlement, Byrnes immediately responded with an impressive, impromptu recital of the advantages Yugoslavia would receive from the Italian treaty. Molotov was unable to refute him, perhaps because at this conference he was handicapped by the Kremlin's desire to woo simultaneously the Italian and Yugoslav Communists. Again, when Molotov unexpectedly proposed a compromise border between the French and Soviet lines, Byrnes was able to detail immediately the liabilities of the suggestion. In addition to learning diplomatic techniques from Molotov and developing expertise on the issues, Byrnes succeeded in Paris because his tightrope walk between public toughness and private negotiation became less difficult. The press appeared to tire of the tedious, complicated, and prolonged discussion, and so did Vandenberg and Connally. Byrnes received only reassurances from the president, and free of his watchdogs, he could successfully return to quid pro quo negotiation.

Byrnes's Paris success was by no means complete. Molotov's refusal to allow the peace conference invitations to be issued until the council agreed on exclusion of China and conference procedure had obviously caught the secretary off guard. In searching for leverage to use against the Soviets, Byrnes apparently did not consider the uncompleted Balkan treaties, nor the nonrecognition of Rumania and Bulgaria. He seemed to have written off the Balkans; all the Paris successes concerned the Italian treaty. In effect, he had agreed to Russian dominance of Eastern Europe without receiving any compensation. His Paris success was also to be short-lived. The reemergence of a viable negotiating climate provided him with only a brief respite before the publicized storm of the peace conference. At his own insistence, the meetings of the conference and its commissions would be open to the press. Byrnes's tightrope act would be required again, but this time it would be impossible.

CHAPTER SIX

THE PARIS PEACE CONFERENCE
29 July–15 October 1946

At the suggestion of a *Washington Post* editorial, thousands of people cheered the American delegates to the Paris Peace Conference as they left National Airport on 27 July 1946. President Truman told the crowd, which included congressional representatives, Supreme Court justices, and cabinet officers, that this "wholehearted send-off" was evidence that the country was behind Mr. Byrnes and his efforts to get a just peace for the world. Secretary Byrnes contrasted the post-World War I situation with the present: "Then we were badly divided"; "this time there is no division between the Executive and the Congress" and "there is no division between the great political parties."[1]

Reporters had described the Paris of 1919 as joyful, with crowds cheering the delegates as they arrived for the Versailles Peace Conference, but in 1946 the 1,500 delegates representing 21 nations found Paris somber. The French government ordered the Luxembourg Palace refurbished and its gardens replanted. Official preparations also included fixing spotlights on Notre Dame, the Place de la Concorde, the Opera House, and the Arch de Triomphe, and the requisitioning of a half dozen of the largest hotels for the delegates and their staffs. The peace conference would sit in the gilded Senate Chamber of the Luxembourg Palace with its three tiers of boxes open to the public.[2]

On 29 July, the opening day of the conference, the Republicaine Garde in brilliant red and white uniforms again lined the ornate stairway leading to the chamber. The minor delegates and experts entered first, and as acquaintances from the San Francisco Conference, greeted each other with handshakes and bows. At exactly 4:00 p.m. the main delegates entered from the rear of the stage in front of the Senate Chamber. Harold Nicolson, a diplomatic veteran of the Versailles Conference, present this time to cover the proceedings for the British Broadcasting Company, observed that Molotov and Vishinsky walked across the stage with "the consciousness of power." Byrnes and the American delegation entered slowly and sedately with all "the consciousness of great virtue"; "and then in trips little Attlee, hesitates on finding himself on the stage, tries to dart back again into the door through which he has come, and is then rescued by an official who leads him across the stage with a hand upon his elbow. A lamentable entry." Bevin was unable to be present at the opening of the conference; he was ill and in bed for several weeks of rest.[3]

After the delegates sat alphabetically in a large horseshoe arrangement, which placed Byrnes at the extreme right and Molotov on the extreme left, a French *huissier* shouted, "Monsieur le Président," and Bidault entered. Nicolson complained that photographers ruined the dignity of the occasion, giving it a "Hollywood effect" with their exploding flashbulbs. Bidault, restoring solemnity, welcomed the delegates to France for the second time in less than thirty years "to discuss the settlement of the post war world." A reporter noted that the only light in the chamber, which was the sunlight coming through a glass dome over the speaker's platform, began to dim as Bidault reminded the delegates of the weakness of the last peace. When the French president said that, "The fundamental cause of their failure was the fact that two great powers which had in turn played a decisive part in the struggle stood aloof from the peace," the light went completely out. Bidault said that "obviously excessive haste is not a charge that can be levelled" at the Four Powers which prepared the draft treaties, but "the difficulties encountered were enormous, because the interests involved were hard to reconcile;" and he concluded what Nicolson characterized as his "short conventional speech" by describing the complexity of the issues facing the conference. "They involve the essential interests of a large number of European nations," he said, and "they give rise sometimes to powerful emotions." Bidault urged the delegates to "tackle these questions with a sincere desire to find, if not ideal, at least reasonable solutions." A *New York Times* reporter, unimpressed with the opening ceremonies, told Nicolson that at Versailles the personalities were those of giants but not here. Nicolson disagreed and maintained that Byrnes was "more effective than President Wilson," Bevin was "a stronger and finer character than Lloyd George," old Orlando couldn't be compared in "force and capacity to Molotov," and "Bidault was a far more suitable person than Clemenceau could ever have been."[4]

After the opening formalities, the peace conference established a Commission on Procedure with a representative from each of the twenty-one nations. The commission met twelve times while the conference held five plenary sessions to hear an opening address from the head of each delegation. The two sets of meetings provided an interesting contrast; the plenary speeches were politely hopeful, while the commission quickly dissolved into bitter wrangling over rules of procedure. From the very first commission meeting at which Belgian Delegate Paul-Henri Spaak won the chairmanship over Edward Kardelj, chief of the Yugoslav delegation, the delegates divided into two rather consistent voting blocs. Molotov was the first to mention the division publicly, when he warned the chief of the Australian delegation, Herbert Evatt, that the Australian proposal to have the conference vote by a simple majority or a three-fifths majority "would have the effect of setting one bloc against another, a majority against a minority." Molotov proceeded to demonstrate his point by organizing what Philip Mosely called "the Slav bloc" and the press referred to as "Six in Hand"—the Soviet Union, Yugoslavia, Poland, Byelorussia, the Ukraine, and Czechoslovakia—to vote consistently together.[5]

Using the six-vote bloc Molotov successfully defeated several proposals: a Greek proposal to allow the conference to discuss, in addition to the treaties, any issue that it voted to discuss by a simple majority; a suggestion by the Netherlands that all twenty-one nations participate in all of the conference's commissions; and a New Zealand recommendation that the French president be elected the permanent chairman of the conference. In defending the recommendation of the Council of Foreign Ministers that they rotate the chairmanship, Molotov argued that those favoring Bidault as permanent chairman were trying to divide the major powers and implied that the council suggestions must be accepted. Dr. Evatt criticized Molotov for questioning the motives of those who opposed him and asked if "every proposal they made [would] be denounced as an attempt to break the unity of the Four Great Powers?" Byrnes demonstrated the division that already existed between the Great Powers when he read from the minutes of the last session of the Council of Foreign Ministers to prove that the rules drawn up were only suggestions. But, having made his point, Byrnes voted with Molotov for a rotating chairmanship as the council had suggested.[6]

The major question before the Commission on Procedure was the vote required for the conference to make a recommendation to the Council of Foreign Ministers. The British delegation, still without Bevin, suggested as a compromise to the simple majority and three-fifths majority proposals that the conference make two types of recommendations, those with a simple majority vote and those with a two-thirds majority vote. The American and the Chinese delegations supported the British proposal, but Molotov charged the British and the Americans with inconsistency for having supported in the council the proposal for a two-thirds majority and then abandoning it now. Molotov and French Deputy Couve de Murville suggested that the conference recommend only agreements passed by a two-thirds vote but that any nation voting for measures that passed with a simple majority might refer them to the council at their own discretion.[7]

Byrnes ignored the acceptable French-Soviet compromise and concentrated instead on documenting his right to consider new procedural proposals by referring again to council minutes. He cited six different times that he had reserved this privilege for the United States, "because I knew the tactics of Mr. Molotov." Byrnes further exacerbated the situation by challenging Molotov to publish the statement that Byrnes had just made in the Soviet Union.[8]

The secretary had a second chance to consider the French-Soviet compromise when Jan Masaryk, cochairman of the Czechoslovak delegation, proposed a subcommittee to suggest a voting compromise from the proposals made. The American and British delegates succeeded, instead, in securing an immediate vote on the British proposal of two types of conference recommendations. Molotov suggested that this vote require a two-thirds majority of the Commission on Procedure, giving Byrnes the opportunity to point out that the Soviet diplomat was now going against the rules suggested by the Council of Foreign Ministers that procedural votes be by a simple majority. "Now, only Mr. Molotov would do that," Byrnes told the commission. The commission passed the British proposal by a vote of fifteen to six, with Byrnes triumphantly believing the Slav bloc had created a Western bloc.[9]

The procedural debate continued when the commission reported its recommendation to the conference on 8 August. Molotov told the conference that the Commission on Procedure had made an "egregious error"; "it had ignored the need to endeavor to obtain unanimous decisions." Molotov blamed the American and British delegations, acting together, for producing this situation and insisted that it be rectified by the conference. Dr. Evatt told the conference that "M. Molotov thinks there's magic in the fraction two-thirds," and pointed out that the procedural commission's vote was by more than a two-thirds majority. The Australian said that all the council was asked to do was to consider the recommendations of a majority of those present and added, "That seems so elementary from the point of view of justice and fair play and democracy that I am amazed that opposition to it is still maintained."[10]

Byrnes needlessly increased the tension of the session by saying in reference to Molotov's inference that he had broken a council agreement: "The repetition of an inaccurate statement will never make it accurate." The secretary's dramatic response to the Soviet allegation that a bloc was operating against Russia was: "Whence comes this talk of blocs? By what right do those who voted, ballot after ballot with the Soviet Union, call those of us who do not always agree with the Soviet Union a bloc? . . . What loose and wicked talk this is!" Couve de Murville tried to restore amity by saying that he "deeply regrets" that "for reasons which I still fail to understand, most of the other delegations" ignored the French compromise on voting, and he offered to propose it again. The conference decided, however, by the same fifteen to six vote to accept the report of the Commission on Procedure on voting rules.[11]

Byrnes considered the results of the procedural battle an American victory. According to his analysis, the smaller nations would now have an opportunity to express themselves fully; the conscience of the world would be demonstrated at the peace conference, and the opinions of the smaller nations would influence the Soviet Union. As he told C. L. Sulzberger, while they drank from a gift supply of Truman's seven and one-half year old bourbon, "The more hell raised by the small powers the better," because they will strengthen the American position "in the jury room." Byrnes, however, had no use for Australian Foreign Minister Evatt who emerged as the leader of the lesser powers; Evatt was "mishandling the ideals of the small nations." Byrnes's criticism of Evatt came, the British delegation believed, because Byrnes wanted to influence and lead the lesser powers himself. In his first address to the conference, he championed the right of small nations to influence the peace by stating their opinions at the conference. "No nation, large or small," he said, "can be insensitive to world opinion," and he pledged that the United States would support in the Council of Foreign Ministers any recommendation of the conference passed with a two-thirds vote.[12]

Prime Minister Attlee echoed the American emphasis on world opinion when he followed Byrnes to the speaker's platform, and he sobered the delegates by reminding them of "a cartoon depicting a statement of the Versailles Treaty saying at the conclusion 'I seem to hear a child cry.' A baby labelled 1939 was in the background." Byrnes complained, nonetheless, that Attlee was "not helpful" and wished Bevin was there.[13]

Molotov, in contrast to the Americans and British, continued to stress the "positive results" the Council of Foreign Ministers had achieved and the necessity of maintaining that unanimity. He warned the conference against "all sorts of reactionary elements who are stuffed with absurd anti-Soviet prejudices and who base their calculations on the frustration of cooperation among the great powers." He also stated the Soviet Union would disregard in the Council of Foreign Ministers any recommendations not passed by a two-thirds majority.[14]

Nicolson, who sided with Molotov in appraising the procedural battle, noted that diplomatic conferences traditionally strived for public unanimity and kept their wrangling private. Nicolson held Byrnes responsible for the public voting innovation at the peace conference and for its immediate consequences: an emphasis on disunity and bloc voting. Byrnes's statements of his desire to have the conference write a "peoples' peace," Nicolson said, "were not always either tactful, lucid, or consistent." Nicolson concluded that "Byrnes's attempt to impress Russia with the force of world opinion has only led Russia to believe that he sought to gang up the small states against her."[15]

Nicolson was even more critical of Byrnes on the issue of publicity, which he considered Byrnes's second innovation at Paris. Byrnes had insisted at the second session of the Paris Conference of the Council of Foreign Ministers that the peace conference be open to the press, and had told the American people in his last radio broadcast that he planned to use his influence to open not only the plenary sessions but also the commissions to journalists. At his initiative the Commission on Procedure had unanimously recommended free access to the press, and the conference had adopted this procedure without debate. Nicolson insisted that a distinction had to be made between open covenants and open covenants openly arrived at, because the latter were impossible. From the beginning of the Paris Conference, Nicolson continued, there was no negotiation and almost no discussion. Each delegate knew that whatever he said would be broadcast to the world, and so he spoke to public opinion, not to the other delegates. As early as 5 August Nicolson described the conference as a "public performance, not a serious discussion."[16]

Byrnes believed that publicizing the conference had positive results, because many people who had earlier believed that "the Foreign Ministers of the western states were unfair to the Soviet Union changed their minds" when they observed Russian tactics and listened to their intemperate statements. Nicolson had a different opinion of this also, believing that the Russians, "not trained in the courtesies of international intercourse," used "highly coloured and highly charged language," and the West took as "deliberate insults remarks which are merely stock-in-trade remarks and part of the current terms of Russian propaganda."[17]

Members of the British delegation criticized Nicolson for being too tolerant of the Russians in his BBC broadcasts, and Nicolson told them, "There is much to be said for the Russian point of view, and we shall achieve nothing by ignoring it." In contrast to Nicolson, Bidault believed the Soviet use of vituperation was more from design. The French president thought the Russians wanted a publicized conference as much as the Americans; it gave them an opportunity to denounce and create a diversionary incident anytime they were at a disadvantage. The Americans, Bidault said, approved of an open conference because it satisfied "their naive love of show and their belief in the virtues of publicity." Bevin decided to avoid public confrontation with the Soviets and to work "things from behind the scenes."[18]

The acrimonious procedural battle did not give the peace conference an auspicious beginning, but as the conference organized itself into eight commissions to begin considering the draft articles of the five treaties, the delegates became aware that potentially the conference could be far more influential—more influential, as Philip Mosely said, "than could have been foreseen at Potsdam almost one year before." This was because the Council of Foreign Ministers brought twenty-six unagreed articles before the conference. A peace conference recommendation on these issues in a divided council would carry great weight. In the Italian treaty the unagreed articles included the borders between Italy and Yugoslavia and the Free Territory of Trieste, reparations to Yugoslavia and Greece, and the details of the international regime to govern Trieste. The most important of the undecided Balkan issues were economic.[19]

The conference decided to hear in plenary session representatives from the former enemy states while the commissions began their work. The first to speak was the Premier and Foreign Minister of Italy Alcide de Gasperi. Byrnes believed de Gasperi "presented his case tactfully but with dignity and courage," but when he left the rostrum to walk down the center aisle of the silent chamber past many who knew him, no one spoke to him. "It impressed me as unnecessarily cruel," Byrnes said, and "when he approached the United States delegation I stood and shook hands with him." Harold Nicolson said, "It was an occasion not unworthy either of the conquerors or the conquered."[20]

The conference decided at Yugoslavia's request to allow discussion of each ex-enemy's remarks; but Byrnes, who chaired the meeting at which the discussion began, told the conference that "he did not propose to allow other members [besides Yugoslavia] to speak on the subject unless the conference took a decision to that effect." Andrei Vishinsky and Dr. Evatt, in their only joint action, challenged Byrnes's decision to limit discussion, and after consulting the minutes of the previous meeting the secretary agreed that he was in error. Molotov's discussion of the Italian statement was so hostile that de Gasperi later asked him why he had attacked Italy so bitterly, and Molotov replied, "Oh, you mustn't take that seriously. That was just polemics." Part of the Soviet polemics involved telling the conference that certain treaty clauses would place Italy under the "tutelage of certain foreign countries and of trusts and cartels." Molotov also referred pointedly to certain Great Powers enriching themselves during the war.[21]

The polemics intensified when the Balkan representatives spoke. The Rumanian foreign minister praised the "glorious Soviet armies," and thanked Russia for limiting its reparations demand, but criticized the severity of the economic clauses providing compensation to Western nationals. The

Bulgarian minister mentioned "the generous assistance of the Soviet Union," and the Hungarian minister also spoke of Soviet "generosity." In addition, the Bulgarian representative opposed Greek claims to Bulgarian territory, and the Ukrainian minister said that "it would not be just to deprive Bulgaria of the territory claimed by Greece, which was merely following the old imperialistic policies." Molotov supported these attacks on the Greek government.[22]

Finally on 15 August Byrnes joined the foray, objecting to "misrepresentation of our position and motives" and to the "Soviet Government giving the impression to the conference that other ex-enemy States are more democratic than Italy, because they have harmonized their viewpoint with the Soviet Union." In his notably emotional speech, the secretary also defended Greece, and in reply to the charge that some Great Powers became rich off the war, he said: "I hope that the Soviet representative was not referring to the United States of America, which came so unhesitatingly to the support of the Soviet Union when in peril." He detailed the $11 billion sent to Russia in Lend Lease supplies, and added, "The United States expenditures during the war aggregated $400 billion dollars."[23]

The Soviet response to this, voiced by Vishinsky, was that "the United States was trying to dominate the world with 'hand-outs.'" The secretary noticed that when Vishinsky made that charge, "he was heartily applauded at the end of his remarks by two of the Czech delegates seated two rows in front of our delegation." Byrnes knew that the Czech government had been given a $50 million credit with a 2⅜ percent interest rate by the United States, and checking into it, further learned that Czechoslovakia had transferred $10 million of this credit to Rumania with a thirteen percent interest rate. The secretary wrote, "I immediately cabled instructions to the state department to stop the extension of credit to Czechoslovakia." In another act of dollar diplomacy, Byrnes told the Italian president at the peace conference that he had just arranged for the United States Army to pay for supplies purchased in Italy during the occupation.[24]

Into the midst of this rancorous situation Byrnes introduced an Iranian-type scenario; this time the villain was

Yugoslavia. The dispute concerned American air travel over the northwestern tip of Yugoslavia, an area directly in the path of the U.S. Army Air Transport Service between Rome and Vienna. The Yugoslav government forbade American planes to cross their territory, but United States transports continued to do so because of the navigational difficulties in that mountainous area. Yugoslavia first charged the United States with 176 separate violations of her borders and then on 9 August attacked and forced down an American plane over Yugoslav territory. On 20 August Byrnes learned that another American transport had been shot down by the Yugoslavs. The crew from the first plane was placed under house arrest in a Belgrade hotel; the five member crew of the second plane did not survive the attack.[25]

"Terribly upset," Byrnes "sent for" the head of the Yugoslav delegation to the peace conference, Vice Premier Edvard Kardelj, and "demanded that he communicate with his government to obtain an explanation." "Upon receiving a very unsatisfactory reply," Byrnes said, "I issued instructions to notify the Yugoslavs that unless we receive a satisfactory reply to our demands within forty-eight hours we would call upon the United Nations Security Council to take appropriate action." His ultimatum, approved in advance by the president, was that Yugoslavia release the imprisoned American crew and give satisfaction for the deaths of the others. News of the Yugoslav-American crisis worsened the already tense atmosphere of the conference, but Byrnes learned with satisfaction that Molotov and Kardelj engaged in an "earnest conversation," with Molotov "doing most of the talking." The Yugoslav government met the American deadline, and Byrnes had the released pilot and copilot flown to Paris to see him. For his efforts, Byrnes received a telegram from Vandenberg which said, "I support you 100%," and four cases of Harper and Old Taylor bourbon from the state department.[26]

Perhaps to bolster the adamancy of the stand the American delegation was taking in Paris, Byrnes issued an "urgent plea" to Vandenberg and Connally to join him at the peace conference. He told Vandenberg that "inasmuch as he had now adopted a 'Republican foreign policy' he is entitled to give the chief Republican conspirator sharing the grief with him." The senators left for "the Paris cockpit" on 23 August in the president's plane to be met at Orly Airport by the secretary of state. Byrnes asked Vandenberg to represent the United States on the Economic Commission, which placed him in the position of arguing for equality of economic opportunity in the Balkan nations and for freedom of commerce and navigation on the Danube. At the second Paris session of the Council of Foreign Ministers, Vandenberg had disagreed with Byrnes on the American demand that the riparian states give other nations the same rights which they enjoyed. Vandenberg said the United States would never do that, but at the peace conference he demanded equal rights for all nations on the Danube. Byrnes appointed Connally to the Political Commission for the Italian treaty where he defended reparations and armed forces limitations although he disagreed with Byrnes's position and said that "on these points Byrnes bowed to Soviet demands." Bidault remarked that soon Vandenberg and Connally became indistinguishable in their appearance, policies, and cigars; both appeared very pleased with themselves, although Bidault thought Vandenberg the better man.[27]

Byrnes finally organized his delegation at the Paris Peace Conference. They met regularly at 9:00 a.m. each day for each commission representative to report on the negotiations in his group. Connally complained, "Secretary Byrnes tended to ignore me at the peace conference but he worked hard to please Senator Vandenberg." Connally said that often he would arrive at a scheduled 9:00 a.m. meeting to find that Byrnes and Vandenberg had already been conferring for fifteen to thirty minutes. Connally said Byrnes did this in order to keep Vandenberg in a good humor. In addition to Connally and Vandenberg, American representatives on the commissions included: Averell Harriman on the Rumanian Commission, Jefferson Caffery on the Bulgarian Commission, and Bedell Smith on the Commission on Hungary. The press commented that the Soviet delegation was also well organized and the largest at the conference. The Soviets arrived at every commission meeting with prewritten arguments on even unimportant points. Altogether the commissions of the conference considered close to 300 amendments to the draft articles of the five treaties.[28]

In the midst of the prolonged, often tedious commission meetings, the American secretary of state presented the conference with another diversion, following the Yugoslav episode. With the encouragement of General Lucius Clay, Byrnes decided to leave the conference, accompanied by Vandenberg and Connally, to go to Stuttgart in the American zone of Germany to make a detailed statement of American policy toward Germany. Byrnes would, in effect, repeat what he had already said at the second session of the Paris meeting of the Council of Foreign Ministers, but he valued the dramatic effect of a speech in Germany to German officials at the height of the publicized East-West divisions. The American party flew from Paris to Berlin and then, joined by Clay and Robert Murphy, traveled to Stuttgart in what had been Adolf Hitler's private, luxuriously equipped train.[29]

There on 6 September, to a capacity audience in the Württemberg Staatstheater, Byrnes made his speech. He had advised the State Department in advance that his remarks might be interpreted as an "attempt to woo Germans" but that it should treat them as a "re-affirmation of United States German policy." Ben Cohen wrote the secretary's speech which Truman saw ahead of time, but enroute Byrnes first added, and then decided to delete as too strong, a statement about American troops staying in Germany as long as other occupation troops were there. Clay so persuasively urged Byrnes to retain this commitment that he attempted to reach the president by telephone to secure his approval. Unable to contact Truman, Byrnes cabled him that he would make the statement unless he heard from the president to the contrary.[30]

Byrnes noticed as he walked onstage in Stuttgart that the band was playing "Stormy Weather" and considered asking General Clay if he had requested appropriate music. In his address Byrnes said, "It is not in the interest of the German people or in the interest of world peace that Germany should become a pawn or a partner in a military struggle for power between the East and the West." Byrnes, who would not have been making this speech if Germany had not already become an East-West issue, restated his concern that Germany was not being administered as an economic unit as agreed at Potsdam and commended the British for agreeing to unite their zone with the American. He also favored German political centralization provided a democratic central government was established, although he understood that this was in opposition to French plans to decentralize Germany economically and politically. In fact, Robert Murphy said that the United States now opposed French desires to internationalize the Ruhr and to annex German territory but did not want to alienate the French government directly, especially since the United States had already sanctioned Polish annexation of Germany territory in the East. Byrnes's Stuttgart speech was, Murphy said, the "clever idea" that his advisers had suggested in order to raise doubts about the validity of Polish annexation of German territory so that the United States could better resist annexation in the West. Accordingly, the secretary said that at Potsdam "the heads of government did not agree to support at the peace settlement the cession of any particular area." Byrnes agreed that France had a right to the Saar, but in reference to the Rhineland and Ruhr he insisted that "the United States will not support any encroachment on territory which is indisputably German or any division which is not genuinely desired by the people concerned." He added, "The United States cannot relieve Germany from the hardships inflicted upon her by the war her leaders started. But the United States has no desire to increase those hardships." Finally, he said, since he had not heard from Truman, the "Security forces will probably have to remain in Germany for a long period. I want no misunderstanding. We will not shirk our duty. We are not withdrawing."[31]

Byrnes received even more publicity from this speech, which he considered his "most effective," than he had from the Yugoslav affair. General Clay said Byrnes's statement was "the first expression by a high American official of our firm intent to maintain our position in Europe." Bevin, who was now well enough to attend the conference, congratulated

Byrnes on his firm stand, as did Churchill, John Foster Dulles, Vandenberg, Connally, and the entire Truman cabinet. French officials did not commend the secretary; they believed Byrnes's Stuttgart speech showed "perfect disregard for France's ambitions in the German field." One of them said, "This time Uncle Sam had kissed Germania on both cheeks with a loud smack." Regardless of French sensibilities, Byrnes believed that the doubts he had raised about Polish acquisition of German territory had forced the Soviet Union to support Polish claims to the detriment of the German Communist party.[32]

Inadvertently, the secretary, immediately after his return to Paris from Germany, provided the peace conference with still another diversion. This one concerned President Truman's Secretary of Commerce Henry Wallace. The former Roosevelt vice-president and secretary of agriculture was one of the last links the Truman administration had with liberal Americans who continued to favor a conciliatory Soviet policy. Wallace had informed Truman of his views on foreign policy in two letters, one written 14 March 1946, and the other 23 July 1946, and Truman had sent this last, twelve-page letter on to Byrnes just before the peace conference convened. In it Wallace had posed the question of how United States actions (a $13 billion defense budget, continued atomic testing and bomb production, plans to arm Latin America, air bases around the world, and an impossible atomic energy control plan) appeared to other nations. Wallace believed the answer was "either (1) that we are preparing ourselves to win the war which we regard as inevitable, or (2) that we are trying to build up a predominance of force to intimidate the rest of mankind."[33]

Neither Truman nor Byrnes appeared to be influenced by Wallace's views, but neither was Wallace deterred from expressing opinions different from those of the administration. On 10 September Wallace had a fifteen-minute conference with the president and told him that he was giving "a sort of tough line with the Soviets" speech in Madison Square Garden on 12 September. Clark Clifford, White House counsel, said Truman only thumbed through a copy of the speech, but at a press conference the afternoon before Wallace was to speak, Truman told reporters, "I approved the whole speech." Wallace began his speech by saying, "I am neither anti-British nor pro-British—neither anti-Russian nor pro-Russian. And just two days ago, when President Truman read these words, he said that they represented the policy of his administration." Truman had the opportunity to withdraw all indication of support before Wallace spoke, as Will Clayton, acting assistant secretary of state during Acheson's vacation, urged after reading an advance copy of the speech following Truman's press conference. Clayton told Charlie Ross, the president's press secretary, that Byrnes "would be very much disappointed" and "would probably feel that the ground had been cut out from under him." Truman chose not to act, and Wallace told his New York audience: "'Getting tough' never bought anything real and lasting—whether for schoolyard bullies or businessmen or world powers. The tougher we get, the tougher the Russians will get. . . . The real peace treaty we now need is between the United States and Russia." Wallace pled for mutual recognition of American-Soviet spheres of influence but with Eastern Europe opened to American trade and with the Soviet Union convinced that the American "primary objective" was no longer "saving the British Empire."[34]

In Paris Byrnes first learned of Wallace's speech and Truman's endorsement from a British newsman. Soon afterward Clayton supplied him with the text of the speech and of Truman's press conference, and Assistant Secretary of State Donald Russell sent voluminous daily press summaries of the resulting furor. The secretary went into seclusion "because I wanted to avoid answering questions about whether the policy of our government had changed." There were many questions to be answered when news of what Russell characterized as "fatuous incompetence in the conduct of the desperately serious business of foreign relations" reached the conferees. Conference delegates wondered in particular if Byrnes in his various public statements had correctly presented American policy. While waiting for the president to contact him and still believing Truman approved Wallace's comments, Byrnes prepared a statement denying either a pro-British or anti-Soviet stand

and defending American interests in Eastern Europe. His statement concluded that Wallace's "criticism threatens to impair the influence of the American Delegation in the making of peace," because "it presents to the world a house divided against itself."[35]

Byrnes held up the release of this statement through 13 and 14 September, but Vandenberg told the press that "the authority of American foreign policy is dependent upon the degree of American unity behind it" and that "rightly or wrongly, Paris is doubtful of this unity this morning." "We can only cooperate with one Secretary of State at a time." Senator Connally told reporters that "while we are striving desperately for peace there should be no controversy or bickering or strife at home." The evening of the fourteenth Clayton advised Byrnes that the president wanted no statements from Paris because he planned a press conference that day. At his press conference the president offered what *Time* magazine called a "clumsy lie"; he said that what he had endorsed was Wallace's right to make his speech, not the content of the speech. Wallace, in response, not only told the press that he intended to continue speaking out on foreign policy, but also that he would release to the press his 23 July letter to the president.[36]

By 17 September after five days had passed without any direct Truman-Byrnes communication, Byrnes learned through Clayton that the president had an appointment with Wallace the next day. He then sent a teletyped letter to Truman to be "delivered before the President sees Wallace." He told the president that the Wallace "incident has impaired the prestige of the delegation here at the Peace Conference," and "if it is not completely clear in your own mind that Mr. Wallace should be asked to refrain from criticizing foreign policy, I must ask you to accept my resignation immediately." All that Byrnes's gesture secured was an "approved" statement which Wallace read to the press after his two hour and twenty minute appointment with Truman, in which he said that he would refrain from speaking on foreign policy until after the peace conference ended. Wallace's statement caused Vandenberg to write Dulles, "The situation here the last few days has been tragic. Just about *all* the American prestige which we have painfully built up the last two years has crashed. Europeans are more bewildered than ever."[37]

On 19 September the president and his beleaguered secretary of state finally had direct communication, in a teletype conversation. Byrnes told Truman that "Wallace's agreement not to speak during this conference . . . promised only a moratorium from criticism." He explained that this conference was only one of several that would follow to complete the treaties and to begin work on the German, Austrian, and Japanese treaties. During these conferences Byrnes said that he would be confronted with Wallace's statements conflicting with his and that he "would then have to insist upon being relieved." It would be better to come home now, Byrnes argued, because the work of the delegation was at a standstill, with the other delegations wondering if the administration would permit Wallace to make another speech attacking us. Truman reassured Byrnes that there was no agreement that Wallace was to resume foreign policy statements after the peace conference, only that he would be quiet until then. The president said, "The situation will be made perfectly clear tomorrow. . . . You have done an excellent job. Nobody appreciates it more than I do and I shall continue to support you with everything I have." The next morning Truman asked for Wallace's resignation and told the press that afternoon that "no change in our foreign policy is contemplated. . . . I have complete confidence in Mr. Byrnes and his delegation now representing this country at the Paris Peace Conference." Byrnes wrote, "Our delegation want back to work."[38]

By mid-September, the peace conference commissions had made little progress, and with the U.N. General Assembly scheduled to meet in New York on 23 September, the Council of Foreign Ministers decided to meet concurrently with the conference to decide what to do to accelerate the work of the delegates. Byrnes had mentioned the possibility of the council meeting while the conference was in session in his last radio speech, and when Mackenzie King, Prime Minister of Canada, suggested the same thing in an address to the conference, the secretary quickly agreed. Altogether the council held seven informal sessions, with each of the foreign ministers missing at least one meeting. The ministers met first on 29 August at Bevin's suggestion to instruct their deputies to examine proposed amendments to the draft treaties and to see if there were any the ministers might agree to support. The deputies met ten times to carry out this decision but almost invariably agreed to oppose suggested amendments to their agreed articles.[39]

Molotov proposed that the ministers ask the United Nations to postpone their meeting until November or December, but Byrnes and Bevin were hesitant about doing so because the council had already requested postponement once. The secretary argued that "to postpone the General Assembly because of the convenience of twenty-one [nations] would create a bad impression among the other thirty," but Molotov asked "how much of the world's surface was represented by the twenty-one nations." Byrnes had already been informed by Acheson that the American delegation to the U.N. opposed postponement, and Byrnes agreed to support them. Not surprisingly, the four ministers found themselves supporting four different positions on this question: Molotov wanted to request postponement, Byrnes opposed postponement, Bevin wanted the U.N. to discuss minor issues at first so the ministers need not attend, and Bidault suggested either concurrent U.N.-peace conference meetings or a conference recess. The ministers did agree to invite China to participate in their last two meetings on the U.N. Molotov held out the possibility that the peace treaties might be signed in Paris before the General Assembly met if the others agreed to postponement, but Bevin wanted a definite prior agreement on when the German and Austrian treaty discussion would begin. The ministers finally, with Byrnes neither agreeing nor disagreeing, decided to request the U.N. Secretary General Trygie Lie to ascertain the views of the other members on postponement to 23 October. Lie called Byrnes at 11:45 p.m. the evening of 9 September to request categorical assurances that the ministers would not request a third postponement. Byrnes's staff refused to awaken him, but the next morning he gave the requested assurances.[40]

The last three meetings of the Council of Foreign Ministers, again excluding China, were held to discuss measures to expedite the work of the conference. Bevin suggested that the commissions be instructed to complete their work by 5 October and that plenary sessions begin that day to consider their recommendations. The British delegation also wanted the final conference vote on commission suggestions completed by 15 October so the conference could adjourn then. Molotov agreed to the dates but wanted the ministers to agree that only the issues voted on by the commissions by 5 October would be brought before the conference. Bevin responded that he did not wish to "play in the hands of those" who did not intend to act in the spirit of all them there. The council agreed to support these dates before the conference, while avoiding the appearance of "dictating" to the other delegates, and to instruct their deputies to report to the ministers if any commission appeared unable to complete its voting by 5 October.[41]

Byrnes approached Molotov on 3 October to suggest limitations on the debate in the closing plenary sessions, and while Molotov agreed, he wanted minority rights protected because "he expected to be speaking for the minority view, which was harder than speaking for the majority as Mr. Byrnes would be doing." Molotov also wanted the council to meet in New York during the General Assembly meeting to complete the treaties because he no longer believed that the drafts could be completed before the U.N. meeting. Byrnes agreed and the two took their suggestions to the council that evening. The other ministers accepted the idea of limiting debate and decided to allot thirty minutes on each treaty to each delegation. At their last council meeting in Paris the ministers agreed to meet in New York on 4 November to complete the treaties and to discuss Germany.[42]

The temper of these council meetings was considerably more relaxed than that of the peace conference itself, but even the peace conference atmosphere was beginning to improve. The change appeared to originate with a press interview that Stalin had held in Moscow at the end of the Wallace debate. In it he had said that he no longer believed the West desired "capitalist encirclement" of the Soviet Union, and so there was "no real danger" of a new war occurring between East and West. Byrnes reciprocated these sentiments in a 3 October address to the American Club in

Paris, agreeing that talk of encirclement was "unwarranted" and mentioning again his German demilitarization treaty. About this same time Molotov left the conference to consult with Stalin at the Kremlin, while the American delegation speculated that Stalin had come to believe Molotov's abrasive tactics at the conference had made more enemies for the Soviet Union. Whatever occurred in Moscow, Molotov returned prepared to cooperate in bringing the conference to a speedy conclusion, knowing that this would involve confirmation of the Soviet minority position.[43]

The American secretary of state with his majority influence at the peace conference was pleased with the results of the commission reports. The Italian Political Commission recommended that Trieste and the 300 surrounding square miles be internationalized under U.N. protection and that Yugoslavia get the bulk of the adjoining disputed area. Of the 3,500 square miles in controversy, Connally said, Italy only got about 500 square miles, and added: "I wanted to hold out for better terms for Italy. But Byrnes was anxious to finish the conference, return to the United States and say, 'Look what I've done.'" Byrnes also got conference approval for a much stronger Security Council appointed governor for Trieste than the Soviets and Yugoslavs had advocated, although this "created the anomaly of the western democracies advocating appointment by the Security Council of a governor having almost dictatorial powers, while the eastern dictatorships sought to place control in a popularly elected legislature." Yugoslavia responded to its defeat by threatening not to sign the Italian treaty and not to withdraw troops from the area of Trieste it occupied. In response, Connally succeeded in having the conference pass a resolution limiting the benefits of the treaties to the signatories.[44]

Vandenberg also fared well in the Balkan Economic Commission, securing provisions in each treaty requiring nondiscriminatory treatment on a reciprocal basis in trade and guarantees for equal economic opportunity in carrying on business within each ex-enemy nation. Vandenberg also secured adoption of a resolution convening an international conference to establish a traffic regime for the Danube.

Molotov even complimented Vandenberg for his speech in support of economic equality in the Balkans, but the Soviet diplomat effectively rebutted the principle of economic equality by pointing out that "if American capital were given a free hand in the small states ruined and enfeebled by the war . . . American capital would buy up the local industries, appropriate the more attractive Rumanian, Yugoslav, and all other enterprises, and would become the master in these small states." Bevin, who privately agreed with Molotov on the Danube issue, told Nicolson that the Americans were "tiresome" on the subject and that their position was weak because of Panama and Suez. "All we ought to ask for," Bevin said, "is full access to ocean-going ships."[45]

On the issue of reparations the American and British delegations again resorted to the tactic of submitting claims against Italy for $20 billion and $11 billion respectively which neither intended to press. This strategy partially succeeded in convincing the lesser powers to lower their reparations claim. The conference voted that Albania's claim against Italy should be denied altogether and that Italy should pay $100 million to the Soviet Union, Yugoslavia, and Greece and $25 million to Ethiopia. The United States failed to secure lower reparation figures for Hungary and Finland, but the conference did award Greece and Yugoslavia $125 million from Bulgaria despite the Slav bloc arguing that the figure was too high.[46]

Altogether the seventy-nine day peace conference made fifty-three recommendations to the Council of Foreign Ministers by a two-thirds majority vote and forty-one by a simple majority. Bloc voting dominated the closing plenary sessions as it had the earlier Commission on Procedure, but the rhetoric was not as inflamed. The peace conference adjourned on schedule on 15 October. Bidault thanked the delegates for having made Paris "for the past two and one-half months the political center of the world," and Nicolson commented that every conference began like a tortoise and ended like a greyhound.[47]

A large crowd, but not the president, welcomed the American delegation home and caused Vandenberg to ask whether "Henry" had made any more speeches. Byrnes drove from National Airport to the State Department, where he received an invitation to visit Truman at the White House. The secretary said the president "received me cordially, but did not mention the Wallace affair."[48]

Byrnes spoke to the American people on 18 October, but in less detail than after previous conferences. In an interesting rationalization, he emphasized that the United States and the Soviet Union voted together on many peace conference issues; since the Soviets insisted on prior agreement in the Council of Foreign Ministers to all issues which they regarded as fundamental, the American-Soviet differences at the conference "were not questions that were fundamental from the Soviet viewpoint." He freely admitted that the public display of American-Soviet tension was real, but added that "it is better that the world should witness and learn to appraise clashes of ideas rather than clashes of arms." He concluded with an oblique reference to the debate over foreign policy within the Truman administration: "In our efforts at Paris we have been criticized by some for being too 'soft' and at times for being too 'tough.' I dislike both words. Neither accurately describes our earnest efforts to be firm but patient."[49]

Vandenberg emphasized this sentiment in a supportive radio statement in which he urged to policy of "friendly firmness" toward the Soviet Union. Both Byrnes and Vandenberg stressed their opposition to the idea of the inevitability of war between the Soviet Union and the United States, and Truman joined them in his 23 October speech to the U.N. General Assembly. The president said, "Above all, we must not permit differences in economic and social systems to stand in the way of peace, either now or in the future." Even Stalin repeated his earlier statement that relations between the United States and the Soviet Union had not deteriorated, and Molotov told the press that the Soviet Union would meet the United States "half-way." Thus, the most publicized East-West division since the end of the war, the Paris Peace Conference, concluded with both sides denying the seriousness of their differences.[50]

Byrnes correctly concluded that the peace conference could not be considered a "failure"; Molotov correctly added that the conference was "unsatisfactory." Since the London meeting of the Council of Foreign Ministers, Byrnes had fought to gain Soviet acceptance of a peace conference. The conference, like the council and the German disarmament treaty, became the secretary's ideas, and he wanted the political credit which their success would bring. Ostensibly, he wanted a peace conference so the peace would be a "peoples' peace," but in order to gain Soviet compliance, he had agreed to a restricted conference with only sixteen other nations having only recommending power. His objective at the conference was to influence the Soviet Union with public opinion, but he learned in Paris that while he had majority influence, he did not have majority control. The victories the secretary heralded on Trieste and reparations actually were French compromise suggestions, not the original American or British proposals. If Byrnes had been less interested in demonstrating American toughness and more interested in diplomacy, he might also have agreed to the French compromise on voting procedure. Byrnes, however, believed he could better influence the Soviet Union if the world could see Russian diplomacy in action and in a minority position. Nicolson, who by the end of the conference had changed his mind about the superiority of the 1946 American delegation over the 1919 group, said that he had the impression that the Americans in Paris "were animated by some vague conception of righteousness and benevolence, striped with bands of improvisation."[51]

Byrnes clearly enjoyed the peace conference, with the exception of the Wallace interlude, and even then he fought to keep the job from which he had already resigned by stressing in his comments to Truman the lengthy conferences still to be held in order to complete the peace treaties. Byrnes must also have realized that despite the furor over Wallace's remarks they were not inconsistent with the positions he himself had taken in the Paris sessions of the Council of Foreign Ministers. They were contradictory only to the hard line he took publicly, and at the peace conference the public stand was the only stand. A French diplomat commented that "never once in our hearing did he utter a word of criticism of either his President or of Wallace. This shows that he was a loyal man—but also, which is perhaps better, that he is a damn smart politician." Byrnes was in his element at the conference, for it provided him with a parliamentary setting, not unlike the United States Senate, in which he could influence votes and play to the galleries. He not only insisted that the conference be open to the press; he supplied the press with news releases, press conferences, and, as the tedious negotiations began to lose public interest, with Yugoslav and Stuttgart diversions. By publicizing the Soviet minority position and championing the role of small powers in the peacemaking, Byrnes also gained bargaining clout for his last conference of the Council of Foreign Ministers. Undoubtedly, he succeeded in marshalling public opinion against the Soviet Union, but without fully realizing the cost involved. What the American secretary of state saw as the conscience of the world speaking, Molotov saw as American-organized opposition to the USSR. At first, Molotov reminded Byrnes of the principle of unanimity within the Council of Foreign Ministers, but when that failed to influence American strategy, he resorted to using the press as Byrnes had. The result was the lowest point in American-Soviet negotiations to date. The Paris Peace Conference proved that inflamed rhetoric was a poor substitute for diplomacy.[52]

CHAPTER SEVEN

THE NEW YORK CONFERENCE OF
THE COUNCIL OF FOREIGN MINISTERS
4 November–12 December 1946

By the end of 1946 events both domestic and foreign had further entrenched the Truman administration's hard line, anti-Soviet stance. The catalytic factor on the domestic scene was a report summarizing American relations with the Soviet Union, which the president had asked his Special Counsel Clark Clifford to prepare during the Paris Peace Conference. In carrying out this directive, Clifford consulted with the secretaries of state, war and navy, the attorney general, and with military and intelligence leaders and reported to Truman by the end of September the "remarkable agreement" among these officials. The premise of the report was that American-Soviet relations — "the gravest problem facing the United States"—would determine "whether or not there would be a third world war." Clifford wrote that "Soviet leaders appear to be conducting their nations on a course of aggrandizement designed to lead to eventual world domination by the USSR." Citing George Kennan's analysis of Soviet motivation, the report accepted the Kremlin's belief in the inevitability of conflict with capitalist nations, "while at the same time they strive to postpone the inevitable conflict in order to strengthen and prepare the Soviet Union."

In reference to the peace treaties, Clifford's statement noted the "disillusionment over the achievements of peace conferences," because of the Soviet record of reneging on earlier conference agreements, and because "the longer the peace settlements are postponed the longer Red Army troops can 'legally' remain in 'enemy' countries." In reference to future American policy, the report recommended aiding nations threatened by the USSR, avoiding disclosure of scientific and technical information, increasing instead of dismantling American military preparedness, and recognizing the limitations of diplomacy. The analysis concluded that "compromise and concessions are considered, by the Soviets, to be evidences of weakness and they are encouraged by our 'retreats' to make new and greater demands." "Conferences and negotiations may continue to attain individual objectives," Clifford allowed, "but we cannot talk the Soviets into changing the character of their philosophy and society."[1]

In 1946 American-Turkish relations illustrated the adherence of the Truman administration to the recommendation of the Clifford report of supporting nations believed threatened by Soviet expansion. Stalin had proposed the revision of the Montreux Convention governing the Dardenelles at the Potsdam Conference, and the Big Three Powers had agreed to discuss the matter individually with Turkey if they so chose. During the summer of 1946 the Soviet Union had proposed excluding all nations from the straits except the Black Sea Powers and placing the straits under joint Russo-Turkish defense. The Truman administration interpreted this move as "an open bid to obtain control of Turkey;" and the American ambassador to Turkey, Edwin C. Wilson, further warned that if the Soviet Union gained control of Turkey, Persian Gulf and Suez areas would be threatened. The Departments of State, War and Navy, supported by the Joint Chiefs of Staff, brought Truman "a unanimous recommendation that we take a strong position." When the president agreed, the Army Chief of Staff Dwight Eisenhower asked if Truman understood that if the Russians did not back down, war might come. The president assured Eisenhower that he did and instructed Assistant Secretary of State Acheson to inform the Ankara government of American support in resisting Soviet demands. As proof, the American government immediately ordered naval units to the eastern Mediterranean, and in the fall of 1946 announced their permanent stationing there.[2]

The second evidence of American adherence to the Clifford report concerned the American plan to establish international control of atomic energy. The committee to draw up a proposal to submit to the U.N. Atomic Energy Commission, chaired by Dean Acheson, quickly produced the Acheson-Lilienthal report. David Lilienthal, chairman of the Tennessee Valley Authority and head of the technical consultant group advising Acheson, believed the plan had "a good chance of being accepted, especially by the Russians." Byrnes suggested that Truman appoint Bernard Baruch, seventy-six-year-old adviser to several presidents, as the American representative to the U.N.A.E.C., because the conservative Baruch would make the control plan politically palatable to Congress. Baruch, however, insisted on a policy-making, not just a policy-representing, role and significantly altered the American proposal by prohibiting use of the Security Council veto on atomic energy matters and by imposing sanctions against any nation violating the rules established. When Baruch presented his plan to the United Nations during the summer of 1946 in words analogous to, or perhaps illustrative of, Byrnes's dramatic "loose and wicked talk," he said, ". . . we are here to make a choice between the quick and the dead." In the ensuing debate the Soviet representative, Andrei Gromyko, countered with a disarmament proposal to precede an international control plan and demanded that atomic production be stopped and stockpiles be destroyed. Truman responded, "We should not under any circumstances throw away our gun until we are sure the rest of the world can't arm against us." With neither side willing to trust the other, compromise was impossible in the prolonged debate, which continued through the fall and winter of 1946. The Atomic Energy Commission finally approved the American plan on 30 December 1946, with Russia and Poland not voting; but when the issue returned to the Security Council, the Soviet Union's veto effectively killed further consideration of the plan. According to the Clifford report no international plan was preferable to one which the United States could not control.[3]

The final Clifford dictate—no diplomatic concessions or compromises—applied to Byrnes and his last meeting of the

Council of Foreign Ministers. As agreed in Paris, the ministers gathered in New York City on 4 November to meet concurrently with the U.N. General Assembly. The council's plan was to consider peace conference recommendations in drawing up the final draft of the Italian, Balkan, and Finnish treaties, and to discuss German issues. The New York meeting of the Council of Foreign Ministers was the first peace conference to be held in the United States since the end of the Russo-Japanese War in 1905 when the Treaty of Portsmouth was written. If New York City was not Portsmouth, it was not Paris either. Unlike the French government which prepared for the arrival of the ministers by gilding the Luxembourg Palace and lining its ornate stairways with sword-saluting guards, Byrnes on behalf of the United States as host government concerned himself with telephone switchboards, mimeographing procedure, and map folding techniques. Just finding a place for the council to meet proved difficult as the U.N. delegates arrived first. Byrnes finally persuaded the president of the Waldorf-Astoria to move out of his thirty-seventh floor suite and to provide seventy-three other rooms for offices. "For reasons of security as well as national prestige," Byrnes requested 50 military guards from the Secretary of War, Robert Patterson, and had 150 military policemen assigned to conference security. The only international mugging incident recorded in New York City concerned a Ukrainian delegate to the U.N. and led to charges of "political banditry" which Byrnes handled by telling Molotov that if the secretary of state "inspired political shootings, an unknown clerk would be in no danger; but the chief delegate of the Soviet Union might be, if he continued his practice of making long speeches."[4]

The first New York Conference of the Council of Foreign Ministers began pleasantly with Byrnes presiding and extending a "hearty welcome" to the gentlemen of the council. Unlike every other council meeting, this time there was no dispute over the agenda, because the ministers immediately agreed to begin their discussion with the peace conference recommendations on the Italian treaty. However, harmony in the council ended with that decision, and Byrnes (later describing the meeting) tested the credulity of his readers by recording his surprise that Molotov "entirely disregarded the recommendations of the conference and argued just as he had been arguing for the past thirteen months." Not only was it difficult to credit him with believing Molotov would respect the peace conference suggestions that he opposed, but it was also difficult to believe that the meeting actually began with the anomaly of Molotov supporting a recommendation and Byrnes and Bevin opposing it.[5]

The first conference proposal was that Yugoslavia be heard on the question of the statute and borders of the Free Territory of Trieste. Molotov wanted to hear Yugoslavia and even Italy again, but Byrnes and Bevin feared the Soviets intended to renege on the whole Trieste settlement by allowing Yugoslavia and Italy to reopen the entire discussion. Despite his public position as the champion of a people's peace and of all two-thirds vote recommendations, Byrnes argued to limit the meaning of this resolution. He said that the recommendation, passed by a two-thirds majority, stated that the Yugoslav representative "may present his views," but it did not say that he "should be heard or that any of us need listen to him." Molotov called this a "difference in language," a "second-rate question," and insisted that both nations be heard, adding that "it goes without saying that hearing does not mean agreeing." Bevin's suspicions continued and he bluntly asked Molotov, "If we can be frank with one another—exactly what is it we are trying to do?" The Soviet diplomat assured Bevin, "There should be no reproaches that the Soviet delegation has departed from any of the agreements made," and secured the agreement of the ministers to hear Yugoslavia and Italy.[6]

Of the three other conference recommendations considered at this first meeting, Molotov accepted one with amendments and refused the other two, which gave him a two-two record for the meeting. The first refused was an Austro-Italian agreement, which Molotov did not consider necessary to record in the treaty; and when Byrnes insisted that the conference had approved this agreement by a two-thirds vote, the Russian tartly responded that "this fact only goes to show that not all the recommendations adopted by two-thirds vote are satisfactory decisions." The other rejected recommendation, which was far more important, suggested Italian reparations to the lesser powers. The ministers deferred discussion on the latter and adjourned in affirmation of Byrnes's "I want to see if we can't agree to step into the next room to have a cocktail."[7]

For the next five meetings the ministers continued to review the ninety-four peace conference recommendations, completed their discussion of the Italian treaty, and then went through the other four treaties. The large number of recommendations, their varying significance, and their increasing technicality led Byrnes to state, "I confess it was tiresome." Vandenberg and Connally, again advising the secretary, but dividing their time between U.N. and council meetings, turned to doodling during the discussions, while Ben Cohen sketched the diplomats present. The only respites the ministers had from their work occurred when the Yugoslav and Italian ministers spoke and when Molotov went to Washington to celebrate the anniversary of the Soviet October Revolution at the Russian embassy. Byrnes asked Acheson to meet the Soviet foreign minister at Union Station and to offer to drive him to the embassy. "In those days of man's innocence about the Russians," Acheson recalled, "Mr. Byrnes did not want minor irritations to add unnecessarily to major ones." Molotov refused the assistant secretary's offer of a ride, only to have flames begin to shoot out from under the hood of the Soviet limousine. Happily, the swarm of security agents on the scene discovered the trouble was mechanical, not political, and Molotov agreed to ride with Acheson.[8]

On the first reading of the Italian treaty, the ministers deferred consideration of eleven recommendations because they could not agree; they sent three recommendations to their deputies to work out minor language disagreements, and they agreed on four peace conference proposals. Great Britain made possible what Couve de Murville, representing Bidault for the entire New York conference, called a "happy event": acceptance of the first important peace conference suggestion by the council. Bevin had withdrawn the British objection to a minor clause on which the others agreed and had pointed out that "Britain still leads in some things." On the next recommendation Molotov withdrew the Soviet objection to allow adoption and said that the Soviets did not wish "to lag behind Great Britain." Byrnes soon followed suit, changed an American abstention to approval, and said, "I join the concession class." On a more substantive peace conference proposal for Italy to compensate up to seventy-five percent for damages inflicted on U.N. property, the Soviet and American delegations united in opposition to strong British-French support for the recommendation, which was one vote short of being a two-thirds vote recommendation. The Americans and Soviets combined in support of another Italian issue, a minor peace conference recommendation which the British and French opposed, but Byrnes's unique argument that "the Soviet-American bloc was supported by the peace conference" eventually led to British and French acceptance of the proposal.[9]

On the Balkan and Finnish treaties, the ministers deferred on their first reading to the vast majority of the peace conference recommendations. Bevin, who had decided like Byrnes to support all two-thirds majority recommendations, became angry at Molotov's persistent and predictable refusal to be influenced by the peace conference on Balkan issues. Bevin, first using sarcasm on the Soviets, said, "Wouldn't it be nice if we adopted a majority resolution now and again," and then told Molotov that he was "treating the Conference almost with contempt." Byrnes, trying a different tactic, interrupted a council meeting to ask for two minutes of silence in honor of the war dead in hopes that "it may help us to reach agreement on our common objectives, objectives for which our boys gave their lives." The council observed two minutes of silence and then resumed their disagreements.[10]

On a military limitations clause in the Bulgarian treaty which Molotov opposed, the commission vote was eleven for and seven against, with three abstentions. Molotov concluded, to the consternation of the British and Americans, that "consequently this article was adopted only by a majority of one vote." On a later Hungarian reparations article that Byrnes opposed and Molotov supported, the

Russian urged that the council should support the majority vote of twelve for, two against, and eight abstaining. Bevin responded, "If the abstentions were counted as argued this morning it was only carried by two votes." There was not the same degree of divergence of position on the first reading of the Balkan and Finnish recommendations as there was on the Italian treaty. The Americans and British almost always supported the peace conference recommendations, and the Soviets almost always opposed them.[11]

The ministers began a second reading of the peace conference resolutions, but when they came to the borders and statute of the Free Territory of Trieste, they wisely decided to change their procedure and concentrate on this major issue instead of the myriad of lesser proposals. News of direct Yugoslav-Italian negotiations to settle the problems between them initiated this procedural change. Molotov and Couve de Murville encouraged the possibility of Yugoslav-Italian assistance in solving the Trieste issue, but Byrnes and Bevin again suspected that Molotov was trying to renege on the council decision to establish a Free Territory despite his assurances to the contrary. By a two-thirds majority vote the peace conference had accepted a French compromise proposal on the statute, although the Soviet Union had opposed it. Now, Molotov frankly told the council that he accepted the French draft "as a basis" for discussion, but that the could not "adopt it in its entirety without some amendments." In answer to Byrnes's question of how many amendments Molotov proposed, the foreign minister said, "A whole box of them," and the secretary responded, "Let's see what you have in the box."[12]

Thus began ten of the most difficult meetings the Council of Foreign Ministers ever held. From 12 November to 23 November the council literally sat as a constitutional convention for the Free Territory of Trieste. Molotov held the initiative from the beginning, impervious to the American and British insistence that the peace conference had already decided the statute and that the conference proposal was in itself a compromise, not the British or American proposition. Tirelessly, the Soviet foreign minister suggested amendment after amendment to the French proposal and forced Bevin and Byrnes into a defensive position, which illustrated the wisdom of his unanimity comments in Paris.[13]

Molotov's first objective was to limit the powers of the governor of Trieste, and so he repeated his Paris arguments that the French draft was "not sufficiently democratic" and that it created "not a Governor but a Dictator." He proposed limiting the governor's legislative suspension right to laws that contradicted the statute, administering foreign affairs in cooperation with elected officials, and electing the judiciary instead of having the governor appoint judges. The most important of the Soviet amendments to the governor's powers concerned control of the police, which Molotov wanted in the hands of the legislature except in times of emergency when the governor could assume control. Molotov agreed that the governor should be a foreigner and that he should have the power to appoint the chief of police from legislature nominees.

Byrnes and Bevin fought back, while de Murville attempted to assume Bidault's former position as middle man. While maintaining in reference to the governor "that if any man hunted the job we must have a psychiatrist interview him first of all," Byrnes insisted that he remain the strongest element in the government. He wanted to clarify who would decide if an emergency situation existed in Trieste and who "would have the power to hire and fire the police force;" and Bevin wanted the statute to specify who would settle disputes between the governor and the legislature. In reference to Molotov's second objective of insuring immediate troop withdrawal from the area, Byrnes and Bevin assured the Soviets that no one "had reason to be afraid that these troops would remain one minute longer than was necessary." Molotov also wanted special zones under the exclusive jurisdiction of Yugoslavia and Italy provided by the Free Port Administration and special Yugoslav privileges in the control of Trieste railroads and customs union. Finally, Molotov wanted the council to establish, subject to Security Council approval, a provisional regime to govern Trieste until the statute went into effect.

The ministers resorted to their old device of informal meetings while discussing the Trieste statute. Although the complexity and the importance of the issues were equaled by

Molotov's indefatigable pursuit of Yugoslav advantage, tempers remained calm, and the ministers even reached some agreement. They decided that the territory shoud be neutral and demilitarized and that only the Security Council could send troops into the area in an emergency. The ministers also agreed to leave to the legislature the procedure of choosing a judiciary, and the adoption of a constitution for the area. The council finally agreed to limit the legislation suspension power of the governor and to establish a provisional regime. These agreements, although painstakingly slow in coming, were substantial and significant. They were made possible not only by Molotov's prodigious efforts but also by the willingness of the others to negotiate their differences.

Byrnes was the first to tire of this laborious process, saying that "if we can't agree, we just don't agree, that's all" and "if we can't agree to make it free let's admit it to the world instead of we four men, the top man in each of our Governments sitting here discussing it after the hours and hours we have spent on it." On the twelfth and worst day of the discussion, the ministers heard a report from the deputies on the still unagreed articles that had been referred to them. Byrnes commented that "as I understand the report, the Deputies did nothing. If we argue these points, we would be here until Christmas." "If we work like the Deputies did this morning on these questions, we will be here until 1950." Molotov said that he did not have "such a pessimistic view" of the deputies' work and proceeded to agree on the next issue, the Italian-Yugoslav frontier, and to offer agreement on the Austro-Italian agreement in exchange for agreement on Yugoslav-Trieste railroads. This exchange followed:

> Mr. Bevin: This seems like horse trading to me.
> Mr. Molotov: I do not know how to horse trade.
> Mr. Byrnes: Find me a horse trader as hard as you are, and I will give him a gold medal.
> Mr. Molotov: I am learning.
> Mr. Bevin: God help us when you have learned!

Before the council met again, Molotov came to Byrnes's suite in the Waldorf for a private conversation on the status of the council's work. Byrnes said that he was "greatly discouraged at the lack of progress," and added that he had almost "come to the conclusion that it would be better to admit frankly that they could not agree and announce their disagreements to the world." In his book, *Speaking Frankly*, written in 1947 immediately after his resignation as secretary of state, Byrnes maintained that his pessimistic note was the hallmark of this conversation and that Molotov tested his sincerity the next day be sending the Yugoslav ambassador to offer a boundary-reparations trade on the Italian treaty. He believed that if he "showed willingness to negotiate," Molotov would think he had not meant "what I had said to him about ending our efforts to reach agreement." Accordingly, he refused the Yugoslav offer and wrote that at the next council session Molotov "announced his agreement to some of the peace conference recommendations and proposed slight modifications for others. He realized that I meant what I had said and that he could secure no further concessions."[14]

Chip Bohlen's account of this conversation largely supports Byrnes's version, although Bohlen remembered that he and Byrnes went to see Molotov in his Ritz Hotel suite at Byrnes's initiative. Bohlen wrote that Byrnes "called me one day and in typical fashion—he had obviously made up his mind—said, 'Come on, Chip, we'll go see Molotov. I have an idea.'" His idea, Bohlen said, was to tell Molotov, "'In thinking the whole matter over, I really believe the wisest thing for us all to do is admit failure and to disband this meeting.'" Byrnes was "smooth"; he told Molotov that Molotov would be able to justify adjourning because he had tried hard on Yugoslavia's behalf but Yugoslavia was "ungrateful." Molotov, Bohlen said, started to stutter as he always did when he was excited and said, "'No, no, Mr. Byrnes, don't take hasty actions. Just wait until this afternoon's meeting and you will see developments.'" On the way out in the elevator, Byrnes said, "'Well, I hope that works,'" and Bohlen concluded that it did because that afternoon "Molotov handed out concessions like cards from a deck."[15]

Since these accounts vary enough from the State Department record of the conversation, *Foreign Relations* adds a footnote to the memorandum: "This appears to be the same conversation described, in somewhat different terms, in James F. Byrnes' *Speaking Frankly*." According to the State Department account, Byrnes did not threaten adjournment; he suggested that the council proceed to the German questions and see what the Yugoslav-Italian negotiations produced. And when Molotov responded that he was not as pessimistic as Byrnes and that "their chief difficulty was to do something, even a little something, to meet the Yugoslav objection," Byrnes was ready to negotiate again. Molotov told Byrnes that he wanted to give the Yugoslavs "something so that there would be no excuse for their not signing" and that "if something could be achieved along that line, he did not think it would be too difficult to settle the outstanding points." Byrnes offered to agree to Allied troop reduction during the period of the provisional government, with the governor deciding when the troops should leave. Molotov thought that "would be acceptable and helpful and he thought would please the Yugoslavs." Byrnes then asked Molotov to accept the French proposal on the other outstanding issues, and Molotov "remarked that insofar as the permanent statute went they were virtually in complete agreement." As to the provisional regime, the two ministers agreed to apply the relevant parts of the permanent statute to the unsettled articles. Byrnes and Molotov even agreed on a common stand on the compensation-percentage of damages to Allied property to present to Britain and France. These agreements contrast considerably with Byrnes's version that "I closed our conversation on a strong note of resignation to the impossibility of securing treaties."[16]

The secretary initiated a luncheon meeting the next day in his suite for only the ministers and their translators. The other ministers tentatively accepted the agreements that Byrnes and Molotov had reached, and the council made considerable progress in agreeing on troop withdrawal and on an election date for the legislature. Byrnes later boasted to the press that at this meeting he used on his colleagues the tactic he had used in Congress to get compromises, a bullbat session. In the South the idea was that if men with differences gathered "to strike a blow for liberty" between twilight and dark when the bullbats began circling the chimneys, they well might reach agreement. This was as good a story as the one about threatening Molotov with adjournment and as much of an exaggeration. This was a luncheon with liquor served, but there was no easy relaxed airing of views; it was a tough negotiating session, and the tentative agreements reached required eight more council sessions before final agreement was possible. And instead of being lulled into agreement by circling bullbats, Molotov established a connection between revising the peace confer- ence recommendations on reparations and settling the Danubian and compensation questions. The Russian diplo- mat told the ministers that "if they could agree on the reparations the Soviet Delegation would accept 50% for compensation, but only in that case. Otherwise, they would insist on 25%." Molotov added that "if they could get agreement . . . there was no reason why they could not agree on the Danube." The meeting ended with Molotov making the not so veiled threat that if Yugoslavia were not placated, "it would be difficult to oust the Yugoslav troops from the areas in which they were now." So much for the Southern bullbat tradition.[17]

The issue of interest to the Soviet delegation, second only to Trieste, was reparations, not for the USSR but for the lesser powers. The peace conference by a two-thirds majority had voted that Italy should pay $100 million to Yugoslavia and to Greece, but Molotov argued that Yugoslavia should receive twice the amount Greece received. He couched his argument in terms of Yugoslavia's larger population and area and greater damages inflicted by Italy; he also insisted that Italy pay Albania $25 million, although the peace conference rejected this proposal. In reference to Bulgarian reparations, the peace conference suggested $125 million, to be divided equally between Yugoslavia and Greece, although Yugoslavia had only requested $25 million. When Molotov asked the Council of Foreign Ministers to reduce Bulgarian reparations, Byrnes suggested giving Yugoslavia the $25 million it wanted and Greece the $62,500,000 awarded by the conference. Molotov wanted a total of $25 million from Bulgaria divided into $16 million to Yugoslavia and $9 million to Greece and described the "strange situation" that would result if the council imposed reparations "four times as great as that suggested by them." Byrnes missed the opportunity to respond that adopting the conference recommendation on Bulgarian reparations was the "something" the council could do to placate Yugoslavia. In pressing his demands, Molotov changed his figures several times and offered at one time to accept $150 million for Yugoslavia and $100 million for Greece from Italy and $20 million each for Yugoslavia and Greece from Bulgaria. Bevin consistently refused to lower the Greek reparations, and Byrnes argued that Italian property in the areas ceded to Yugoslavia should be counted as part of Yugoslavia's payments. The secretary also countered by arguing for a lowering of Hungarian reparations to the Soviet Union, but, leaving the fate of Hungary's payments up to Molotov's "careful and prayerful consideration," said, "If after he has prayed, he did not reduce them, I would agree to it." Molotov did not reduce Hungary's reparations. It apparently did not occur to Byrnes to connect the Trieste and reparations issues to gain bargaining clout against Molotov.[18]

Byrnes finally offered to raise Yugoslav reparations from Italy to $125 million and to leave Greece's at $100 million and to lower Bulgarian reparations to $45 million for Greece and $20 million for Yugoslavia. Both Bevin and Molotov opposed the secretary's proposal, but Molotov again lowered his demand to Italian payments of $130 million for Yugoslavia, $100 million for Greece, and $15 million for Albania, with Bulgaria paying $20 million to Yugoslavia and $30 million to Greece. Bevin still refused, and Byrnes would not agree to Albania receiving reparations. Couve de Murville initiated still another juggling of Soviet and American figures, but confusion, not agreement, resulted from so many arithmetic proposals. Molotov did accept, eventually, the principle of equal reparations for Yugoslavia and Italy if Albania also received payment. The discussion bordered on the ludicrous as the haggling continued, with Molotov maintaining "that the principle of equality is unjust to Yugoslavia"; and Bevin asking, "Why if we are just, should we be so mean to Greece?" Couve de Murville finally suggested that since the ministers accepted equal payments, they should decide on a combined Italian-Bulgarian total payment and then work on the division of that total between Yugoslavia and Greece. This exchange followed:

> Mr. Bevin: I will accept $155 million.
> Mr. Molotov: I will agree to $145 million.
> Mr. Bevin: I cannot accept it.
> Mr. Couve de Murville: I hardly dare suggest the middle figure of $150 million

Molotov interjected that they had forgotten about Albania; "where figures should be there is a blank," he said. Byrnes responded, "I am in favor of giving them just that—blank." The secretary did introduce a unique, if unacceptable, solution for Albania: give Yugoslavia more than it wanted from Bulgaria so the Yugoslavs could award the surplus to Albania.[19]

At this juncture Molotov again connected the reparations settlement to the Danubian and compensation issues. In reference to the Danube, Molotov agreed to the peace conference proposal that a conference be held to establish an international regime for the river; but he wanted to exclude Greece and include the Ukraine, and he did not want the equal user's rights stated in the Balkan treaties. On compensation for damage to Allied property, Molotov stayed with his 25 percent threat after the United States moved to 50 percent. Both the French and British continued to support the peace conference recommendation of 75 percent, although Bevin asked, "Does anyone propose 100%?" Finally, on 5 December the ministers settled all three issues. The council excluded Greece from the Danubian conference, but placed the principle of free navigation in the Balkan treaties. On compensation, the ministers compromised at payment of $66^{2/3}$ percent of the value of the damage caused, and the final reparations settlement was that Yugoslavia and Greece would receive a total of $150 million each from Italy and Bulgaria and that Italy would pay Albania $5 million.[20]

With agreement on the major issues of Trieste, reparations, the Danube, and compensation, the ministers held seven more meetings to settle the outstanding minor points and to plan for the discussion of the German and Austrian treaties. They quickly agreed to hold a session of the Council of Foreign Ministers in Moscow on 10 March without China present, but Molotov again resisted Byrnes's efforts to appoint special deputies to begin work immediately on the German and Austrian treaties. The Soviet diplomat argued that they should reach some agreements first so that the deputies "would have a real prospect of fruitful work." This time Byrnes countered by suggesting that the deputies hear the views of the other nations directly interested in the German treaty before the council convened, particularly on the subject of German frontiers. Molotov said that he was apprehensive that nations would state their claims to parts of Germany and, that there would "be agitation and a whetting up of appetites," which would "produce disquiet in Germany." When Bevin and de Murville added their support to the Americn proposal and Byrnes leaked information to the press that the Russians were holding up the right of Allied nations to present their views on Germany, Molotov capitulated. He complained to the council that he had hardly spoken before the press reported his views "in a sense unfavorable to the Soviet Union," but he agreed to the appointment of special deputies. The ministers decided that the deputies should meet in London on 14 January to begin work on the German and Austrian treaties and to hear presentations from other nations. The council also established an agenda for its March meeting, beginning with a report by the Allied Control Authority in Germany on its progress, considering a provisional political organization for Germany, preparing a German peace treaty, discussing again Byrnes's German disarmament treaty, and finally working on the Austrian treaty.[21]

The Council of Foreign Ministers ended their New York Conference by instructing their deputies to prepare final drafts on the Italian, Balkan, and Finnish treaties and to submit these documents to the signatory nations in Paris on 10 February 1947. As chairman of their last meeting on 12 December, Molotov said that it seemed to him that they had completed their work. "This being so, permit me," he said, "to congratulate the members of the Council of Foreign Ministers on finishing a long and hard work in drafting the five peace treaties." Molotov was one of the few to congratulate the ministers on the completion of their protracted negotiations; the council's success, unlike its difficulties, went largely unnoticed. For the first time, and without explanation, Byrnes did not make a radio report to the American people on the work of a conference of the Council of Foreign Ministers. The conference simply ended, and the foreign ministers went on to other responsibilities.[22]

To this day Byrnes's account of the New York meeting of the Council of Foreign Ministers has gone unchallenged, because historians have joined his contemporaries in ignoring the conference or in accepting Byrnes's version that his ultimatum to Molotov made possible the completion of the treaties. In New York, according to Robert Murphy, Byrnes "almost single-handedly pushed through their acceptance when another deadlock threatened." The minutes of the council meetings indicate that the secretary's description of the presumed stalemate, threat, and resulting compliance was exaggerated. What Byrnes described to the press, to the cabinet, and for posterity as Molotov's obdurance was, in fact, the Soviet diplomat's continuing determination to write treaties favorable to the Soviet Union. In New York Byrnes paid for ignoring the principle of unanimity at the Paris Peace Conference. Molotov, on the other hand, used the peace conference compromises on the important issues as the basis for his demands, insisting in effect on compromises on top of compromises. Molotov, like Byrnes, did not want a New York deadlock; he wanted the treaties completed because the Soviet Union would gain from their completion. The Italian treaty specified American and British troop withdrawals before the end of 1947, and the Balkan treaties ended the Allied Control Councils there while allowing Soviet troops to stay until the completion of the Austrian and German treaties. The Finnish Treaty allowed Russian troops to stay permanently.[23]

As difficult as it is to believe that Byrnes thought Molotov would accept the peace conference proposals, that was one of the alternative explanations of his actions. Another possibility was that the secretary expressed publicly his expectation of Soviet acceptance in order to pressure Molotov, and still another was Byrnes's impatience with the prolonged negotiations and his desire to produce results. In the background still influencing Byrnes was the Clifford report with its no compromises pronouncement. Perhaps the best interpretation of Byrnes's New York performance was that publicly he continued to do obeisance to the desire of the administration and the nation to be "tough" with the USSR, hence the exaggeration of the stalemate and ultimatum. Privately, he continued to negotiate, eventually producing treaties that all four nations could accept, but which he could no longer present on the radio to the American people as American triumphs. The Council of Foreign Ministers accepted a total of forty-seven of the fifty-three two-thirds majority peace conference recommendations and twenty-four of the forty-one simple majority suggestions. The bulk of those accepted were either insignificant or considerably amended by Molotov.[24]

Byrnes stayed in New York after the council meeting to give a speech on disarmament to the U.N. General Assembly. When the Assembly adjourned on 16 December, he returned to Washington to report to the president and the cabinet on the New York Conference. On 19 December he returned to the White House to see the president and to resign as secretary of state. This was the third time the president and he talked about his resignation: the first was in April after a medical checkup and before he left for the first session of the Paris Conference of the Council of Foreign Ministers; the second time was during the Wallace affair when he had threatened to resign unless Truman muzzled Wallace. This time Byrnes reminded Truman that in April he had told him that he would resign after the completion of the treaties, anticipating then the date of 1 July. Now that the council had completed the treaties, and although his health was better, he asked to be relieved. He said that Truman gave him several reasons why he should stay on but once he convinced the president that he was serious, Truman asked his opinion of George Marshall as a successor. Byrnes characterized Marshall as a "splendid appointment" and left with the understanding of 10 January as his resignation date. He spent the Christmas holidays in Bermuda and returned to

Washington to learn on 7 January that news of his resignation had reached the press. He suggested that Truman go ahead and announce his resignation and Marshall's appointment; only hours later Truman released to the press Byrnes's two letters of resignation and the president's acceptance letter. Truman's letter said in part:

> I realize full well how arduous and complex have been the problems which have falled to you since you took office in July 1945. Big events were then impending and the months that have ensued have presented problems of the utmost moment, with all of which you have dealt with rare tact and judgment and—when necessary—firmness and tenacity of purpose.[25]

Reaction to Byrnes's resignation was, predictably, mixed. Vandenberg and Dulles complained about "the Administration's dangerous habit of annually changing Secretaries of State," and Vandenberg said, "Continuity of foreign policy is rather difficult under such itinerant auspices." Connally registered his surprise at what he considered Byrnes's abrupt resignation, because he believed that Byrnes was secure as secretary of state. Dulles and Joseph Davies both doubted that illness was Byrnes's reason for resigning, as it, of course, was not. After Byrnes's physical examination in April showing additional heart damage, he received a second opinion indicating doubt about the extent of the trouble. In January 1947 after Truman accepted his resignation, a third physical examination showed "no indication of additional myocardial damage about which they had warned me." Undoubtedly, the secretary resigned because his relationship with the president, difficult from the first, had worsened with the Wallace trouble. Also, he realized that the German and Austrian negotiations would involve even longer and more arduous meetings, not to mention political hazards, than the first five treaties. Understanding his reasons for resigning was considerably easier than understanding his staying on would have been. As he said at this juncture, "Any man who would want to be Secretary of State would go to hell for pleasure."[26]

Politically, Byrnes's resignation was well-planned. *Time* magazine had just named him its "Man of the Year," and it did so in terms Byrnes would most appreciate: "A nervous nation found a firm and patient voice." Byrnes "managed to get over to the Russians and the world that the U.S. had planted the weight of its power in the path of the Russian advance." Moreover, Byrnes left office after formally completing the work that had occupied him during his entire term as secretary of state, and in the old State Department building he signed the peace treaties on his last day in office. Both the new secretary, George Marshall, and Vandenberg, the incoming Chairman of the Senate Foreign Relations Committee, agreed that Byrnes should attend the Congressional hearings on the treaties. Vandenberg said, "They are *your* treaties. *You* are more responsible for them than anybody else."[27]

CHAPTER EIGHT

CONCLUSION

James F. Byrnes served as secretary of state for eighteen months from July 1945 to January 1947, a crucial period in United States history, which began with the end of World War II and ended with the onset of the cold war. This period should have been a great opportunity for a statesman, but Byrnes was not a statesman; he was a politician with vast governmental experience and with equally vast diplomatic ignorance. A statesman would have understood the value of possessing a long-range international perspective, of recognizing the legitimate interests of other nations, and of rising above personal political gain. A statesman might even have possessed principles to guide him and, instead of being motivated by public opinion, might have attempted to educate the public about international reality. Byrnes's perspective was short-term and nationalistic, and he was as ignorant of the interests of other nations as he was aware of the political value of being credited with writing the peace. He simply believed that since the United States had emerged from the war the wealthiest and the most powerful nation the world had ever known, it could write its postwar vision into the treaties. He had little opportunity or inclination to prepare for the critical work he had to do. He brought to the State Department established work habits characterized by a remarkable sense of self-confidence, reliance on a select group of advisers, and improvised solutions to problems of unfathomed complexity. These habits led to his ignoring State Department resources and expertise and to personalizing American foreign policy. At a time when the United States needed all its diplomatic talent concentrated on its postwar problems, one man dominated the determination of American foreign relations.

Byrnes's skills were as explicit as his limitations. He brought to his diplomatic post formidable talents as a practitioner of compromise, a finder of middle ground between opposing views. His easygoing, even-tempered personality was another asset; a gregarious extrovert, he knew the value of personal relations and humor in easing difficult situations. An energetic worker, he tirelessly continued to pursue solutions that he could present to the American people as personal triumphs. Being a remarkably candid secretary of state, he single-handedly ended the secretiveness of American wartime diplomacy. Undoubtedly, he sincerely believed in the right of the American people to know what their diplomats were doing, but he also understood the political value of referring to a "people's peace" and being identified in the mind of the public with the writing of that peace. Finally, he was an intelligent man; he had an alert, inquiring mind, and he learned quickly.

The problem was that there was so much to be learned. The postwar world expected by the United States did not materialize, and Byrnes and the American people learned this during the writing of the peace by the Council of Foreign Ministers. He made the State Department idea of a council to write the first drafts of the peace treaties his and from the beginning had a vested interest in its success. The Council of Foreign Ministers originated as part of the American desire to avoid the mistakes of the Versailles Peace Conference, and to create an interim collective security organization until the United Nations could begin to function. The idea was not only to allow the alliance that won the war to write the peace but also to perpetuate the alliance. What Byrnes considered to be the easy acceptance by the British and the Soviets of the American proposal for a Council of Foreign Ministers at Potsdam increased his confidence in the success of the council. However, the objections over the inclusion of China and France and over discussion privileges versus voting rights, though initially smoothed over, became built-in flaws of the proposal. The necessity of unanimity within the council allowed the most reluctant of the participants to determine the progress of the negotiations and provided new horizons for Byrnes's talents for compromise. Adding to the difficulties of the Council of Foreign Ministers was that the device which allowed the wartime alliance to maintain a unanimous front, postponement of issues on which agreement was impossible, was not available to the council.[1]

Byrnes went to the London Conference of the Council of Foreign Ministers with only a vague conception of what the United States wanted written into the treaties, but with the firm assumption that American military and economic power would allow the United States to dictate the treaties. The secretary understood that the American people wanted the treaties written quickly so that the troops could come home, and he did not expect much difficulty in doing this. After all, the cumbersome Versailles Conference had completed its work in six months; surely, the Council of Foreign Ministers could work more quickly. In London Byrnes learned that the Soviet Union wanted its status as a victorious Great Power acknowledged in treaties giving it control of the Balkans, reparations with which to rebuild, bases in the Mediterranean, a share in the control of Japan, and benefits for its client state of Yugoslavia. These explicit Russian demands directly conflicted with the American goals of national self-determination, freedom of trade, collective security, and American predominance. Not wanting to be blamed for spoiling the peace, and contrary to his later account that he broke off the conference rather than accede to Molotov's demands, Byrnes tried to conciliate the Soviet diplomat, but Molotov refused to compromise. Embarrassed, Byrnes publicly blamed the diplomatic failure on the Soviets and described the Russian bid for equal power status as a threat to the United States and as an effort to dominate Europe.

Still eager to write the treaties, the secretary initiated a meeting in Moscow where he successfully used a new approach to the USSR, quid pro quo negotiations. The Moscow agreement lacked substance, but he had renewed diplomatic contact with the Soviet Union and the Council of Foreign Ministers could resume its work. Returning home from the Moscow Conference, he reaped the harvest of telling the American people too much about American-Soviet differences and of not telling the president of the United States enough. His open diplomacy changed American public opinion toward the USSR, and it in turn changed American foreign policy. Truman not only insisted on more presidential control over American international affairs, he also responded to the public's demand for a firm Soviet policy.

Truman intuitively distrusted the Soviet Union. This natural inclination, plus the change in public opinion and his own desire to appear decisive, led to new strictures on Byrnes's efforts to write the peace treaties. The president's relationship with Byrnes was understandably strained from the beginning, but Truman, angered by political differences with Byrnes after his resignation as secretary of state, exaggerated in his memoirs his lecturing of the secretary after Moscow. Inasmuch as Byrnes found it possible to maintain a friendly relationship with Molotov, his relationship with Truman was as correct as Byrnes said it was. Although he kept Truman better informed about American foreign relations after the Moscow conference, his policy-making powers remained intact. The only real post-Moscow change in his diplomacy was that now he had to do public obesiance to the desire of the public and the administration that he get tough with the Soviet Union. Since he understood the incompatibility of intransigence and compromise, and since he still wanted credit for writing the peace, he decided to be publicly tough and privately yielding. He characterized his new approach as "patience with firmness" and later as "firmness with patience," but the patience was always visible within the council and the firmness appeared in public statements. At both sessions of the Paris Conference of the Council of Foreign Ministers, he successfully employed his tactic of public intransigence and private diplomacy. Only at the Paris Peace Conference did he yield totally to the emerging dictum of compromise equals appeasement; at the peace conference there was no privacy. In New York he found it possible to return again to his contradictory, but success-ful, public-private attitudes, and the Council of Foreign Ministers completed the five peace treaties.

The treaties were reasonably good treaties, perhaps the best that could have been written under the circumstances. They did not so much settle the fate of the belligerents as they settled the struggle for power among the victors by acknowledging postwar reality in Europe. Although the Americans and British set out to weaken Soviet control of the Balkans, and the Soviets attempted to lessen American-British influence in Italy, both failed. The Soviet effort to gain naval bases in the Mediterranean for its trade failed as did the American effort to penetrate the Balkans economical-ly. Although the treaties included equal trade clauses, they were unenforceable. The Soviet Union received more reparations than the United States wanted, but less than it desired. If the USSR appeared to gain the most from the treaties, that was because its goals were more realistic than those of the Americans, and the treaties reflected reality. The only real winners were Yugoslavia and Italy, both of whom received much better treatment than either had a right to expect.[2]

Writing the treaties was a major accomplishment, perhaps even a symbol of what might have been if persistent, tenacious, face-to-face negotiations had continued. The Council of Foreign Ministers negotiated under a near impossible situation created by the simultaneous influence of the Iranian-Yugoslav-Turkish crises, the ever escalating rhetoric, and the atomic bomb. The foreign ministers involved were provincial nationalists, with their perspec-tives limited to their own nation's welfare, and with one of their number, Molotov, clearly dominating the others. Unhindered by the press, public opinion, or Congress, aided by definite goals, and aware of the American desire to maintain the alliance, Molotov introduced first the council and then the world to a new brand of diplomacy. Chain-smoking Russian cigarettes and stroking his mustache, Molotov manipulated the others like a puppet master, time after time reducing Bevin to fury, Byrnes to impatience, and Bidault to new compromise suggestions. Bevin — suffering from angina, slow to comprehend, and easily distracted —

understood his dependence on the United States but grated under it, complaining frequently that Britain was being ignored, which it was. A strong French Communist party forced Bidault into his role as council mediator, and he succeeded far better in presenting compromise proposals than he did in protecting French interests. Bidault was no statesman, but he was the closest the Council of Foreign Ministers came to having one.[3]

Also handicapping the Council of Foreign Ministers was the Potsdam decision to begin first with the lesser treaties and then to deal with Austria and Germany. Bidault said, "The troubles of the war-shattered world are like a tangled skein. The threads have to be straightened out; but this cannot be done by pulling at the end of one thread after another. The skein is full of knots, and the main knot is Germany." Germany was not just a French obsession; Nicolson wrote, "To approach this central problem tentatively, and from the easiest end, was to be stung by each of the nettles without firmly grasping a single one." Since American-Soviet confrontation over the peace settlement had to come, it was better to have it over Germany immediately, because a settlement there would be of more value than one on the lesser treaties. Discussing Germany first might have led to a general European settlement, a frank acknowledgment of existing spheres of influence and, if not the avoidance, at least the easing, of a Soviet-American encounter. Certainly beginning with Germany would have strengthened the American-British position because they controlled two-thirds of Germany and their military power was there, not in Eastern Europe. Since the Soviet strength was in Eastern Europe, all Byrnes could do was protest and criticize and by so doing, estrange the Soviets. Pointing this out in an article summarizing the work of the council, the American journalist, Walter Lippmann, characterized the decision to begin with satellite treaties "a gigantic blunder," which challenged the Russians "first of all on the ground where they were most able to be, and were most certain to be, brutal, stubborn, faithless and aggressive."[4]

As intriguing as historical might-have-beens are, historians must concern themselves with what happened, and what happened was that the fragility of American-Soviet relations did not withstand the threat of peace. Stalin had said as early as Yalta, "It is good to have an alliance of the principal Powers during a war. It would not be possible to win the war without the Alliance. But an Alliance against the common enemy is something clear and understandable. Far more complicated is an alliance after the war for securing lasting peace and the fruits of victory."[5] American leaders understood after World War II that it was in the national interest to maintain good relations with the Soviet Union, but when the USSR frustrated American postwar expectations, U.S. officials decided, with benevolent arrogance, that it was in American and world interests to restrain the Soviet Union. The United States government incorrectly interpreted Soviet insistence on a sphere of influence as a renewal of the Communist ideological imperative to foment world revolution, overthrow capitalist governments, and install the Soviet political system. Outmaneuvered by Molotov in the Council of Foreign Ministers, Byrnes's decision to resort to open diplomacy hardened American suspicions of Russian goals into conviction. By publicly displaying the Russian intemperate diplomacy in a minority position at the Paris Peace Conference, Byrnes sought not only to pressure the USSR into compliance by outvoting and marshalling public opinion against it, but also to justify his personal inability to produce the kind of treaties the American people expected. Apparently impervious to American military and economic superiority, the Kremlin decided that the price it would have to pay for continued friendship with the United States was too high. Better to rebuild with reparations, protect Soviet security with a ring of satellite nations, and continue political repression inside Russia by replacing the Fascist enemy with the old capitalist enemy.

Chip Bohlen accurately wrote that Byrnes "had to deal with possibly the most difficult period of any since World War II."[6] With his critical lack of international experience, Byrnes attended eight different diplomatic conferences, spending 245 of his 562 days as secretary of state outside the United States. He presided over the implementation of a drastic departure in traditional American diplomacy: protecting American security, not by avoiding entangling alliances, but by continuous involvement in international affairs. The American public accused Byrnes simultaneously of being too soft and too hard on the Soviet Union, of being too quick to accept any compromise and of rejecting legitimate Soviet demands. He was guilty on all counts, but Byrnes and the Council of Foreign Ministers did write the peace treaties, which was half of what he expected to do. He failed to realize his other objective of perpetuating the alliance, and this failure occurred partly because of the means he used to write the treaties. James F. Byrnes's public intransigence and private compromise diplomacy allowed him both to demonstrate an alternative to Soviet-American estrangement and to encourage the impetus toward the cold war.

NOTES

CHAPTER ONE

[1]Cabel Phillips, *The Truman Presidency. The History of a Triumphant Succession* (New York: Macmillan, 1966); Barton J. Bernstein, ed., *Towards a New Past: Dissenting Essays in American Past* (New York: Pantheon, 1968); Barton J. Bernstein, ed., *Politics and Policies of the Truman Administration* (Chicago: Quadrangle, 1970); Robert Allen and William V. Shannon, *The Truman Merry-Go-Round* (New York: Vanguard Press, 1950); Tris Coffin, *Missouri Compromise* (Boston: Little, Brown, 1947); Walt Rostow, *The United States in the World Arena* (New York: Harper & Row, 1960); John Spanier, *American Foreign Policy Since World War II* (New York: Praeger, 1960).

[2]Diary of Henry Stimson, 18 April 1945, Yale University Library; Dean Acheson, *Present at the Creation: My Years in the State Department* (New York: Norton, 1969), p. 731; Harry Truman, *Mr. Citizen* (New York: Random House, 1960), p. 261; Charles Bohlen, *Witness to History, 1929-1969* (New York: Norton, 1973), p. 212; Arthur Vandenberg, Jr., *The Private Papers of Senator Vandenberg* (Boston: Houghton Mifflin, 1952), pp. 167-68.

[3]James F. Byrnes, *Speaking Frankly* (New York: Harper and Brothers, 1947); James F. Byrnes, *All In One Lifetime* (New York: Harper and Brothers, 1958); George Curry, *James F. Byrnes* (New York: Cooper Square Publishers, 1965).

[4]Phillips, *The Truman Presidency*, p. 40; Byrnes, *All In One Lifetime* pp. 222-30; Harry Truman, *Year of Decisions* (Garden City, N.Y.: Doubleday, 1955), pp. 22-23, 192; Margaret Truman, *Harry S. Truman* (New York: Simon and Schuster, 1973), pp. 186-87; 13; Samuel Rosenman, Oral History Interview, 15 October 1968, Harry S. Truman Library; Allen and Shannon, *Truman Merry-Go-Round*, p. 13.

[5]Curry, *James F. Byrnes*, p. 101; Phillips, *The Truman Presidency*, p. 83. Others explained that Byrnes accompanied Roosevelt to Yalta because the president wanted to utilize Byrnes's knowledge of shorthand to keep a record (Coffin, *Missouri Compromise*, p. 247); that Roosevelt was grooming Byrnes as secretary of state to replace Stettinius, (Lloyd C. Gardner,

Architects of Illusion, Men and Ideas in American Foreign Policy, 1941-1949 [Chicago: Quadrangle, 1970], p. 85); that Roosevelt wanted him as an expert on economic matters (Byrnes, *Speaking Frankly,* p. 21); and that Roosevelt wanted him to interpret conference results to Congress (John Gaddis, *The United States and the Origins of the Cold War, 1941-1947* [New York: Columbia University Press, 1972], p. 160).

   [6]Margaret Truman, *Harry S. Truman,* p. 236; Curry, *James F. Byrnes,* p. 102; Truman, *Year of Decisions,* p. 22; Phillips, *The Truman Presidency,* pp. 83-84. The transcript of Byrnes's shorthand notes that Truman received is the only transcript ever made. Byrnes kept the original notes in a secret compartment under his telephone in his Spartanburg office until he gave his papers to Clemson University. The original notes are now at Clemson; the one transcription is at the Truman Library.

   [7]Truman, *Year of Decisions,* p. 23; Coffin, *Missouri Compromise,* p. 247. The Senate unanimously approved Byrnes as secretary of state.

   [8]Truman, *Year of Decisions,* p. 23; Tom Connally, *My Name Is Tom Connally* (New York: Crowell, 1954), p. 289; Coffin, *Missouri Compromise,* p. 246; Vandenberg, *Private Papers,* pp. 224-25.

   [9]Coffin, *Missouri Compromise,* pp. 245-46; Rostow, *United States in the World Arena,* p. 180; *Time,* 49 (6 January 1947), 25-27; Connally, *My Name Is Tom Connally,* p. 289; Cyril Clemens, *The Man From Missouri. A Biography of Harry S. Truman* (New York: J.P. Didier, 1945), p. 139; Gardner, *Architects of Illusion,* p. 84; Curry, *James F. Byrnes,* pp. 87-104; Richard D. Burns, "James F. Byrnes" in *An Uncertain Tradition: American Secretaries of State in the Twentieth Century,* ed. Norman Graebner (New York: McGraw Hill, 1961), pp. 224-27.

   [10]Speeches of 6 January, 15 March, and 27 May 1941 in *The Public Papers and Addresses of Franklin D. Roosevelt,* ed. Samuel Rosenman, Vols. 9-13, 1940-45 (New York: Random House, 1941-1950), IX, p. 672, 10 pp. 69, 192; Roosevelt Press Conferences, 24 November 1942, *ibid.,* XI, p. 492; Robert E. Sherwood, *Roosevelt and Hopkins: An Intimate History* (New York: Harper, 1950), p. 266; Robert Divine, *Second Chance: The Triumph of Internationalism in America During World War II* (New York: Atheneum, 1967), pp. 34, 67-69.

   [11]These include: Walter Lefeber, *America, Russia, and the Cold War, 1945-1967* (New York: Wiley, 1967); Diane Shaver Clemens, *Yalta* (New York: Oxford University Press, 1970); Gar Alperovitz, *Atomic Diplomacy: Hiroshima and Potsdam* (New York: Simon & Schuster, 1965); Barton J. Bernstein, "American Foreign Policy and the Origins of the Cold War," in *Politics and Policies of the Truman Administration,* ed. Bernstein; D. F. Fleming, *The Cold War and Its Origins, 1917-1960* (Garden City, N.Y.: Doubleday, 1961) 2 vols.; and Elliott Roosevelt, *As He Saw It* (New York: Duell, Sloan & Pearce, 1946).

   [12]Truman, *Year of Decisions,* p. 12; Jonathan Daniels, *The Man of Independence* (Philadelphia: Lippincott, 1950), pp. 229, 258-59; William Hillman, ed., *Mr. President: The First Publication from the Personal Diaries, Private Letters, Papers and Revealing Interviews of Harry S. Truman, Thirty-Second President of the United States of America* (New

York: Farrar, Straus & Young, 1952), pp. 51-52; Alfred Steinberg, *The Man From Missouri: The Life and Times of Harry S. Truman* (New York: Doubleday, 1962), p. 186; Gabriel Kolko, *The Politics of War: The World and the United States Foreign Policy, 1943-1945* (New York: Harper & Row, 1968), pp. 380-81; Herbert Feis, *Churchill, Roosevelt, Stalin: The War They Waged and the Peace They Sought* (Princeton: Princeton University Press, 1957), pp. 596-600; William H. McNeill, *America, Britain, and Russia: Their Cooperation and Conflict* (New York: Harper, 1953), pp. 579-80.

[13]Truman, *Year of Decisions*, pp. 37-39, 49-50, 70-72, 77-82; Bohlen memorandum on Truman-Harriman Conversation, 20 April 1945 in *Foreign Relations of the United States Diplomatic Papers* (Washington, D.C.: Government Printing Office, 1960), V, 231-34, hereafter referred to as *FR: 1945;* Forrestal Diary, 23 April 1945, in *The Forrestal Diaries,* ed. Walter Millis (New York: Viking, 1951), p. 49; Bohlen memorandum of Truman meeting with advisers, 23 April 1945, *FR: 1945,* V, 252-55; William Leahy, *I Was There* (New York: McGraw Hill, 1950), pp. 409-13; Bohlen memorandum of Truman-Molotov meeting, *FR: 1945,* V, 256-58; Charles Bohlen, *Witness to History,* p. 213.

[14]Leahy, *I Was There,* pp. 315-16; Morgenthau Diary, 10 January 1945, in John Morton Blum, *From the Morgenthau Diaries: Years of War, 1941-1945* (Boston: Houghton Mifflin, 1967), pp. 305-06; Grew to Kennan, 27 January 1945, *FR: 1945,* V, pp. 968-70; Grew to Harriman, 26 January 1945, *ibid.,* pp. 967-68.

[15]Vandenberg, *Private Papers,* pp. 177-78, 181, 185-86; Davies to Byrnes, 10 May 1945, Davies Diary, 13 and 18 May 1945, Joseph E. Davies Papers, Library of Congress, Boxes 16 and 17; Henry L. Stimson and McGeorge Bundy, *On Active Service in Peace and War* (New York: Harper, 1947), pp. 605-11; Davies's report to Truman on Conversations with Churchill, 12 June 1945 in *Foreign Relations of the United States: The Conference of Berlin (The Potsdam Conference),* 1945, 2 vols. (Washington, D.C.: Government Printing Office, 1960), I, 64-65, hereafter referred to as *FR: Potsdam;* Truman, *Year of Decisions,* pp. 257-58, 261; Sherwood, *Roosevelt and Hopkins,* pp. 885-87; Bohlen's notes of Hopkins-Stalin meeting of 27 May 1945, *FR: Potsdam,* pp. 889-90; Bohlen, *Witness to History,* pp. 214-19.

[16]Byrnes, *Speaking Frankly,* p. 70; Leahy, *I Was There,* p. 242.

[17]*FR: Potsdam,* I, 162-63; Memorandum for the President from Byrnes, 11 June 1945, James F. Byrnes Papers, Correspondence File, Clemson University.

[18]Stettinius to Grew, 19 June 1945, *FR: Potsdam,* I, 283; Memorandum for the Potsdam Conference, Record Group 59, General Records of the Department of State, Decimal File 1945-1949, National Archives.

[19]*FR: Potsdam,* I, 263.

[20]Byrnes, *Speaking Frankly,* pp. 70-71.

[21]Alperovitz, *Atomic Diplomacy,* p. 174; Byrnes, *Speaking Frankly,* pp. 71, 257-63; Truman, *Year of Decisions,* pp. 415-19.

[22]Byrnes, *Speaking Frankly,* p. 67.

[23]Bohlen, *Witness to History,* pp. 228, 231; Truman, *Year of Decisions,* pp. 344-49; Thompson and Cohen Minutes, 17 July 1945, *FR: Potsdam,* II,

52–63; Byrnes, *Speaking Frankly,* p. 72; Diary of William Leahy, 17 July 1945, p. 111.

²⁴Thompson Minutes, First Meeting of the Foreign Ministers, 18 July 1945, *FR: Potsdam,* II, 66–70.

²⁵Thompson and Cohen Minutes, 18 July 1945, *FR: Potsdam,* II, 88–95; Winston Churchill, *The Second World War: Triumph and Tragedy* (Boston: Houghton Mifflin, 1953), p. 650; Byrnes, *Speaking Frankly,* p. 72.

²⁶Thompson Minutes, Second Meeting of the Foreign Ministers, 19 July 1945, *FR: Potsdam,* II, 101–2; United States Delegation Memorandum, 19 July 1945, *ibid.,* p. 108; Text approved by the Heads of Government, 20 July 1945, *ibid.,* pp. 612–13.

²⁷Thompson Minutes, 19, 20, and 21 July 1945, *FR: Potsdam,* II, 101–2, 167–68, 186–87, 203–4, 614–15; Leahy, *I Was There,* p. 405.

²⁸Charles L. Mee, *Meeting at Potsdam* (New York: M. Evans, 1975), pp. 14–15, 76, 82, 126–27, 129, 168–69; Proposal by the United States Delegation, 17 July 1945, *FR: Potsdam,* II, 609–19. Mee's laboriously contrived, air-castle of a thesis reaches its perfection on page 247 when he quotes from V. M. Molotov's speech of 10 October 1946, without realizing that Molotov made his remarks to the Paris Peace Conference convened by the Council of Foreign Ministers.

²⁹Page Minutes, 24 July 1945, *FR: Potsdam,* II, 354–55; Byrnes, *Speaking Frankly,* p. 72; *Department of State Bulletin,* 13 (12 August 1945), 209.

³⁰Joint Communiqué on the Potsdam Conference, 2 August 1945, printed in *Voices of History,* 1945–1946, p. 394.

³¹Byrnes, *Speaking Frankly,* p. 71. These issues included an American proposal for the internationalization of inland waterways, troop withdrawals from Iran, disposition of the Italian colonies, and revision of the Montreux Convention on the Black Sea Straits.

CHAPTER TWO

¹Balfour to Byrnes, 15 August 1945, *FR: 1945,* II, 99.

²James Byrnes, *Speaking Frankly,* pp. 92; George Curry, *James F. Byrnes,* p. 148; *ibid.,* p. 130; Charles Bohlen, *Witness to History,* p. 225. Bohlen disagreed with Byrnes's intention to inform Truman directly about foreign affairs because Byrnes seldom had the time to do so, and Bohlen saw Truman as badly needing State Department expertise.

³Theodore Achilles, Oral History Interview, Dulles Oral History Project, Princeton University; James Byrnes, Oral History Interview, Dulles Oral History Project; *Council of Foreign Ministers, London, September 1945,* John Foster Dulles Papers, Princeton University, I, 1–4, hereafter referred to as *CFM—London.*

⁴Dean Acheson, *Present at the Creation: My Years in the State Department* (New York: Norton, 1969), p. 163; Tris Coffin, *Missouri Compromise,* p. 246; Joseph M. Jones, *The Fifteen Weeks (February 21–June 5, 1947)* (New York: Macmillan, 1955), pp. 105–7; Graham H. Stuart, *The Department of State* (New York: Macmillan, 1949), pp. 425, 440.

⁵Byrnes, *Speaking Frankly,* p. 261; Truman, *Year of Decisions,* p. 87; Journal of Joseph E. Davies, 29 July 1945, Davies Papers, Library of Congress, Box 19; Oppenheimer to Stimson, 17 August 1945, quoted in Richard G. Hewlett and Oscar E. Anderson, Jr., *A History of the United States Atomic Energy Commission: The New World, 1939-1945* (University Park: Pennsylvania State University Press, 1962), p. 417; Byrnes, *Speaking Frankly,* p. 265; Diary of Henry Stimson, 12 August-4 September 1945, quoted in Gaddis, *The United States and the Origins of the Cold War,* p. 264; Minutes of the Meeting of the Secretaries of State, War, and Navy, 10 October 1945, *FR: 1945,* II, 55-56. "Bomb in pocket" must have been the in-joke of 1945, with Molotov making as many as Byrnes (Memorandum to Truman, 29 September 1945, Davies Papers; Byrnes, *ibid.,* pp. 266-67).

⁶Truman, *Year of Decisions,* pp. 46, 98; Bohlen Memorandum on Truman-Molotov Conversation, 23 April 1945, *FR: 1945,* V, 256-57; Herbert Feis, *Between War and Peace: The Potsdam Conference* (Princeton: Princeton University Press, 1960), p. 27; Fredrick J. Dobney, ed., *Selected Papers of Will Clayton* (Baltimore: Johns Hopkins Press, 1971), pp. 150-51; Francis Williams, *A Prime Minister Remembers* (London: Heinemann, 1961), pp. 127-33; Alexander Werth, *France, 1940-1955* (London: Robert Hale, 1956), pp. 257-58; Curry, *James F. Byrnes,* p. 148.

⁷Byrnes, *Speaking Frankly,* pp. 92-93; Memorandum, 8 September 1945, *CFM—London,* II, pt. 1, pp. 38-43, pt. 2, p. 470; Byrnes, *ibid.,* pp. 92-93; Press Conference Transcript, 11 September 1945, Press Clippings Folder, James F. Byrnes Papers, Clemson University.

⁸Edward Weintal, Oral History Interview, Dulles Oral History Project; Adam Ulam, *The Rivals. America and Russia Since World War II* (New York: Viking Press, 1971), p. 27; John Foster Dulles, *War or Peace* (New York: Macmillan, 1950), pp. 28-29; Williams, *A Prime Minister Remembers,* p. 149; Clement Attlee, *As It Happened* (London: Heinemann, 1954), p. 169; Conversations Between Byrnes and Bidault, 23 and 24 August 1945, Correspondence Folder, Byrnes Papers.

⁹Record of the First Meeting of the Council of Foreign Ministers, 11 September 1945, *FR: 1945,* II, 112-23.

¹⁰*Ibid.;* Letter from Dulles to Phillip Jessup, 10 October 1945, Correspondence Folder, Dulles Papers; Acheson to Achilles, 11 September 1945, General Records of the State Department, Record Group 59, File Number 1945-1949, Box C-226; Theodore Achilles, Oral History Interview, Dulles Oral History Project; Acheson to Achilles, 12 and 28 September 1945, General Records of the State Department, Record Group 59, File Number 1945-1949, Box C-226; Byrnes to the State Department, 14 September, 1 October 1945, *ibid.*

¹¹Record of the First Meeting of the Council of Foreign Ministers, 11 September 1945, *FR: 1945,* II, 96-124.

¹²Record of the Second Meeting of the Council of Foreign Ministers, 12 September 1945, *ibid.,* pp. 125-31; Record of the Third Meeting of the Council of Foreign Ministers, 14 September 1945, *ibid.,* pp. 158-63; Byrnes, *Speaking Frankly,* p. 93; Memorandum by the United States Delegation, 12 September 1945, *FR: 1945,* II, 134-35; "Suggested Directives to the Deputies," 14

September 1945, *ibid.,* pp. 179–81; Record of the Third Meeting of the Council of Foreign Ministers, *ibid.;* Record of the Sixth Meeting of the Council of Foreign Ministers, 17 September 1945, *ibid.,* p. 204; Record of the Seventh Meeting of the Council of Foreign Ministers, 17 September 1945, *ibid.,* pp. 210–12; Record of the Twelfth Meeting of the Council of Foreign Ministers, 19 September 1945, *ibid.,* p. 256; Philip Mosely, *The Kremlin and World Politics. Studies in Soviet Policy and Action* (New York: Vintage, 1960), p. 252; John W. Wheeler-Bennett and Anthony Nicholls, *The Semblance of Peace. The Political Settlement After the Second World War* (London: Macmillan, 1972), p. 403, maintains that the London agreements were "distinguished only for their insignificance;" *New York Times,* 17 September 1945; Davies Diary, 12 September 1945.

[13]Record of the Third Meeting of the Council of Foreign Ministers, *FR: 1945,* II, p. 162; Record of the Sixth Meeting of the Council of Foreign Ministers, *ibid.,* pp. 203–4; U.S. Delegation Minutes of the Sixth Meeting, 17 September 1945, *ibid.,* II, 204–9.

[14]Memorandum of Conversation, 14 September 1945, *ibid.,* II, 163–66.

[15]Record of the Fourth Meeting of the Council of Foreign Ministers, 15 September 1945, *FR: 1945,* II, 166–75; Record of the Fifth Meeting of the Council of Foreign Ministers, 15 September 1945, *ibid.,* pp. 186–94.

[16]Memorandum of Conversation, 16 September 1945, *FR: 1945,* II, 200–1; Byrnes, *Speaking Frankly,* p. 96. Byrnes learned that Stettinius had told the Soviet delegation at San Francisco during the discussion of a U.N. trusteeship system that the Soviet Union was "eligible" to receive a territory to administer under trusteeship. Separating a statement of eligibility from an American commitment to support a Soviet request for a trusteeship, the secretary later told Molotov that "in the United States any citizen is eligible to become President, but that does not mean every citizen is going to be President."

[17]Minutes of the Cabinet, 15 September 1945, 128/3, pp. 1–2, Public Records Office, hereafter referred to as CAB.

[18]*Ibid.,* p. 2.

[19]*Ibid.,* p. 4.

[20]*Ibid.,* pp. 5–7; see also CAB 128/1, 3 September 1945, and CAB 128/1, 11 September 1945.

[21]Record of the Seventh Meeting of the Council of Foreign Ministers, 17 September 1945, *FR: 1945,* II, 212–16; Record of the Twelfth Meeting of the Council of Foreign Ministers, *ibid.,* pp. 257–58.

[22]Record of the Seventh Meeting, *ibid.,* p. 210; Record of the Eighth Meeting of the Council of Foreign Ministers, 18 September 1945, *ibid.,* II, 229; Record of the Ninth Meeting of the Council of Foreign Ministers, 18 September 1945, *ibid.,* II, 227; Statements by Representatives of the Yugoslav Government, *ibid.,* pp. 229–32; Statement by the Italian Foreign Minister, *ibid.,* pp. 232–36; Record of the Tenth Meeting of the Council of Foreign Ministers, 18 September 1945, *ibid.,* pp. 240–42; Record of the Eleventh Meeting of the Council of Foreign Ministers, 19 September 1945, *ibid.,* pp. 248–54; Record of the Twelfth Meeting, *ibid.,* pp. 254–55; Byrnes, *Speaking Frankly,* p. 97.

²³Record of the Second Meeting, *FR: 1945,* II, *ibid.,* p. 131; Memorandum by Leslie Squires, 11 October 1945, *ibid.,* II, p. 182; Memorandum by Cavendish Cannon, 14 September 1945, *ibid.,* pp. 182-85; Memorandum by the United Kingdom Delegation, 17 September 1945, *ibid.,* pp. 219-22 and 18 September 1945, pp. 227-29; Acheson to Byrnes, 18 September 1945, *ibid.,* pp. 236-38.

²⁴Potsdam Briefing Book, 29 June 1945, United States Department of State, *Foreign Relations of the United States, Conference of Berlin, 1945,* 2 vols. (Washington, D.C.: Government Printing Office, 1960), I, 357-62; C. L. Sulzberger, *A Long Row of Candles, 1934-1954* (New York: Macmillan, 1969), p. 267.

²⁵*CFM—London,* II, pt. 1, pp. 232-33.

²⁶Memorandum of Conversation, 16 September 1945, *FR: 1945,* II, pp. 194-202.

²⁷Memorandum of Conversation, 19 September 1945, *ibid.,* II, pp. 243-47.

²⁸Memorandum by the United States Delegation, 19 September 1945, *ibid.,* II, pp. 263-67.

²⁹Memorandum of Conversation, 20 September 1945, *ibid.,* pp. 267-69.

³⁰Record of the Thirteenth Meeting of the Council of Foreign Ministers, 20 September 1945, *ibid.,* II, pp. 269-75; Record of the Fourteenth Meeting of the Council of Foreign Ministers, 20 September 1945, *ibid.,* pp. 275-83.

³¹U.S. Delegation Minutes of the Fifteenth Meeting of the Council of Foreign Ministers, 21 September 1945, *ibid.,* II, pp. 288-98; U.S. Delegation Minutes of the Sixteenth Meeting 21 September 1945, *ibid.,* II, pp. 300-10.

³²Byrnes, *Speaking Frankly,* p. 102; Memorandum of Conversation, 22 September 1945, Correspondence Folder, Byrnes Papers; Herbert Feis, *Contest Over Japan* (New York: Norton, 1967), p. 42, accepted Byrnes's account of this conversation and concluded that Byrnes's negative response to an Allied Control Council motivated Molotov to protest France and China discussing the Balkan treaties. Not only does *Foreign Relations* not mention introduction of a Japanese Control Council by Molotov until 24 September, but also the Balkan issue had been building for days and the Byrnes-Molotov flare-up occurred 21 September, leaving Byrnes's refusal to recognize Rumania and Bulgaria the more likely source of Molotov's motivation on 22 September. Byrnes, *ibid.,* p. 102; Curry, *James F. Byrnes,* pp. 152-53; Memorandum of Conversation, 22 September 1945, *FR: 1945,* II, pp. 313-15; *CFM—London,* II, pt. 2, p. 261.

³³U.S. Delegation Minutes of the Seventeenth Meeting, 22 September 1945, *FR: 1945,* II, pp. 316-23; Memorandum by Cohen, 22 September 1945, *ibid.,* pp. 330-31.

³⁴Truman, *Year of Decisions,* pp. 516-18; Byrnes, *Speaking Frankly,* p. 103; Diary of William Leahy, 22 September 1945, Library of Congress; Truman to Stalin, 22 September 1945, *FR: 1945,* II, p. 328; Truman to Stalin, 22 September 1945, *ibid.,* p. 329; Stalin to Truman, 22 September 1945, *ibid.,* p. 331; Attlee to Truman, 23 September 1945, *ibid.,* pp. 331-33; Stalin to Truman, 24 September 1945, *ibid.,* p. 334.

³⁵*CFM—London,* II, pt. 2, p. 261.

³⁶CAB 128/3, 25 September 1945, pp. 1-2; CAB 129/3, 23 September 1945, pp. 53-56.

[37]CAB 128/3, 25 September 1945, pp. 1-2.

[38]Memorandum of Conversation, 26 September 1945, *FR: 1945,* II, pp. 381-84; Memorandum of Conversation, 25 September 1945, *ibid.,* pp. 265-70; Memorandum of Conversation, 26 September 1945, *ibid.,* pp. 410-12; Memorandum of Conversation, 27 September 1945, *ibid.,* pp. 417-18; Memorandum of Conversation, 27 September 1945, *ibid.,* pp. 418-21; Memorandum of Conversation, 27 September 1945, *ibid.,* II, pp. 425-48.

[39]*CFM—London,* II, pt. 2, pp. 297-98; 308-13; Memorandum of Conversation, 28 September 1945, *FR: 1945,* II, pp. 435-39.

[40]*CFM—London,* II, pt. 2, pp. 318-24; W. Averell Harriman and Elie Abel, *Special Envoy to Churchill and Stalin, 1941-1946* (New York: Random House, 1975), pp. 508-9, 488, 504.

[41]U.S. Delegation Minutes of the Twenty-eighth Meeting, 29 September 1945, *FR: 1945,* II, pp. 445-56.

[42]*CFM—London,* II, pt. 2, p. 231; Achilles Oral History Interview, Dulles Oral History Project; Daniel Yergin misinterpreted Dulles's objections as opposition to recognizing the Balkans, which Dulles actually favored, Daniel Yergin, *Shattered Peace: The Origins of the Cold War and the National Security State* (Boston: Houghton Mifflin, 1977), p. 129.

[43]*CFM—London,* II, pt. 2, pp. 345-46; Byrnes, *Speaking Frankly,* pp. 105-6; U.S. Delegation Minutes of the Twenty-ninth Meeting, 20 September 1945, *FR: 1945,* II, pp. 476-87; Bohlen, *Witness to History,* p. 247; Harriman, *Special Envoy,* p. 507.

[44]Memorandum of Conversation, 30 September 1945, *FR: 1945,* II, pp. 487-89.

[45]Memorandum of Conversation, 30 September 1945, *ibid.,* pp. 489-92; U.S. Delegation Minutes of the Thirtieth Meeting, 30 September 1945, *ibid.,* pp. 493-508.

[46]*Ibid.;* Bevin to Byrnes, 30 September 1945, *ibid.,* pp. 515-17.

[47]Record of a Conversation at the Soviet Embassy on 1 October 1945, CAB 129/3, 4 October 1945, pp. 1-4.

[48]U.S. Delegation Minutes of the Thirty-first Meeting, 1 October 1945, *ibid.,* II, pp. 519-29; U.S. Delegation Minutes of Thirty-second Meeting, 2 October 1945, *ibid.,* pp. 529-40; U.S. Delegation Minutes of the Thirty-third Meeting, 2 October 1945, *ibid.,* pp. 541-55.

[49]*Department of State Bulletin,* 13 (14 October 1945), p. 567; *New York Times,* 29 September 1945, 3 October 1945, 4 October 1945; *Department of State Bulletin,* 13 (7 October 1945), p. 507; Bohlen, *Witness to History,* p. 247; Dulles, *Report on the London Meeting of the Council of Foreign Ministers,* 6 October 1945, Dulles Papers.

[50]Bohlen, *Witness to History,* p. 247; Davies Journal, 9 October 1945, Box 22. Contrary to Churchill's account of the percentage plan, Averell Harriman stated that he was not present at the Churchill-Stalin 9 October 1944 meeting. According to what Churchill told Harriman on 12 October, the British and Soviet leaders agreed to 90 percent Soviet influence in Rumania, 90 percent British influence in Greece, 50 percent division of influence in Yugoslavia and Hungary, and 75 percent Soviet influence in Bulgaria. Harriman told Churchill that he "was certain both Roosevelt and

Hull would repudiate" the plan but did not add whether he ever informed the president of the spheres of influence arrangement. Harriman, *Special Envoy*, pp. 356-8. Byrnes knew that Churchill and Stalin had reached an "informal understanding" about Soviet predominance in Rumania and British predominance in Greece at their 1944 meeting. Byrnes, *Speaking Frankly*, p. 53.

[51]Yalta Conference Communiqué, 12 February 1945, United States Department of State, *Foreign Relations of the United States: The Conferences at Malta and Yalta, 1945* (Washington, D.C.: Government Printing Office, 1955), pp. 977-78; Leahy, *I Was There*, pp. 315-16; Byrnes, *Speaking Frankly*, p. 53; McNeil, *America, Britain and Russia*, p. 699. Harriman offers a different interpretation of Stalin's motivation on promising free elections. Harriman, *Special Envoy*, pp. 413-15.

[52]Minutes of the Meeting of the Secretaries of State, War, and Navy, 16 October 1945, *FR: 1945*, II, pp. 59-61; Stettinius Calendar Notes, 28 September 1945, Stettinius Papers, Box 247, quoted in John Gaddis, *Origins of the Cold War*, p. 266; John Morton Blum, ed. *The Price of Vision: The Diary of Henry A. Wallace, 1942-1946* (Boston: Houghton Mifflin, 1973), pp. 501-2.

[53]Byrnes, *Speaking Frankly*, p. 99; *New York Times*, 22 September 1945, 23 September 1945, 24 September 1945.

[54]Dulles, *War or Peace*, pp. 27, 29; Byrnes, *Speaking Frankly*, pp. 277-78.

[55]Adam Ulam, *Stalin, The Man and His Era* (New York: Viking, 1973), pp. 628-32; Adam Ulam, *The Rivals*, pp. 6, 25, 82.

[56]Lloyd C. Gardner, *Architects of Illusion*, pp. 94-95; Gaddis, *Origins of the Cold War*, pp. 265-66; Alperovitz, *Atomic Diplomacy*, p. 226, supports Balkan motivation; Feis, *Contest Over Japan*, p. 42, supports Japanese motivation; McNeil, *America, Britain, and Russia*, p. 697, and Mosely, *The Kremlin and World Politics*, pp. 215-216, supports the idea that no recognition motivated introduction of Japan; Bohlen, *Witness to History*, p. 246.

[57]Quoted in Gregg Herken, "American Diplomacy and the Atomic Bomb" (Ph.D. diss., Princeton University, 1973), pp. 75, 100-2, 120-21.

[58]Harriman, *Special Envoy*, pp. 509, 519; Mosely, *The Kremlin and World Politics*, pp. 251, 300.

CHAPTER THREE

[1]Byrnes, *Speaking Frankly*, p. 107; *New York Times*, 30 September and 14 October 1945.

[2]George Curry, *James F. Byrnes*, p. 157; Mark Ethridge and C. E. Black, "Negotiating on the Balkans, 1945-1947," in Raymond Dennett and Joseph E. Johnson, eds., *Negotiating with the Russians* (Boston: World Peace Foundation, 1951), pp. 184-203; Byrnes's News Conference Transcript, 10 October 1945, Press Clippings Folder, Byrnes Papers, Clemson University; Byrnes, *Speaking Frankly*, p. 107; Curry, *James F. Byrnes*, p. 157; Ernest R. May, *"Lessons" of the Past: The Use and Misuse of History in American*

Foreign Policy (London: Oxford University Press, 1973), pp. 28–29, notes that Ethridge received biased information directly from the very American representatives in Rumania and Bulgaria on whose objectivity he was to check.

³Byrnes to Harriman, 12 October 1945, United States Department of State, *FR: 1945,* II, pp. 562–63; Harriman to Byrnes, 13 October 1945, *ibid.,* p. 563 and 18 October 1945, *ibid.,* p. 564; Memorandum of Conversation, 24 and 25 October 1945, *ibid.,* pp. 567–78; Byrnes, *Speaking Frankly,* p. 108; Curry, *James F. Byrnes,* p. 158.

⁴Memorandum of Press and Radio News Conferences, Press Clippings, Folder, Byrnes Papers; James F. Byrnes, *All In One Lifetime,* p. 310; Byrnes, *Speaking Frankly,* p. 108; Curry, *James F. Byrnes,* pp. 158–59.

⁵*Public Papers of the Presidents: Harry S. Truman, 1945-1947* (Washington, D.C.: Government Printing Office, 1961–63), pp. 381–82, 437; Hewlett and Anderson, Jr., pp. 456–70; Vannevar Bush, *Pieces of the Action* (New York: Simon & Schuster, 1970), pp. 296–97; Byrnes, *Speaking Frankly,* pp. 108–9; Curry, *James F. Byrnes,* pp. 159–60; *New York Times,* 22 November 1945; Gaddis, *The United States and the Origins of the Cold War,* pp. 268–73; Barton J. Bernstein, "The Quest for Security: American Foreign Policy and International Control of Atomic Energy, 1942–1946," *Journal of American History,* 60 (March 1974), pp. 1003–24.

⁶*New York Times,* 5 November 1945; Dunn to Byrnes, 17 October 1945, State Department Records, File Number 1945–1949, Box 3833; Byrnes, *Speaking Frankly,* p. 109; Curry, *James F. Byrnes,* pp. 161–2.

⁷Byrnes to Harriman, 23 November 1945, *FR: 1945,* II, p. 578; Byrnes, *All In One Lifetime,* pp. 318–19; Harriman to Byrnes, 24 November 1945, *FR: 1945,* II, p. 579; Harriman, *Special Envoy,* p. 515.

⁸Byrnes to Winant, 25 November 1945, *FR: 1945,* II, p. 580; Winant to Byrnes, 26 November 1945, *ibid.,* p. 581; Harriman, *Special Envoy,* p. 509.

⁹Record of Trans-Atlantic Teletype Conference, 27 November 1945, *ibid.,* pp. 582–85.

¹⁰Winant to Byrnes, 27 November 1945, *ibid.,* p. 585; Byrnes to Winant, 29 November 1945, *ibid.,* pp. 587–89; Bevin to Byrnes, 28 November 1945, *ibid.,* pp. 585–86; Memorandum of Conversation, 29 November 1945, *ibid.,* pp. 590–91; Memorandum of Conversation, 4 December 1945, *ibid.,* pp. 593–95; Halifax to Byrnes, 6 December 1945, *ibid.,* p. 597; Joseph Davies Diary, 11 December 1945, Davies Papers, Library of Congress, Box 19, CAB 128/4, 6 December 1945, pp. 1–2.

¹¹Robert Murphy, *Diplomat Among Warriors* (Garden City: Doubleday, 1964), p. 300; Lloyd C. Gardner, *Architects of Illusion,* p. 98; Byrnes saw Truman "for a possible thirty minutes" the night before he left for Moscow. Harry Truman, *Year of Decisions,* p. 55; Byrnes to Winant, 29 November 1945, *FR: 1945,* II, p. 587; Harriman to Byrnes, 11 October 1945, *ibid.,* p. 560; Byrnes to Harriman, 8 December 1945, *ibid.,* p. 603; Murphy, *Diplomat Among Warriors,* p. 300; Bohlen, *Witness to History, 1929-1969,* p. 248.

¹²Russell D. Buhite, *Patrick J. Hurley and American Foreign Policy* (Ithaca: Cornell University Press, 1973), Chapter 11.

¹³Diary of William Leahy, 13 November 1945, William Leahy Papers, Library of Congress; Vandenberg, *The Private Papers,* pp. 226–29;

Newsweek, 26 (26 November 1945), p. 34; Connally, *My Name Is Tom Connally,* pp. 289-90; Bernstein, "Quest for Security," pp. 1027-28.

[14]Memorandum for the President, 6 December 1945, State Department Records, File Number 1945-1949, Box C-226; For Byrnes from Acheson, 15 December 1945, *ibid.;* Dean Acheson, *Present at the Creation,* pp. 135-36; Davies Journal, 8 December 1945, Davies Papers.

[15]Byrnes, *Speaking Frankly,* p. 108; Gaddis, *Origins of the Cold War,* pp. 276-78; Byrnes to Winant, 29 November 1945, *FR: 1945,* II, pp. 587-89.

[16]Harriman to Molotov, 7 December 1945, *ibid.,* II, pp. 599-600; Molotov to Harriman, 7 December 1945, *ibid.,* II, pp. 600-1; Halifax to Byrnes, 6 December 1945, *ibid.,* II, pp. 597-98.

[17]Byrnes to Harriman, 8 December 1945, *FR: 1945,* II, p. 604; James B. Conant, *My Several Lives,* pp. 476-79; Memorandum of Conversation, 7 December 1945, *FR: 1945,* II, pp. 601-2.

[18]Bohlen, *Witness to History,* pp. 247-48; George Kennan, *Memoirs, 1925-1950* (Boston: Little, Brown, 1967), pp. 285-86; *New York Times,* 15 December 1945; Byrnes, *Speaking Frankly,* p. 110.

[19]U.S. Delegation Minutes, First Formal Session, 16 December 1945, *FR: 1945,* II, pp. 610-21; Conant, *My Several Lives,* p. 480; Kennan, *Memoirs,* p. 287; Harriman, *Special Envoy,* pp. 523-24.

[20]Record of Conversation, 17 December 1945, *FR: 1945,* II, pp. 629-32.

[21]U.S. Delegation Minutes, Second Formal Session, 17 December 1945, *FR: 1945,* II, pp. 632-40; Memorandum of Conversation, 18 December 1945, *ibid.,* II, pp. 643-47; Byrnes, *Speaking Frankly,* pp. 112-13.

[22]U.S. Delegation Minutes, Third Formal Session, 18 December 1945, *FR: 1945,* II, pp. 647-60; U.S. Delegation Minutes of an Informal Meeting, 19 December 1945, *ibid.,* II, pp. 666-71.

[23]Kennan, *Memoirs,* p. 279; Memorandum of Conversation, 19 December 1945, *FR: 1945,* II, pp. 680-84; Byrnes, *Speaking Frankly,* pp. 114-15; Curry, *James F. Byrnes,* pp. 170-2.

[24]Byrnes to Caffery, 20 December 1945, *FR: 1945,* II, p. 706; *ibid.,* pp. 706-7; Footnotes 73 and 77, *ibid.;* Acheson to Byrnes, 20 December 1945, *ibid.,* II, pp. 707-8; Byrnes to Acheson, 22 December 1945, *ibid.,* II, p. 725; U.S. Delegation Minutes of an Informal Meeting, 21 December 1945, *ibid.,* II, pp. 718-19; Robinson to Byrnes, 23 December 1945, *ibid.,* II, pp. 759-60; Caffery to Byrnes, 24 December 1945, *ibid.,* II, p. 761; Harriman to Acheson, 24 December 1945, *ibid.,* II, p. 760; *New York Times,* 25 and 26 December 1945.

[25]Kennan, *Memoirs,* p. 286; Memorandum of Conversation, 18 December 1945, *FR: 1945,* II, pp. 643-45.

[26]Memorandum by the U.S. Delegation, 18 December 1945, *ibid.,* II, pp. 700-1; *ibid.,* pp. 701-2; U.S. Delegation Minutes of an Informal Meeting, 22 December 1945, *ibid.,* II, pp. 727-34.

[27]Memorandum of Conversation, 23 December 1945, *ibid.,* II, pp. 750-56; Harriman, *Special Envoy,* p. 525. Bevin later complained about "much previous consultation between the United States and Soviet Governments" (Minutes of the Cabinet, 1 January 1946, Public Records Office, 128/5, p. 3, hereafter referred to as CAB).

[28]CAB 128/5, 1 January 1946, p. 4; U.S. Delegation Minutes of an Informal Meeting, 24 December 1945; *ibid.,* II, pp. 761-69; *ibid.,* 25 December 1945, pp.

781-95; *ibid.,* 26 December 1945, pp. 801-5; Bohlen, *Witness to History,* p. 249; Kennan, *Memoirs,* p. 284.

[29]Memorandum of the U.S. Delegation, 16 December 1945, *FR: 1945,* II, pp. 623-24; *ibid.,* pp. 624-26; *ibid.,* pp. 626-27; U.S. Delegation Minutes, Third Formal Session, 18 December 1945, *ibid.,* II, pp. 647-62; *ibid.,* Fourth Formal Session, 19 December 1945, II, pp. 672-75; *ibid.,* Fifth Formal Session, 20 December 1945, II, pp. 692-96; *ibid.,* Informal Meeting, 21 December 1945, II, pp. 710-18; Matthews to Byrnes, 18 October 1945, Files of John Hickerson, State Department Records, Box 3; Feis, *Contest Over Japan,* pp. 103-4; Conant, *My Several Lives,* p. 483; Kennan, *Memoirs,* pp. 289-90.

[30]U.S. Delegation Minutes, First Formal Session, 16 December 1945, *FR: 1945,* II, pp. 618-21; *ibid.,* Second Formal Session, 17 December 1945, pp. 639-43; *ibid.,* Fifth Formal Session, 20 December 1945, pp. 696-700; *ibid.,* Informal Meeting, 21 December 1945, pp. 716-21; Memorandum by the U.S. Delegation, 16 December 1945, *ibid.,* II, pp. 628-29; U.S. Delegation Minutes of an Informal Meeting, 19 December 1945, *ibid.,* II, pp. 666-69.

[31]Memorandum of the Soviet Delegation, 21 December 1945, *ibid.,* II, pp. 719-20; U.S. Delegation Minutes of an Informal Meeting, 23 December 1945, *ibid.,* II, pp. 747-50; Memorandum of Conversation, 23 December 1947, *ibid.,* II, pp. 756-58; Curry, *James F. Byrnes,* pp. 175-76; Ulam, *Stalin,* p. 631, says Byrnes should have told Stalin that if he really wanted to aid his East European friends, he should pull Russian troops out of those nations as Stalin had suggested Americans do to help Chiang.

[32]U.S. Delegation Minutes, First Formal Session, 16 December 1945, *FR: 1945,* II, p. 616; Memorandum of Conversation, 17 December 1945, *ibid.,* II, pp. 630-31; Byrnes, *All In One Lifetime,* p. 333; Memorandum of Conversation, 19 December 1945, *FR: 1945,* II, pp. 684-87; Gary Hess, "The Iranian Crisis of 1945-46 and the Cold War," *Political Science Quarterly,* 89 (March 1974), pp. 126-30.

[33]Record of the United Kingdom Delegation, 19 December 1945, *ibid.,* II, pp. 688-90; *ibid.,* 20 December 1945, pp. 708-9; *ibid.,* 24 December 1945, p. 771; Memorandum of Conversation, 23 December 1945, *ibid.,* II, pp. 750-52; United Kingdom Record of Conversation, 24 December 1945, *ibid.,* II, pp. 774-75; Memorandum of Conversation, 25 December 1945, *ibid.,* II, pp. 778-79; Byrnes, *Speaking Frankly,* pp. 118-21.

[34]U.S. Delegation Minutes of an Informal Meeting, 25 December 1945, *FR: 1945,* II, pp. 795-97; *ibid.,* 26 December 1945, pp. 805-8; Hess, "The Iranian Crisis," p. 131.

[35]Davies to Byrnes, 11 December 1945, Davies Papers; Winant to Byrnes, 5 November 1945, State Department Records, File Number 1945-1949, Box C-226; Kerr to Bevin, 3 December 1945, *FR: 1945,* II, pp. 82-84; Footnote 30, *ibid.,* p. 82; Harriman, *Special Envoy,* p. 521.

[36]Memorandum of Conversation, 17 December 1945, *FR: 1945,* II, p. 632; Memorandum by the U.S. Delegation, 18 December 1945, *ibid.,* II, pp. 663-66.

[37]Conant, *My Several Lives,* pp. 480-81; Kennan, *Memoirs,* p. 287; Footnote 43, *FR: 1945,* II, p. 664; U.S. Delegation Minutes, Sixth Formal Session, 22 December 1945, *ibid.,* II, pp. 736-37; *ibid.,* Informal Meeting, 23

December 1945, *FR: 1945,* II, pp. 744-47; Memorandum of Conversation, 23 December 1945, *ibid.,* II, p. 756; U.S. Delegation Minutes of an Informal Meeting, 24 December 1945, *FR: 1945,* II, pp. 762-63, 769; Byrnes, *Speaking Frankly,* pp. 267-68; Bernstein, "Quest for Security," p. 1029.

[38]Kennan, *Memoirs,* p. 289; Byrnes, *Speaking Frankly,* pp. 118, 268; Conant, *My Several Lives,* p. 482; Bohlen, *Witness to History,* p. 249.

[39]U.S. Delegation Minutes, Seventh Formal Session, 26 December 1945, *FR: 1945,* II, pp. 813-14; Footnote 4, *ibid.,* p. 813; Byrnes, *Speaking Frankly,* p. 121.

[40]*New York Times,* 25, 26, 27, 28 and 30 December 1945; *London Times,* 28 December 1945; *Izvestia,* 28 December 1945; Acheson to Byrnes, 22 December 1945, State Department Records, File Number 1945-1949, Box 3833; Davies to Byrnes, 28 December 1945, Davies Papers; Acheson to Bohlen, 26 December 1945, State Department Records, File Number 1945-1949, Box 3833; Harriman to Acheson, 27 December 1945, *FR: 1945,* II, p. 815; Cabell Phillips, *The Truman Presidency. The History of a Triumphal Session* (New York: Macmillan, 1966), p. 148; Byrnes to Acheson, 17 December 1945, *FR: 1945,* II, p. 610; footnote 78, *ibid.,* p. 707; footnote 81, *ibid.,* p. 709; Bohlen, *Witness to History,* pp. 250-51; Byrnes to Acheson, 22 December 1945, *FR: 1945,* II, p. 725; Harriman to Acheson, 24 December 1945, *ibid.,* II, p. 760; Byrnes, *All In One Lifetime,* p. 340; footnote 60, *FR: 1945,* II, p. 684; Acheson, *Present at the Creation,* pp. 135-37; Memorandum of Press and Radio News Conferences, 19 December 1945, Press Clippings Folder, Byrnes Papers.

[41]Acheson Interview, Princeton Seminars, 1953, Truman Library, pp. 12-14.

[42]Margaret Truman, *Harry S. Truman,* pp. 323-25; Byrnes, *All In One Lifetime,* p. 343; Truman, *Year of Decisions,* p. 550; Acheson, *Present at the Creation,* p. 136; Byrnes, *Speaking Frankly,* pp. 237-38.

[43]*New York Times,* 30 December 1945; Byrnes, *All In One Lifetime,* p. 345; Leahy Diary, 31 December 1945, Leahy Papers; Jonathan Daniels, *The Man of Independence* (Philadelphia: Lippincott, 1950), pp. 309-11.

[44]Truman, *Year of Decisions,* pp. 550-52; Curry, *James F. Byrnes,* pp. 189-90; Hillman, *Mr. President,* p. 103.

[45]Truman, *Year of Decisions,* pp. 551-52; Gaddis, *Origins of the Cold War,* pp. 280-81; Davies to Byrnes, 11 December 1945, Davies Papers.

[46]In reference to publishing the Ethridge report, Stalin told Byrnes that if he did, the Soviet Union would ask the Soviet publicist, Ilya Ehrenburg, "who was also an impartial man and visited these countries, to publish his views." (Memorandum of Conversation, 23 December 1945, *FR: 1945,* II, p. 753); McNeill, *America, Britain, and Russia,* p. 116, says about Byrnes's offer of economic assistance to the Balkans, "An argument less likely to persuade Stalin can hardly be imagined. He must have interpreted Byrnes's words to mean: 'We must have peace treaties to re-establish capitalist exploitation of Rumanian oil wells and Finnish nickle mines; but Byrnes apparently believed that the hard plight of Eastern Europeans . . . would prey on Stalin's mind and make him eager to have American help to relieve the suffering.'" For a conflicting analysis of Byrnes's diplomacy, see Joyce

and Gabriel Kolko, *The Limits of Power, The World and United States Foreign Policy, 1945-1954* (New York: Harper and Row, 1972), p. 42, which states, "Byrnes was no compromiser, either before or after the Moscow Conference." Kennan, *Memoirs,* pp. 287-88.

CHAPTER FOUR

[1]Hadley Cantril and Mildred Strunk, eds. *Public Opinion, 1935-1946* (Princeton: Princeton University Press, 1951), pp. 371, 963, 1060.

[2]Vandenberg to John W. Blodgett, 24 December 1945, Correspondence Folder, Arthur Vandenberg Papers, The University of Michigan; Vandenberg to C. E. Hutchinson, 29 December 1945, *ibid.; New York Times,* 29 December 1945; Leahy Diary, 28 December 1945, Leahy Papers; Vandenberg to Brien McMahon, 2 January 1946, Correspondence Folder, Vandenberg Papers; Edward Weintal, Oral History Interview, The John Foster Dulles Oral History Project, Princeton University.

[3]Bevin had earlier advised the Iranians not to bring the issue before the United Nations (Minutes of the Cabinet, 1 January 1946, Public Records Office, 128/5, p. 5, hereafter referred to as CAB). *New York Times,* 17, 23, 26 February and 2 March 1946; Vandenberg, *The Private Papers,* p. 250.

[4]Phillips, *The Truman Presidency,* p. 258; *New York Times,* 22 January 1946; Elbridge Durbrow, *Comment on Stalin's "Election" Speech,* 11 February 1946, State Department Records, File No. 1940-1947, Box 17; *New York Times,* 11 February 1945; Acheson, *Present at the Creation,* p. 150; Phillips, *The Truman Presidency,* pp. 358-59; Leahy Diary, 21 February 1946.

[5]Byrnes, *Speaking Frankly,* p. 123; Curry, *James F. Byrnes,* pp. 194, 197; *New York Times,* 11, 17 February 1946; Hewlett and Anderson, *A History of the United States Atomic Energy Commission,* p. 501; Leahy Diary, 20, 21 February 1946.

[6]Kennan to Byrnes, 22 February 1946, United States Department of State, *FR: 1945,* VI, pp. 696-707; Kennan, *Memoirs, 1925-1950,* pp. 68-69, 292-93. The president read Kennan's telegram; the State Department commended Kennan, and Secretary of the Navy James Forrestal made it required reading for the highest officers in the armed services.

[7]*Department of State Bulletin,* 14 (10 March 1946), pp. 355-58.

[8]Byrnes, *All In One Lifetime,* p. 349; Leahy Diary, 3 March 1946; Williams, *A Prime Minister Remembers,* pp. 162-63; *Vital Speeches,* 12 (15 March 1946), pp. 329-32.

[9]Byrnes to Molotov, 5 March 1946, United States Department of State, *FR: 1946,* VII, pp. 340-42; *New York Times,* 6, 13, 20 March and 7 April 1946; Rossow to Byrnes, 5 March 1946, *FR: 1946,* VII, p. 340; Memorandum by Edward Wright, 16 August 1965, *ibid.,* pp. 346-48; Byrnes to Molotov, 8 March 1946, *ibid.,* p. 348; Kennan to Byrnes, 15 March 1946; *ibid.,* p. 356.

[10]George V. Allen Papers, Harry S. Truman Library, Box 1; Byrnes, *All In One Lifetime,* p. 351; Curry, *James F. Byrnes,* pp. 205-7; Herbert Feis, *From Trust to Terror, The Onset of the Cold War, 1945-1950* (New York: Norton,

1970), p. 85; Memorandum of Conversation, 1 May 1946, *FR: 1946,* II, p. 204; Vandenberg, *Private Papers,* p. 251; Adam Ulam, *The Rivals,* pp. 118-19; Hess, "The Iranian Crisis," pp. 117-46.

¹¹Dunn to Byrnes, 15 January 1946, *FR: 1946,* II, pp. 7-8; footnote 17, *ibid.,* p. 7; Reinstein to Collado, 24 January 1946, State Department Records, File No. 1945-49, Box 3833; Byrnes to Dunn, 23 March 1946, *ibid.,* Box C-227; Byrnes to Dunn, 5 April 1946, *ibid.*

¹²Mosely, *The Kremlin and World Politics,* pp. 253-54; Philip Mosely, "Some Techniques of Negotiation," in Dennett and Johnson, eds., *Negotiating With the Russians,* pp. 281-87; Collado to Reinstein, 6 February 1946, State Department Records, File No. 1945-1949, Box C-227; Dunn to Byrnes, 19 February 1946, *FR: 1946,* II, footnote 30, p. 13; Dunn to Matthews, 27 February 1946, *ibid.,* pp. 16-19.

¹³Byrnes to Dunn, 5 March 1946, *FR: 1946,* II, pp. 22-23; Byrnes, *Speaking Frankly,* p. 124.

¹⁴Memorandum of Conversation, 6 March 1946, *FR: 1946,* II, p. 25; Dunn to Byrnes, 8 March 1946, *ibid.,* p. 26; Halifax to Byrnes, 9 March 1946, *ibid.,* pp. 27-28; Byrnes to Gallman, 21 March 1946, *ibid.,* pp. 33-34; Halifax to Byrnes, 22 March 1946, *ibid.,* pp. 34-35; Byrnes to Gallman, 22 March 1946, *ibid.,* p. 35; Bevin to Byrnes, 23 March 1946, *ibid.,* p. 36; Byrnes to Dunn, 18 March 1946, *ibid.,* pp. 29-30; Dunn to Byrnes, 21 March 1946, *ibid.,* pp. 30-31; Dunn to Byrnes, 21 March 1946, *ibid.,* pp. 32-33.

¹⁵Byrnes to Dunn, 6 March 1946, *ibid.,* pp. 25-26; Dunn to Byrnes, 13 March 1946, *ibid.,* pp. 28-29; *New York Times,* 17 March 1946; Memorandum, State Department Records, File No. 1945-1949, Box C-227.

¹⁶Bevin to Byrnes, 5 April 1946, *FR: 1946,* II, p. 46; Molotov to Byrnes, 6 April 1946, *ibid.,* p. 46; Caffery to Byrnes, 9 April 1946, *ibid.,* pp. 46-47; Dunn to Byrnes, 18 April 1946, *ibid.,* pp. 70-72.

¹⁷*New York Times,* 15, 17, 18, 19, 20, 21, 22, and 23 April 1946; The British Embassy to the State Department, 13 April 1946, *FR: 1946,* II, pp. 53-55; Department of State to the British Embassy, 18 April 1946, *ibid.,* pp. 68-69; Sulzberger, *A Long Row of Candles,* p. 310. In Paris Byrnes aided Bidault right before the French elections by calling Truman and getting assurances that a U.S. loan to France would be quickly concluded (Memorandum of Conversation, 1 May 1946, *FR: 1946,* II, p. 206.)

¹⁸Vandenberg to Dulles, 15 April 1946, Correspondence Folder, John Foster Dulles Papers.

¹⁹*New York Herald Tribune,* 24 April 1946; Byrnes to Smith, 16 April 1946, *FR: 1946,* III, pp. 62-63.

²⁰Byrnes, *All In One Lifetime,* pp. 353-55; Acheson, *Present at the Creation,* p. 163; Acheson Interview, Princeton Seminars, 1953, Harry S. Truman Library, pp. 14-16; Curry, *James F. Byrnes,* pp. 207-9; Truman, *Year of Decisions,* pp. 552-53.

²¹Vandenberg, *Private Papers,* pp. 262-64; *New York Times,* 25 April 1946. Truman approved the movement of U.S. troops into Paris to prevent possible Communist uprisings during the 5 May elections, but Acheson with support from the Secretaries of War and Navy got him to rescind the order. (Leahy Diary, 3 and 4 May 1946); *FR: 1946,* II, pp. 94-104; *ibid.,* Fourth

Meeting, 29 April 1946, pp. 153–55, 165–73.

[22]U.S. Delegation Record, Second Meeting, 26 April 1946, *FR: 1946,* II, pp. 114–21; Vandenberg Diary, 26 April 1946, Vandenberg Papers; Vandenberg, *Private Papers,* pp. 264–65; U.S. Delegation Record, First Informal Meeting, 2 May 1946, *FR: 1946,* II, p. 218.

[23]Vandenberg, *Private Papers,* p. 267; U.S. Delegation Record, Fourth Meeting, 29 April 1946, *FR: 1946,* II, pp. 155–63, 163–65; Byrnes, *Speaking Frankly,* p. 127.

[24]Mosely to Dunn, 23 April 1946, State Department Records, File No. 1945–1949, Box C–227; Vandenberg, *Private Papers,* pp. 268–69; U.S. Delegation Records, Fourth Meeting, 29 April 1946, *FR: 1946,* II, pp. 178–84; Record of Decisions, Eighth Meeting, 3 May 1946, *ibid.,* pp. 222–23; The Secretary of State to the President and the Acting Secretary of State, 4 May 1946, *ibid.,* pp. 224–25; Vandenberg Diary, 3, 4 May 1946; U.S. Delegation Record, Ninth Meeting, 4 May 1946, *ibid.,* pp. 225–35; *ibid.,* Tenth Meeting, 4 May 1946, pp. 237–46; Byrnes, *Speaking Frankly,* pp. 127–28.

[25]*Ibid.,* pp. 125–27; Bohlen, *Witness to History,* p. 253; Byrnes, *All In One Lifetime,* pp. 357–58; Curry, *James F. Byrnes,* p. 214.

[26]Vandenberg, *Private Papers,* pp. 263, 268; Memorandum for the President, 11 June 1945, Correspondence Folder, Byrnes Papers; Murphy, *Diplomat Among Warriors,* p. 301; Memorandum of Conversation, 28 April 1946, *FR: 1946,* II, p. 146.

[27]U.S. Delegation Record, Fourth Meeting, 29 April 1946, *ibid.,* pp. 166–73; *New York Times,* 2 May 1946; CAB 128/5, 13 May 1946, p. 42. John Gimbel argued convincingly that Byrnes first proposed his twenty-five year treaty to secure French abandonment of its plans to separate the Ruhr and Rhineland from Germany (John Gimbel, "The United States, France, and the American Treaty on German Disarmament, 1946: A Study in Cold War Mythmaking," Paper delivered to the American Historical Association, December 1977).

[28]Memorandum of Conversation, 1 May 1946, *FR: 1946,* II, p. 204; Vandenberg *Private Papers,* pp. 269, 272; U.S. Delegation Record, Seventh Meeting, 2 May 1946, *FR: 1946,* II, pp. 212–13; *ibid.,* First Informal Meeting, 2 May 1946, pp. 214–22.

[29]Teletype Transcript, 2 May 1946, Paris Conference Folder, Byrnes Papers.

[30]Memorandum of Conversation, 5 May 1946, *FR: 1946,* II, pp. 247–49; Curry, *James F. Byrnes,* pp. 217–18; Byrnes, *Speaking Frankly,* pp. 128–29; Vandenberg, *Private Papers,* pp. 276–78; Bohlen, *Witness to History,* p. 254; U.S. Delegation Record, Second Informal Meeting, 6 May 1946, *FR: 1946,* II, pp. 251–56.

[31]*Ibid.,* Eleventh Meeting, 7 May 1946, pp. 258–70; *ibid.,* Twelfth Meeting, 7 May 1946, pp. 272–83; *ibid.,* Thirteenth Meeting, 8 May 1946, pp. 300–1.

[32]*Ibid.,* pp. 301–7; *ibid.,* Fourteenth Meeting, 9 May 1946, pp. 312–19; *ibid.,* Fifteenth Meeting, 10 May 1946, pp. 323–32; Byrnes, *Speaking Frankly,* p. 129. The next day, Bevin reported to his cabinet the lack of progress in the council and the impatience of the dominions about the postponement of the peace conference. The cabinet instructed him to continue his resistance to the Soviet demand of approved drafts. (CAB 128/5, 9 May 1946, p. 34.)

33U.S. Delegation Record, Third Informal Meeting, 10 May 1946, *FR: 1946,* II, pp. 333-41; *ibid.,* Fourth Informal Meeting, 11 May 1946, pp. 341-46; Vandenberg, *Private Papers,* pp. 278-80; CAB 128/5, 13 May 1946, p. 41.

34U.S. Delegation Record, Sixth Informal Meeting, 13 May 1946, *FR: 1946,* II, pp. 362-66.

35*Ibid.,* Seventeenth Meeting, 14 May 1946, pp. 387-91; *ibid.,* Seventh Informal Meeting, 15 May 1946, pp. 394-99; *ibid.,* Eighth Informal Meeting, 16 May 1946, pp. 426-33; *ibid.,* Ninth Informal Meeting, 16 May 1946, pp. 434-36; *ibid.,* Eighteenth Meeting, 15 May 1946, pp. 408-16.

36CAB 128/5, 13 May 1946, p. 41; Conversation with M. Bidault, 15 May 1946, CAB 129/9, 17 May 1946, p. 1.

37Vandenberg, *Private Papers,* p. 283; Curry, *James F. Byrnes,* p. 222; *FR: 1946,* II, p. 104; James F. Byrnes, *Paris Meeting of Foreign Ministers,* 20 May 1946, State Department Records, File No. 1945-1949, Box C-227.

38Vandenberg, *Private Papers,* pp. 273, 284-87; Vandenberg to Gordon McDonald, 28 May 1946, Correspondence Folder, Vanderberg Papers; Vandenberg to Howard C. Laurence, 28 May 1946, *ibid.;* Vandenberg to Henry Luce, 28 May 1946, *ibid.*

39Vandenberg Diary, 7 and 8 May 1946, *ibid.;* Connally, *My Name Is Tom Connally,* p. 297.

40Vandenberg, *Private Papers,* p. 286; Memorandum of Conversation, 1 May 1946, *FR: 1946,* II, p. 204; *New York Times,* 24 November 1974. ; 41Joyce and Gabriel Kolko, *The Limits of Power,* p. 48, accepts American public intransigence and does not mention Byrnes's concessions; Wheeler-Bennett and Nicholls, *The Semblance of Peace,* p. 430 notes only Byrnes's public firmness, stating Byrnes "had shed his proclivity towards appeasement of Russia and was now a protagonist of a robust policy of resistance."

42*New York Times,* 12 May 1946; Vandenberg Diary, 15 May 1946, Vandenberg Papers; for Bevin's report to the Cabinet on the conference see Memorandum by the Secretary of State for Foreign Affairs, CAB 129/10, 22 May 1946, p. 1.

CHAPTER FIVE

1Memorandum, 10 June 1946, Joseph Davies Papers; V. M. Molotov, *Problems of Foreign Policy. Speeches and Statements, April, 1945-November, 1948* (Moscow: Foreign Languages Publishing House, 1949), pp. 37-50; *New York Times,* 27 May and 2 June 1946; Smith to Byrnes, 10 June 1946, United States Department of State, *FR: 1946,* II, pp. 480-81; Bevin to Byrnes, 29 May 1946, *ibid.,* pp. 452-53; footnote 12, *ibid.,* p. 452.

2*New York Times,* 22 May, 14 and 15 June 1946; Vandenberg to Arthur Summerfield, 4 June 1946, Vandenberg Papers, The University of Michigan.

3Vandenberg, *Private Papers,* pp. 290-1; Acheson to Byrnes, 15 June 1946, *FR: 1946,* II, pp. 506-7; Smith to Acheson, 15 June 1946, *ibid.,* p. 507; Caffery to Acheson, 15 June 1946, *ibid.,* p. 508.

4U.S. Delegation Record, Nineteenth Meeting, 15 June 1946, *ibid.,* pp. 493-504.

[5]Smith to United States Delegation, 17 June 1946, *ibid.*, pp. 527-28; *ibid.*, 25 June 1946, p. 528 in footnote 38.

[6]U.S. Delegation Record, Twentieth Meeting, 17 June 1946, *ibid.*, pp. 520-24; *ibid.*, Twenty-first Meeting, 18 June 1946, p. 531; Joyce and Gabriel Kolko, *The Limits of Power,* p. 47.

[7]U.S. Delegation Record, Twenty-third Meeting, 20 June 1946, *FR: 1946,* II, pp. 554-55; *ibid.*, Tenth Informal Meeting, 20 June 1946, pp. 557-63.

[8]*Ibid.*, Twenty-ninth Meeting, 28 June 1946, pp. 675-78; Memorandum of Conversation, 30 June 1946, *ibid.*, p. 700; U.S. Delegation Record, Thirty-third Meeting, 3 July 1946, *ibid.*, pp. 738-42; Kolko, *Limits of Power,* p. 48, accepts the colonial settlement as a Soviet concession, only failing to realize that the American, British, and French delegations also compromised; Richard D. Burns, "James F. Byrnes, 1945-1947" in *An Uncertain Tradition,* ed. Graelner, p. 239, erroneously states that Byrnes won British control of Italy's colonies from the Soviets; Minutes of the Cabinet, 1 July 1946, Public Record Office, 128/6, p. 159, hereafter referred to as CAB.

[9]Byrnes to United States Delegation, 7 June 1946, *FR: 1946,* p. 478; U.S. Delegation Record, Twenty-first Meeting, 18 June 1946, *ibid.*, pp. 529-35.

[10]James Byrnes, *Speaking Frankly,* p. 132; Memorandum of Conversation, 24 June 1946, *FR: 1946,* II, p. 599; Vandenberg Diary, 21 June 1946, Vandenberg Papers.

[11]U.S. Delegation Record, Eleventh Informal Meeting, 21 June 1946, *FR: 1946,* II, pp. 570-74; Bevin, preferring a permanent international regime, reluctantly agreed to the French plan for a temporary regime (CAB 128/6, 1 July 1946, p. 161).

[12]Memorandum of Conversation, 21 June 1946, *ibid.*, pp. 574-76; Byrnes, *Speaking Frankly,* pp. 132-33; Vandenberg Diary, 21 June 1946, Vandenberg Papers; Caffery to Acheson, 22 June 1946, *FR: 1946,* II, p. 582.

[13]Memorandum of Conversation, 24 June 1946, *ibid.*, pp. 598-601; *ibid.*, 25 June 1946, pp. 614-16; U.S. Delegation Record, Thirteenth Informal Meeting, 26 June 1946, *ibid.*, pp. 641-46; Bevin had reported to his cabinet on 24 June that the council would complete its work by 28 June (CAB, 128/5, 24 June 1946, p. 143).

[14]U.S. Delegation Record, Twenty-eighth Meeting, 27 June 1946, *FR: 1946,* II, pp. 648-62.

[15]Bevin had earlier complimented Molotov on his resourcefulness in postponing a Dodecanese solution, and Molotov had responded that he would accept the compliment if the Greek government had empowered Bevin to represent them but so far as he had received no information that they had; Byrnes, *All In One Lifetime,* p. 359; Vandenberg, *Private Papers,* pp. 292-93.

[16]U.S. Delegation Record, Thirtieth Meeting, 29 June 1946, *FR: 1946,* II, pp. 689-95. Vandenberg filed a memorandum with Byrnes stating his opposition to any international scheme for Trieste "so there can be no doubt if I am forced to ultimately dissent." Vandenberg Diary, 29 June 1946, Vandenberg Papers; U.S. Delegation Record, Twelfth Informal Meeting, 22 June 1946, *FR: 1946,* II, pp. 580-82; *ibid.*, Twenty-ninth Meeting, 29 June 1946, p. 680. The Council eventually had the United Nations meeting

postponed. Kolko, *Limits of Power,* p. 47, erroneously states that the Paris Council of Foreign Ministers awarded $225 million to the other nations Italy damaged.

[17]Memorandum of Conversation, 30 June 1946, *FR: 1946,* II, pp. 698–700; U.S. Delegation Record, Thirty-first Meeting, 1 July 1946, *ibid.,* pp. 703–12; Byrnes, *Speaking Frankly,* p. 134; Vandenberg, *Private Papers,* p. 294.

[18]*Ibid.;* Vandenberg Diary, 2 and 3 July 1946, Vandenberg Papers; Bohlen, *Witness to History,* p. 254; U.S. Delegation Record, Thirty-second Meeting, 2 July 1946, *FR: 1946,* II, pp. 715–21; Memorandum of Conversation, 2 July 1946, *ibid.,* pp. 722–25; Key to Acheson, 2 July 1946, *ibid.,* pp. 728–29; Proposal by the United States Delegation, 3 July 1946, *ibid.,* pp. 752–53; U.S. Delegation Record, Thirty-third Meeting, 3 July 1946, *ibid.,* pp. 731–38. Burnes, "James F. Byrnes," p. 239, accepts the Trieste settlement as a "substantial concession" Byrnes won from the Soviets, not realizing internationalization was far from what the American delegation originally wanted for Trieste.

[19]*Ibid.,* pp. 742–51; Vandenberg Diary, 3 July 1946, Vandenberg Papers.

[20]*Ibid.,* 4 July 1946; U.S. Delegation Record, Thirty-fourth Meeting, 4 July 1946, *FR: 1946,* II, p. 754; *ibid.,* Fourteenth Informal Meeting, 4 July 1946, pp. 771–74; Byrnes, *Speaking Frankly,* p. 754. Kolko, *Limits of Power,* pp. 48–49 incorrectly states the Soviet Union agreed to American procedure for the peace conference in exchange for a reparations settlement; Molotov agreed only to a specific date for the conference.

[21]U.S. Delegation Record, Thirty-fourth Meeting, 4 July 1946, *FR: 1946,* II, pp. 755–69; United States Proposal, 4 July 1946, *ibid.,* pp. 774–75; Byrnes, *All In One Lifetime,* p. 360; as a part of the peace conference date-reparations settlement, Bevin agreed to sacrifice his claim on British assets in Rumania to the Soviet Union (CAB, 128/6, 15 July 1946, p. 198). Bidault tried several times to postpone this long meeting so he could keep an appointment with the President of the Provisional Government of Viet Nam, Ho Chi Minh, but was ignored and finally just left (Vandenberg Diary, 4 July 1946, Vandenberg Papers).

[22]Byrnes, *Speaking Frankly,* p. 136; U.S. Delegation Record, Thirty-fifth Meeting, 5 July 1946, *FR: 1946,* II, pp. 781–99; Byrnes, *All In One Lifetime,* p. 360.

[23]Vandenberg Diary, 5 and 6 July 1946, Vandenberg Papers; Bohlen, *Witness to History,* p. 255; U.S. Delegation Record, Thirty-sixth Meeting, 6 July 1946, *FR: 1946,* II, pp. 801–15.

[24]Byrnes, *Speaking Frankly,* p. 42.

[25]U.S. Delegation Record, Fifteenth Informal Meeting, 8 July 1946, *FR: 1946,* II, pp. 823–33.

[26]Vandenberg, *Private Papers,* pp. 296–97; Curry, *James F. Byrnes,* pp. 232–33; U.S. Delegation Record, Fifteenth Informal Meeting, 8 July 1946, *FR: 1946,* II, pp. 833–36.

[27]John Gimbel, *The American Occupation of Germany: Politics and the Military, 1945-1949* (Stanford: Stanford University Press, 1968), chapters 1–4; Murphy to Byrnes, 24 February 1946, *FR: 1946,* V, pp. 505–7; *ibid.,* 19 March 1946, pp. 527–28; Byrnes, *Speaking Frankly,* p. 171; Potsdam

Conference Protocol, 1 August 1945, United States Department of State, *FR: Potsdam,* II, pp. 1481-87; Lucius Clay, *Decision in Germany* (New York: Doubleday, 1950), pp. 120-25.

[28]U.S. Delegation Record, Thirty-eighth Meeting, 9 July 1946, *FR: 1946,* II, pp. 842-50.

[29]Clay, *Decision in Germany,* pp. 126-27; Byrnes, *Speaking Frankly,* pp. 174-78.

[30]U.S. Delegation Record, Thirty-ninth Meeting, 10 July 1946, *FR: 1946,* II, pp. 860-77.

[31]Vandenberg Diary, 10 July 1946, surprisingly agreed with Molotov that it would be futile to appoint special deputies to begin work on a German treaty as there was not agreement among the ministers on the subject; Walter Bedell Smith, *My Three Years in Moscow* (Philadelphia: J.B. Lippincott, 1950), pp. 235-36.

[32]Byrnes, *All In One Lifetime,* p. 366; Curry, *James F. Byrnes,* pp. 233-37; Murphy, *Diplomat Among Warriors,* pp. 301-2; U.S. Delegation Record, Fortieth Meeting, 11 July 1946, *FR: 1946,* II, pp. 880-98; Clay, *Decision In Germany,* pp. 130-31.

[33]U.S. Delegation Record, Forty-first Meeting, 12 July 1946, *FR: 1946,* II, pp. 907-16; *ibid.,* Forty-second Meeting, pp. 935-37; Vandenberg Diary, 11 July 1946, Vandenberg Papers; CAB, 128/6, 15 July 1946, p. 197.

[34]U.S. Delegation Record, Forty-first Meeting, 12 July 1946, *FR: 1946,* II, pp. 913-16; Proposal by the Soviet Delegation, 12 July 1946, *ibid.,* pp. 939-40; U.S. Delegation Record, Forty-second Meeting, 12 July 1946, *ibid.,* pp. 928-37; Press Clippings, Byrnes Papers; Vandenberg Diary, 12 July 1946, Vandenberg Papers; CAB, 128/6, 15 July 1946, p. 197.

[35]Cohen to Truman, 11 July 1946, *FR: 1946,* II, pp. 903-4; Curry, *James F. Byrnes,* p. 376, footnote 24 mentioned "The Secretary had not been well during the week and had stayed in bed most of that morning (21 July)"; Byrnes, *Speaking Frankly,* p. 137; Byrnes, *All In One Lifetime,* p. 325; William Leahy Diary, 14 July 1946, Leahy Papers, Library of Congress; *New York Times,* 15 July 1946; *Department of State Bulletin,* 15 (28 July 1946), p. 167.

[36]*Senate Miscellaneous Documents. Senate Documents, Seventy-ninth Congress, Second Session* (Washington, D.C.: Government Printing Office, 1947), pp. 133-45, 190-215.

[37]*Ibid.,* p. 3; Dean Acheson, *Sketches from Life of Men I Have Known* (New York: Norton, 1961), pp. 126-27.

CHAPTER SIX

[1]Byrnes, *Speaking Frankly,* pp. 138, 236; Byrnes, *All In One Lifetime,* pp. 360-61; George Curry, *James F. Byrnes,* p. 239; William Leahy Diary, 27 July 1946, Leahy Papers, Library of Congress; *Department of State Bulletin,* 15 (4 August 1946), pp. 202-10.

[2]*New York Times,* 31 March, 28 July 1946.

[3]Nigel Nicolson, ed., *Harold Nicolson, The Later Years, 1945-1962* (New York: Atheneum, 1968), pp. 69-70, referred to hereafter as Nicolson Diary;

Nicolson found himself the only Versailles veteran at the conference "except for a dotard in the Brazilian delegation whose memory is unreliable."

[4]Nicolson Diary, 29 July 1946; Verbatim Record, First Plenary Meeting, 29 July 1946, United States Department of State, *FR: 1946,* III, pp. 26-29; Paris Peace Conference Newspaper Clippings, 30 July 1946, James F. Byrnes Papers, Clemson University.

[5]Verbatim Record, Second Plenary Session, 30 July 1946, *FR: 1946,* III, pp. 33-41; *ibid.,* Third Plenary Session, 31 July 1946, pp. 48-64; *ibid.,* Fourth Plenary Session, 1 August 1946, pp. 68-81; *ibid.,* Fifth Plenary Session, 2 August 1946, pp. 86-101; *ibid.,* Sixth Plenary Session, 3 August 1946, pp. 105-22; Byrnes, *Speaking Frankly,* pp. 139-40; U.S. Delegation Journal, First Meeting, Commission on Procedure, 30 July 1946, *FR: 1946,* III, pp. 32-33; *ibid.,* and U.S. Delegation Minutes, Second Meeting, 31 July 1946, pp. 44-45; *ibid.,* Third Meeting, 1 August 1946, p. 65; Mosely, *The Kremlin and World Politics,* p. 259; *New York Times,* 31 August 1946.

[6]U.S. Delegation Journal and Minutes, Fourth Meeting, Commission on Procedure, 2 August 1946, *FR: 1946,* III, pp. 84-85; *ibid.,* Fifth Meeting, 3 August 1946, pp. 104-5; *ibid.,* Sixth Meeting, 5 August 1946, pp. 123-24; Curry, *James F. Byrnes,* pp. 241-42.

[7]U.S. Delegation Journal, Seventh and Eighth Meetings, Commission on Procedure, 5 August 1946, *FR: 1946,* III, pp. 124-25; *ibid.,* Ninth and Tenth Meetings, 6 August 1946, pp. 125-26; *ibid.,* Eleventh Meeting, 6 August 1946, pp. 128-29; *ibid.,* Twelfth Meeting, 7 August 1946, pp. 130-31.

[8]Neither of Byrnes's accounts of the Paris Peace Conference, nor that of George Curry, mentions the French compromise on voting which Molotov accepted: *New York Times,* 11 August 1946, reported that within forty-eight hours Moscow press and radio carried Byrnes's full speech.

[9]McNeill, *America, Britain, and Russia,* p. 721; Byrnes, *Speaking Frankly,* p. 140.

[10]Verbatim Record, Seventh Plenary Session, 8 August 1946, *FR: 1946,* III, pp. 131-471.

[11]*Ibid.,* Eighth Plenary Session, 9 August 1946, pp. 148-62; Byrnes, *Speaking Frankly,* p. 140.

[12]*Ibid.,* p. 139; Sulzberger, *A Long Row of Candles. Memoirs and Diaries,* p. 316; F. S. Northedge, *British Foreign Policy. The Process of Readjustment* (New York: Praeger, 1962), p. 51.

[13]Verbatim Record, Second Plenary Meeting, 30 July 1946, *FR: 1946,* III, pp. 33-39.

[14]*Ibid.,* Third Plenary Meeting, 31 July 1946, pp. 45-52.

[15]Harold Nicolson, "Peacemaking at Paris: Success, Failure or Farce?" *Foreign Affairs,* 25 (January 1947), p. 190; Nicolson Diary, 16 October 1946.

[16]Nicolson, "Peacemaking at Paris," p. 197; Nicolson Diary, 5, 9, and 17 August 1946.

[17]Byrnes, *Speaking Frankly,* p. 140; generally, the American press supported Byrnes throughout the conference. Press Clippings, Byrnes Papers; *New York Times,* 7, 8, 10, 11, and 16 August 1946.

[18]Vera Micheles Dean, *Saturday Review of Literature,* 29 (26 October 1946), 16, reviews Nicolson's book, *The Congress of Vienna* and quotes

Nicolson: "It was indeed true that Russia, having endured harsh suffering and achieved major triumphs, was assuming an attitude of arrogant secretiveness which caused dismay to her partners in the Grand Alliance" as a parallel to Soviet action in Paris; Georges Bidault, *Resistence: The Political Biography of Georges Bidault* (New York: Praeger, 1956), p. 126.

[19]Mosely, *Kremlin and World Politics*, p. 256; McNeill, *America, Britain, and Russia*, p. 720.

[20]Byrnes, *Speaking Frankly*, p. 141; Nicolson Diary, 17 August 1946.

[21]Verbatim Record, Eleventh Plenary Meeting, 11 August 1946, *FR: 1946*, III, pp. 175-85; *ibid.*, Twelfth and Thirteenth Plenary Meetings, 12 August 1946, pp. 186-89; Nicolson Diary, 17 August 1946.

[22]United States Journal, Fifteenth Plenary Meeting, 13 August 1946, *FR: 1946*, III, p. 190; *ibid.*, Verbatim Record Extract, p. 191; *ibid.*, Sixteenth Plenary Meeting, 14 August 1946, pp. 200-9; *ibid.*, Seventeenth Plenary Meeting, 14 August 1946, pp. 210-21.

[23]*Ibid.*, Eighteenth Plenary Meeting, 15 August 1946, pp. 228-32; Byrnes, *Speaking Frankly*, pp. 141-44; Curry, *James F. Byrnes*, pp. 244-46; Byrnes, *All In One Lifetime*, p. 364.

[24]Feis, *From Trust to Terror*, p. 127, maintains, "The discussions at the Peace Conference were almost free of bitterness and recrimination. Rather, they were matter-of-fact and at times torpid."

[25]Byrnes, *Speaking Frankly*, pp. 144-46; Curry, *James F. Byrnes*, pp. 246-47; *New York Times*, 10, 12, and 21 August 1946.

[26]Acheson to Byrnes, 22 August 1946, State Department Records, File Number 1945-1949, National Archives; Vandenberg, *Private Papers*, p. 298; Russell to Byrnes, 5 August 1946, Correspondence Folder, Byrnes Papers.

[27]Vandenberg, *Private Papers*, pp. 298-99; Vandenberg to J. W. Blodgett, 23 August 1946, Correspondence Folder, Vandenberg Papers, The University of Michigan; unfortunately, Vandenberg stopped making daily diary entries during the Paris Peace Conference; Vandenberg Diary, 29 June 1946, Vandenberg Papers; Byrnes, *Speaking Frankly*, pp. 140-1; Connally, *My Name Is Tom Connally*, pp. 299-301; Bidault, *Resistance*, p. 130.

[28]Byrnes, *Speaking Frankly*, p. 141; Connally, *My Name Is Tom Connally*, p. 299; Sulzberger, *A Long Row of Candles*, p. 317, said Mrs. Connally complained to him that Sulzberger too paid more attention to Vandenberg, so Sulzberger invited Connally to lunch and found "Old Tawm sulky"; *New York Times*, 31 August 1946; several women's groups complained to Byrnes that the American delegation did not include a woman; the secretary explained that the delegation was a working delegation of experts, not of civilian representatives; the press noted the Soviet delegation included more women experts than any other; Mabel Griswold to Byrnes, 17 September 1946, Correspondence Folder, Byrnes Papers; Women's International League for Peace and Freedom to Byrnes, 17 September 1946, *ibid.*, World Woman's Party for Equal Rights to Byrnes, 28 July 1946, *ibid.; New York Times*, 1 September 1946.

[29]Byrnes, *Speaking Frankly*, pp. 187-93; Curry, *James F. Byrnes*, pp. 248-52.

[30]Byrnes to State Department 5 September 1946, State Department Records, File Number 1945-1949.

[31]*Department of State Bulletin,* 15 (15 September 1946), pp. 496–501; Murphy, *Diplomat Among Warriors,* pp. 302–3; Byrnes, *All In One Lifetime,* pp. 367–70.

[32]Clay, *Decision in Germany,* pp. 78–81; Clayton to Byrnes, 6 September 1946, Correspondence Folder, Byrnes Papers; Forrestal to Byrnes, 8 September 1946, *ibid.;* Vandenberg to Dulles, 8 September 1946, Correspondence Folder, John Foster Dulles Papers, Princeton University; Dulles to Vandenberg, 7 September 1946, *ibid.;* Dulles Papers; Joseph Davies Diary, 30 September 1946, Davies Papers, Library of Congress, said in reference to the Stuttgart speech, "Jim Byrnes has, I fear, irrevocably sown the dragon's teeth in Europe. . ."; Alexander Werth, *France, 1940-1955* (London: Robert Hale, 1956), pp. 294, 308; *New York Times,* 7, 10, and 17 September 1946.

[33]Truman, *Year of Decisions,* pp. 555–60; Curry, *James F. Byrnes,* pp. 252–73; Vandenberg, *Private Papers,* pp. 300–3; Wallace to Truman, 23 July 1946, Clark Clifford Papers, Harry S. Truman Library, Box 18; Daniels, *The Man of Independence,* p. 314; Phillips, *The Truman Presidency,* pp. 149–54; *New York Times,* 13 September 1946.

[34]Edward L. Schapsmeier and Frederick H. Schapsmeier, *Prophet in Politics: Henry A. Wallace and the War Years, 1940-1965* (Ames: Iowa State University Press, 1970), Chapter 10; interestingly, Joseph Davies Diary, 10 September 1946, records that Truman told Davies, "His policy was simple. He was neither for nor against Russia. He was neither for nor against Britain."

[35]Phillips, *The Truman Presidency,* p. 151; Clayton to Byrnes, 13 September 1946, Correspondence Folder, Byrnes Papers; Russell to Byrnes, 13, 16, 19, and 20 September 1946, *ibid.;* Byrnes, *Speaking Frankly,* pp. 239–43; Byrnes, *All In One Lifetime,* pp. 370–76; Acheson, *Present at the Creation,* pp. 190–92; Millis, ed., *The Forrestal Diaries,* pp. 206–10; Byrnes's Press Statement, Press Clippings Folder, Byrnes Papers.

[36]Vandenberg, *Private Papers,* pp. 300–1; Connally, *My Name Is Tom Connally,* p. 302; Clayton to Byrnes, 14 September 1946, Correspondence Folder, Byrnes Papers.

[37]Clayton to Byrnes, 17 September 1946, Correspondence Folder, Byrnes Papers; Byrnes to Russell, 18 September 1946, *ibid.;* Leahy Diary, 18 September 1946 states Leahy advised Truman Wallace and Byrnes could not both stay in the cabinet; Memorandum for the Files on the Wallace Incident, 19 September 1946, Bernard Baruch Papers, Princeton University, states Baruch threatened to resign as the defender of the American atomic energy proposal before the United Nations Atomic Energy Commission in an interview with Truman right before his appointment with Wallace.

[38]Byrnes, *All In One Lifetime,* pp. 374–76; *Public Papers of the Presidents: Harry S. Truman, 1945-1947,* pp. 431, 426, 428; Russell to Byrnes, 20 September 1946, Correspondence Folder, Byrnes Papers; Blum, ed., *The Price of Vision,* pp. 613–26.

[39]Verbatim Record, Fifth Plenary Meeting, 2 August 1946, *FR: 1946,* III, p. 90; United States Delegation Journal, Sixth Meeting, Commission on Procedure, 5 August 1946, *ibid.,* p. 124; U.S. Delegation Minutes, First Informal Meeting, Council of Foreign Ministers, 29 August 1946, *ibid.,* pp. 313–21.

[40]Acheson to Byrnes, 27 August 1946, State Department Records, File Number 1945-1949; U.S. Delegation Minutes, Second Informal Meeting, Council of Foreign Ministers, 4 September 1946, *FR: 1946,* III, pp. 364-70; *ibid.,* Third Informal Meeting, 6 September 1946, pp. 383-90; *ibid.,* Fourth Informal Meeting, 8 September 1946, pp. 398-404; Memorandum, 10 September 1946, Correspondence Folder, Byrnes Papers.

[41]U.S. Delegation Minutes, Fifth Informal Meeting, Council of Foreign Ministers, 24 September 1946, *FR: 1946,* III, pp. 538-49.

[42]Memorandum of Conversation, 3 October 1946, *ibid.,* pp. 645-48; U.S. Delegation Minutes, Sixth Informal Meeting, Council of Foreign Ministers, 3 October 1946, *ibid.,* pp. 654-59; *ibid.,* Seventh Informal Meeting, 14 October 1946, pp. 856-59.

[43]*New York Times,* 25 September 1946; *Department of State Bulletin,* 15 (13 October 1946), pp. 665-68; Matthews to Leland Harrison, 4 October 1946, State Department Records, File Number 1940-1947, Box 17; Harriman Memorandum, 2 October 1946, *ibid.,* Byrnes, *Speaking Frankly,* p. 147.

[44]Connally, *My Name Is Tom Connally,* pp. 302-3; Byrnes, *Speaking Frankly,* pp. 147-48; Curry, *James F. Byrnes,* pp. 277-78; United States Delegation Journal, Twenty-ninth Plenary Meeting, 7 October 1946, *FR: 1946,* III, pp. 689-91; *ibid.,* Thirty-third Plenary Meeting, 8 October 1946, pp. 697-99; *ibid.,* Thirty-fourth Plenary Meeting, 9 October 1946, pp. 700-2.

[45]Byrnes, *Speaking Frankly,* pp. 148-49; United States Delegation Journal, Thirty-seventh Plenary Meeting, 10 October 1946, *FR: 1946,* III, pp. 758-60; *ibid.,* Thirty-eighth Plenary Meeting, 10 October 1946, pp. 760-62; Nicolson Diary, 6 September 1946.

[46]Byrnes, *Speaking Frankly,* p. 148; Curry, *James F. Byrnes,* p. 279.

[47]Verbatim Record, Thirty-fifth Plenary Meeting, 9 October 1946, *FR: 1946,* III, pp. 702-27; *ibid.,* Thirty-sixth Plenary Meeting, 9 October 1946, pp. 727-58; *ibid.,* Thirty-ninth Plenary Meeting, 10 October 1946, pp. 762-91; *ibid.,* Forty-second Plenary Meeting, 11 October 1946, pp. 796-816; *ibid.,* Forty-fifth Plenary Meeting, 12 October 1946, pp. 822-40; *ibid.,* Forty-seventh Plenary Meeting, 14 October 1946, pp. 843-56; *ibid.,* Forty-eighth Plenary Meeting, 15 October 1946, pp. 859-61; Nicolson, "Peacemaking at Paris," p. 190.

[48]*New York Times,* 18 October 1946.

[49]*Department of State Bulletin,* 15 (27 October 1946), pp. 742-43.

[50]Curry, *James F. Byrnes,* p. 282; *Department of State Bulletin,* 15 (3 November 1946), pp. 890-911; Byrnes, *All In One Lifetime,* p. 380; *New York Times,* 13 November 1946.

[51]*New York Times,* 15, 18 October 1946; Nicolson, "Peacemaking at Paris," pp. 200-1.

[52]*Time,* 49 (6 January 1947), p. 27.

CHAPTER SEVEN

[1]Clifford to Truman, 24 September 1946, Clark Clifford Papers, Harry S. Truman Library; *American Relations with the Soviet Union, A Report to the President by the Special Counsel to the President, ibid.*

²Truman, *Years of Trial and Hope,* pp. 96-98; Wilson to Byrnes, 12 August 1946, United States Department of State, *Foreign Relations of the United States, 1946* (Washington, D.C.: Government Printing Office, 1970), VII, p. 837, hereafter referred to as *FR: 1946*; Acheson to Byrnes, 14 August 1946, *ibid.,* pp. 840-42; Millis, ed., *The Forrestal Diaries,* pp. 192, 211; Acheson, *Present at the Creation,* pp. 195-196.

³Hewlett and Anderson, *A History of the United States Atomic Energy Commission,* pp. 531-58, 576-618; Truman, *Years of Trial and Hope,* pp. 6-11; Acheson, *Present at the Creation,* pp. 151-55; Margaret Coit, *Mr. Baruch* (Boston: Houghton Mifflin, 1957), pp. 563-71; Baruch to Truman, 26 March 1946, Correspondence Folder, Bernard Baruch Papers, Princeton University; Baruch to Byrnes, 21 March 1946, *ibid.;* Byrnes to Baruch, 19 April 1946, *ibid.,* Memorandum of Conversation, 7 June 1946, *ibid.;* Bernard Baruch, *The Public Years* (New York: Holt, Rinehart, & Winston, 1962), pp. 346-67; *The United States and the United Nations: United States Atomic Energy Proposals* (Washington, D.C.: Government Printing Office, 1946), pp. 1-12; Department of State, *International Control of Atomic Energy: Growth of a Policy* (Washington, D.C.: Government Printing Office, 1946); *New York Times,* 20 June 1946; Byrnes, *Speaking Frankly,* pp. 268-75.

⁴Byrnes, *Speaking Frankly,* pp. 150-1; Byrnes, *All In One Lifetime,* pp. 380-2; Burns, "James F. Byrnes, 1945-1947," in *An Uncertain Tradition,* ed. Graebner, p. 239, mistakenly concludes because of the concurrent Council of Foreign Ministers and United Nations meetings that after the Paris Peace Conference, Byrnes "took the conference's recommendations on Italy, Bulgaria, Rumania, and Hungary to the United Nations in New York for its approval"; Byrnes to Patterson, 22 October 1946, State Department Records, File Number 1945-1949, National Archives.

⁵Byrnes, *Speaking Frankly,* p. 151; Byrnes, *All In One Lifetime,* p. 382; Curry, *James F. Byrnes,* pp. 283-4.

⁶U.S. Delegation Minutes, First Meeting, 4 November 1946, United States Department of State, *FR: 1946,* II, pp. 969-88.

⁷*Ibid.*

⁸Byrnes, *Speaking Frankly,* p. 151; U.S. Delegation Minutes, Third Meeting, 6 November 1946, *FR: 1946,* II, pp. 1021-30; Statement by the Yugoslav Minister, 6 November 1946, *ibid.,* pp. 1031-38; Statement by the Italian Ambassador, 6 November 1946, *ibid.,* pp. 1038-42; Acheson, *Sketches From Life of Men I Have Known,* pp. 85-86.

⁹U.S. Delegation Minutes, Second Meeting, 5 November 1946, *FR: 1946,* II, pp. 993-1012; *ibid.,* Third Meeting, 6 November 1946, pp. 1021-30; Byrnes, *Speaking Frankly,* p. 152, mentions Bevin changing his position on the first important peace conference recommendation but does not mention Molotov immediately following suit.

¹⁰U.S. Delegation Minutes, Fourth Meeting, 8 November 1946, *FR: 1946,* II, pp. 1061-69.

¹¹*Ibid.,* Fifth Meeting, 11 November 1946, pp. 1077-93.

¹²*Ibid.,* Seventh Meeting, 12 November 1946, pp. 1111-26.

¹³*Ibid.,* Eighth Meeting, 13 November 1946, pp. 1129-43; *ibid.,* Ninth Meeting, 14 November 1946, pp. 1144-54; *ibid.,* First Informal Meeting, 15 November 1946, pp. 1166-74; *ibid.,* Second Informal Meeting, 16 November

1946, pp. 1174-84; *ibid.,* Third Informal Meeting, 18 November 1946, pp. 1186-94; *ibid.,* Fourth Informal Meeting, 20 November 1946, pp. 1200-11; *ibid.,* Fifth Informal Meeting, 21 November 1946, pp. 1215-26; *ibid.,* Sixth Informal Meeting, 22 November 1946, pp. 1235-51; *ibid.,* Seventh Informal Meeting, 23 November 1946, pp. 1256-64.

¹⁴Memorandum of Conversation, 25 November 1946, *FR: 1946,* II, pp. 1264-69; Byrnes, *Speaking Frankly,* pp. 152-54; Byrnes, *All In One Lifetime,* pp. 382-83.

¹⁵Bohlen, *Witness to History,* pp. 255-56, the afternoon council meeting when Bohlen referred to Molotov dealing out agreements actually produced only one agreement; it concerned the governor's powers; U.S. Delegation Minutes, Eighth Informal Meeting, 25 November 1946, *FR: 1946,* II, pp. 1269-78.

¹⁶Millis, ed., *The Forrestal Diaries,* pp. 233-4, records that Byrnes presented his version of the effectiveness of his threat to Molotov to the cabinet on 16 December 1946; *New York Times,* 5 December 1946 indicates Byrnes gave the story to the press, also, because James Reston wrote that the Byrnes-Molotov conversation was of the "greatest significance" in changing the Soviet diplomat's attitude.

¹⁷U.S. Delegation Minutes, Ninth Informal Meeting, 26 November 1946, *FR: 1946,* II, pp. 1285-96; *New York Times,* 26, 27 November 1946; U.S. Delegation Minutes, Tenth Informal Meeting, 27 November 1946, *FR: 1946,* II, pp. 1304-9; *ibid.,* Tenth Meeting, 28 November 1946, pp. 1324-29; *ibid.,* Eleventh Meeting, 29 November 1946, pp. 1340-2; *ibid.,* Twelfth Meeting, 30 November 1946, pp. 1356-62; *ibid.,* Thirteenth Meeting, 2 December 1946, pp. 1369-78; *ibid.,* Fourteenth Meeting, 3 December 1946, pp. 1382-95; *ibid.,* Fifteenth Meeting, 4 December 1946, pp. 1404-8; *ibid.,* Sixteenth Meeting, 5 December 1946, pp. 1421-26.

¹⁸*Ibid.,* First Meeting, 4 November 1946, pp. 985-87; *ibid.,* 11 November 1946, pp. 1085-87; *ibid.,* Ninth Informal Meeting, 26 November 1946, pp. 1291-93; *ibid.,* Tenth Informal Meeting, 27 November 1946, pp. 1309-10.

¹⁹*Ibid.,* Eleventh Meeting, 29 November 1946, pp. 1342-50; *ibid.,* Thirteenth Meeting, 2 December 1946, pp. 13, 75-78.

²⁰*Ibid.,* Tenth Informal Meeting, 27 November 1946, pp. 1312-13; *ibid.,* Tenth Meeting, 28 November 1946, pp. 1334-37; *ibid.,* Eleventh Meeting, 29 November 1946, p. 1350; *ibid.,* Fifteenth Meeting, 4 December 1946, pp. 1408-14; *ibid.,* Sixteenth Meeting, 5 December 1946, pp. 1427-33; James Reston, *New York Times,* 5 December 1946, the day of the council agreement, ran a story of Bevin telling Molotov of two Irish laborers out on strike reading a newspaper to see if there was "any danger of a settlement." In the reparations settlement Italy paid Yugoslavia $125 million and Greece $105 million, while Bulgaria paid Yugoslavia $25 million and Greece $45 million; Molotov also accepted an eighteen month requirement in the Balkan treaties that they would not discriminate economically among nations. The Americans and British wanted a five year requirement.

²¹U.S. Delegation Minutes, Seventeenth Meeting, 6 December 1946, *FR: 1946,* II, pp. 1453-54; *ibid.,* Eighteenth Meeting, 7 December 1946, pp. 1469-75; *ibid.,* Nineteenth Meeting, 9 December 1946, pp. 1481-90; *ibid.,*

Twentieth Meeting, 10 December 1946, pp. 1494-1505; *ibid.*, Twenty-first Meeting, 11 December 1946, pp. 1509-16; *ibid.*, Twenty-second Meeting, 11 December 1946, pp. 1521-30; *ibid.*, Twenty-third Meeting, 12 December 1946, pp. 1536-51; Memorandum of Conversation, 9 December 1946, *FR: 1946,* II, pp. 1479-81; *New York Times,* 9, 10, 11 December 1946; Murphy, *Diplomat Among Warriors,* p. 304, referred to himself and Lucius Clay as peace circuit riders for Byrnes had again summoned them to advise him on German issues.

[22]U.S. Delegation Minutes, Twenty-third Meeting, 12 December 1946, *FR: 1946,* II, p. 1551; *New York Times,* 13, 14 December 1946; Sulzberger, *A Long Row of Candles,* pp. 339-40, reported that when the treaties were signed in Paris on 10 February in the Salon de l'Horloge of the Quai d'Orsay on the table where the wounded Robespierre lay before being guillotined: "There was strangely little joy in the room or in Paris itself which greeted the event with supreme indifference." Diplomats also signed the covenant of the League of Nations and the Kellog-Briand Pact in this same room. The treaties were flown to Molotov in Moscow and Bevin in London for their signature.

[23]Byrnes, *Speaking Frankly,* pp. 150-55, describes the entire council meeting in just over five pages. Byrnes, *All In One Lifetime,* pp. 381-84, only uses a little over three pages on the New York meeting; Curry, *James F. Byrnes,* pp. 283-91 gives the longest analysis to date, but it is just over eight pages long; historians accepting Byrnes's account of the New York meeting include: Richard S. Kirkendall, *The Truman Period as a Research Field* (Columbia: The University of Missouri Press, 1967), p. 50; Wheeler-Bennett and Nicolls, *The Semblance of Peace,* pp. 436-38; Gaddis, *The United States and the Origins of the Cold War,* pp. 323-24; and Murphy, *Diplomat Among Warriors,* p. 304; Opie Redvers et al., *The Search for Peace Settlements* (Washington: The Brookings Institute, 1951), pp. 93-94; Stephen Kertesz, ed., *The Fate of East Central Europe. Hopes and Failure of American Foreign Policy* (Notre Dame: University of Notre Dame Press, 1956), pp. 10-11; McNeill, *America, Britain and Russia,* pp. 722-23; and Yergin, *Shattered Peace,* p. 250.

[24]*FR: 1946,* III, pp. xix.

[25]Byrnes, *All In One Lifetime,* pp. 385, 387-88; Curry, *James F. Byrnes,* pp. 293-97; McNeill, *America, Britain, and Russia,* p. 659, footnote 2, states, but does not document, that Byrnes "resigned in a huff"; Byrnes to Truman, 19 December 1946, Correspondence Folder, Byrnes Papers; *New York Times,* 7 January 1947; Truman to Byrnes, 7 January 1946, Correspondence Folder, Byrnes Papers.

[26]*New York Times,* 8, 9 January 1947; Byrnes to Stimson, 17 January 1946, Correspondence Folder, Byrnes Papers; Vandenberg to Dulles, 18 January 1947, Correspondence Folder, Dulles Papers; Connally, *My Name Is Tom Connally,* p. 312; Joseph Davies Diary, 7 January 1947, Davies Papers, Library of Congress; Sulzberger, *A Long Row of Candles,* p. 367; Byrnes, *All In One Lifetime,* pp. 355-56; Curry, *James F. Byrnes,* pp. 312-17.

[27]*Time,* 49 (6 January 1947), p. 25; Byrnes, *All In One Lifetime,* p. 388; Marshall to Byrnes, 18 February 1947, Correspondence Folder, Byrnes

Papers; Vandenberg to Byrnes, 17 February 1947, Correspondence Folder, Byrnes Papers; Byrnes's competitors as *Time*'s "Man of the Year" included Joseph Stalin, Ernest Bevin, Georges Bidault, Chiang Kai-shak, and Douglas MacArthur.

CHAPTER EIGHT

[1]Bevin maintained that the council decision to allow armistice signatories to decide treaties caused him "much embarrassment" and "proved a fertile cause of delay." He also characterized as "unfortunate" the fact that Britain had renounced in advance any territorial advantage as a result of the war (Minutes of the Cabinet, 2 January 1947, Public Records Office, 128/9, p. 3).

[2]Bevin insisted in his summary of the treaties to the cabinet that if Britain took full advantage of the Balkan treaties, there was a "good prospect of reestablishing our trading connection." He also believed that the Trieste settlement had prevented an irredentist movement and that the colonial decision at least allowed British administration to continue for a while longer (CAB 128/9, 2 January 1947, p. 4). See also CAB 128/9, 6 January 1947, p. 11.

[3]Acheson, *Sketches From Life of Men I Have Known,* pp. 1-3, 85-86; Biographical Sketches Prepared by Personal Intelligence Section of the Department of State, 5 October 1945, State Department Records, File Number 1945-1949, Box 10B, National Archives.

[4]Georges Bidault, "Agreement on Germany: Key to World Peace," *Foreign Affairs,* 24 July 1946, p. 57; Harold Nicolson, "Peacemaking at Paris: Success, Failure, or Farce?" *Foreign Affairs,* 25 January 1947, p. 194; Walter Lippmann, "A Year of Peacemaking," *Atlantic Monthly,* December 1946, pp. 36-38; Bevin also believed that the British bargaining position was weak from the beginning because of the decision to begin with the lesser treaties. He saw Southeastern Europe "conceded" to the Soviet Union before the council sessions began (CAB 128/9, 2 January 1947, p. 3).

BIBLIOGRAPHY

ARCHIVES AND MANUSCRIPT COLLECTIONS

Allen, George V. Harry S. Truman Library
Baruch, Bernard. Princeton University Library
Byrnes, James F. Clemson University Library.
Clayton, William L. Harry S. Truman Library.
Clifford, Clark. Harry S. Truman Library.
Connally, Tom. Library of Congress.
Davies, Joseph E. Library of Congress.
Dulles, John Foster. Princeton University Library.
Forrestal, James V. Princeton University Library.
Leahy, William D. Library of Congress.
Minutes of the Cabinet, 1945-1946, British Public Records Office.
Truman, Harry S. Harry S. Truman Library.
United States Department of State Archives, 1945-1946. Record Group 43 and 59, National Archives.
Vandenberg, Arthur. University of Michigan Archives.

INTERVIEWS

Dulles, John Foster. Oral History Collection. Princeton University Library.

OFFICIAL DOCUMENTS

British and Foreign State Papers, 1945-1947. Vols. 145-147. London: Her Majesty's Stationery Office, 1953.
Correspondence Between the Chairman of the Council of Ministers of the U.S.S.R. and the Presidents of the U.S.A. and the Prime Ministers of Great Britain During the Great Patriotic War of 1941-1945. 2 vols. Moscow, 1957.
Great Britain, Parliament. *Hansard's Parliamentary Debates.*

Great Britain, Secretary of State for Foreign Affairs. *Selected Documents on Germany and the Question of Berlin: 1944-1961. Index to the Correspondence of the Foreign Office for the Year 1945.* London: Her Majesty's Stationery Office, 1970.

International Control of Atomic Energy. Growth of a Policy. Washington: Government Printing Office, 1946.

Public Papers of the Presidents: Harry S. Truman, 1945-1947. Washington: Government Printing Office, 1961-1963.

The United States and the United Nations. United States Atomic Energy Proposals. Government Printing Office, 1962.

U.S. Congress. *Congressional Record.* 78th through 80th Congress.

U.S. Department of State. *Department of State Bulletin,* Vols. 12-14.

———. *Foreign Relations of the United States. Annual Volumes, 1945-1946.* Washington: Government Printing Office, 1960-1970.

———. *Foreign Relations of the United States: The Conference of Berlin (The Potsdam Conference), 1945,* 2 vols. Washington: Government Printing Office, 1960.

———. *Foreign Relations of the United States: The Conferences at Malta and Yalta, 1945.* Washington: Government Printing Office, 1955.

———. *Foreign Relations of the United States: 1946, Council of Foreign Ministers.* Washington: Government Printing Office, 1970.

———. *Foreign Relations of the United States, 1946, Paris Peace Conference.* 2 vols. Washington: Government Printing Office, 1970.

U.S. Senate. *Senate Miscellaneous Documents. 79th Congress, Second Session.* Washington: Government Printing Office, 1947.

NEWSPAPERS

New York Times, April 1945-January 1947.

BOOKS

Acheson, Dean. *Present at the Creation: My Years in the State Department.* New York: Norton, 1969.

———. *Sketches From Life of Men I Have Known.* New York: Harper and Brothers, 1961.

Allen, Robert and William J. Shannon. *The Truman Merry-Go-Round.* New York: Vanguard Press, 1950.

Alperovitz, Gar. *Atomic Diplomacy: Hiroshima and Potsdam. The Use of the Atomic Bomb and the American Confrontation with Soviet Power.* New York: Simon and Schuster, 1965.

Attlee, Clement. *As It Happened.* London: Heinemann, 1954.

Baruch, Bernard. *The Public Years.* New York: Holt, Rinehart, & Winston, 1962.

Bernstein, Barton J., ed. *Politics and Policies of the Truman Administration.* Chicago: Quadrangle, 1970.

Bidault, Georges. *Resistance. The Political Biography of George Bidault.* New York: Praeger, 1956.

Blum, John Morton. *From the Morgenthau Diaries: Years of War, 1941-1945.* Boston: Houghton Mifflin, 1967.

_____, ed. *The Price of Vision. The Diary of Henry A. Wallace, 1942-1946.* Boston: Houghton Mifflin, 1973.

Bohlen, Charles. *Witness to History, 1929-1969.* New York: Norton, 1973.

Buhite, Russell D. *Patrick J. Hurley and American Foreign Policy.* Ithaca: Cornell University Press, 1973.

Bush, Vannevar. *Pieces of the Action.* New York: Simon and Schuster, 1970.

Byrnes, James F. *All In One Lifetime.* New York: Harper & Brothers, 1958.

_____. *Speaking Frankly.* New York: Harper & Brothers, 1947.

Cantril, Hadley and Mildred Strunk, eds. *Public Opinion, 1935-1946.* Princeton: Princeton University Press, 1951.

Churchill, Winston. *The Second World War. Triumph and Tragedy.* Boston: Houghton Mifflin, 1953.

Clay, Lucius. *Decision in Germany.* New York: Doubleday, 1950.

Clemens, Cyril. *The Man From Missouri. A Biography of Harry S. Truman.* New York: J. P. Didier, 1945.

Clemens, Diane Shaver. *Yalta.* New York: Oxford University Press, 1970.

Coffin, Tris. *The Missouri Compromise.* Boston: Little, Brown, 1947.

Coit, Margaret. *Mr. Baruch.* Boston: Houghton Mifflin, 1957.

Conant, James B. *My Several Lives. Memoirs of a Social Inventor.* New York: Harper and Row, 1970.

Connally, Tom. *My Name Is Tom Connally.* New York: Thomas Y. Crowell, 1954.

Curry, George. *James F. Byrnes.* New York: Cooper Square Publishers, 1965.

Daniels, Jonathan. *The Man of Independence.* Philadelphia: Lippincott, 1950.

Dennett, Raymond and Joseph Johnson, eds. *Negotiating with the Russians.* Boston: World Peace Foundation, 1951.

Divine, Robert. *Second Chance: The Triumph of Internationalism in America During World War II.* New York: Atheneum, 1967.

Dobney, Fredrick, J., ed. *Selected Papers of Will Clayton.* Baltimore: Johns Hopkins Press, 1971.

Dulles, John Foster. *War or Peace.* New York: Macmillan, 1950.

Druks, Herbert. *Harry S. Truman and the Russians, 1945-1953.* New York: Robert Speller, 1966.

Feis, Herbert. *Between War and Peace: The Potsdam Conference.* Princeton: Princeton University Press, 1960.

————. *Churchill, Roosevelt, Stalin: The War They Waged and the Peace They Sought.* Princeton: Princeton University Press, 1957.

————. *Contest Over Japan.* New York: Norton, 1967.

————. *From Trust to Terror. The Onset of the Cold War, 1945-1950.* New York: Norton, 1970.

Fleming, D. F. *The Cold War and Its Origins, 1917-1960.* 2 vols. Garden City: Doubleday, 1961.

Gaddis, John. *The United States and the Origins of the Cold War, 1941-1947.* New York: Columbia University Press, 1972.

Gardner, Lloyd C. *Architects of Illusion. Men and Ideas in American Foreign Policy, 1941-1949.* Chicago: Quadrangle, 1970.

Gimbel, John. *The American Occupation of Germany: Politics and the Military, 1945-1949.* Stanford: Stanford University Press, 1968.

Graebner, Norman, ed. *An Uncertain Tradition: American Secretaries of State in the Twentieth Century.* New York: McGraw-Hill, 1961.

Harriman, W. Averell and Elie Abel. *Special Envoy to Churchill and Stalin, 1941-1946.* New York: Random House, 1975.

Hewlett, Richard G., and Oscar E. Anderson, Jr. *A History of the United States Atomic Energy Commission: The New World, 1939-1946.* University Park: Pennsylvania State University Press, 1962.

Hillman, William, ed. *Mr. President: The First Publication from the Personal Diaries, Private Letters, Papers and Revealing Interviews of Harry S. Truman, Thirty-second President of the United States of America.* New York: Farrar, Straus and Young, 1952.

Jones, Joseph M. *The Fifteen Weeks (February 21-June 5, 1947).* New York: Macmillan, 1955.

Kennan, George. *Memoirs. 1925-1950.* Boston: Little, Brown, 1967.

Kertesz, Stephen, ed. *The Fate of East Central Europe: Hopes and Failures of American Foreign Policy.* Notre Dame: University of Notre Dame Press, 1956.

Kirkendall, Richard S. *The Truman Period as a Research Field.* Columbia: The University of Missouri Press, 1967.

Kolko, Joyce and Gabriel. *The Limits of Power, 1945-1954.* New York: Harper & Row, 1972.

Kolko, Gabriel. *The Politics of War: The World and United States Foreign Policy, 1943-1945.* New York: Harper & Row, 1968.

LeFeber, Walter. *America, Russia, and the Cold War, 1945-1967.* New York: Wiley, 1967.

Leahy, William D. *I Was There.* New York: McGraw Hill, 1950.

McNeill, William H. *America, Britain, and Russia: Their Cooperation and Conflict, 1941-1946.* New York: Harper, 1953.

Mee, Charles L. *Meeting At Potsdam.* New York: M. Evans, 1975.

Millis, Walter, ed. *The Forrestal Diaries.* New York: Viking Press, 1951.

Molotov, V. M. *Molotov Speeches at the Paris Peace Conference.* London: Soviet News Service, 1946.

_____. *Problems of Foreign Policy. Speeches and Statements, April, 1945-November, 1948.* Moscow: Foreign Languages Publishing House, 1949.

Mosely, Philip. *The Kremlin and World Politics. Studies in Soviet Policy and Action.* New York: Vintage Books, 1960.

Murphy, Robert. *Diplomat Among Warriors.* New York: Doubleday, 1964.

Nicolson, Nigel, ed. *Harold Nicolson. The Later Years, 1945-1962.* Vol. III of *Diaries and Letters.* New York: Athenaeum, 1968.

Northedge, F. S. *British Foreign Policy. The Process of Readjustment.* New York: Frederick A. Praeger, 1962.

Phillips, Cabell. *The Truman Presidency. The History of a Triumphant Succession.* New York: Macmillan, 1966.

Redvers, Opie, Joseph W. Ballantine, Jeannette E. Muther, Paul Birdsall, and Clarence E. Bhurber. *The Search for Peace Settlements.* Washington: The Brookings Institute, 1951.

Roosevelt, Elliott. *As He Saw It.* New York: Duell, Sloan, and Pearce, 1946.

Rosenman, Samuel, ed. *The Public Papers and Addresses of Franklin Delano Roosevelt.* Vols. IX-XIII, 1940-45. New York: Random House, 1941-1950.

Rostow, W. W. *The United States in the World Arena. An Essay in Recent History.* New York: Harper & Row, 1960.

Schapsmeier, Edward L., and Frederick H. Schapsmeier. *Prophet In Politics: Henry A. Wallace and the War Years, 1940-1965.* Ames: Iowa State University Press, 1970.

Sherwood, Robert E. *Roosevelt and Hopkins: An Intimate History.* New York: Harper, 1948.

Smith, Walter Bedell. *My Three Years In Moscow.* Philadelphia: J. B. Lippincott, 1950.

Steinberg, Alfred. *The Man From Missouri: The Life and Times of Harry S. Truman.* New York: Doubleday, 1962.

Stimson, Henry L., and McGeorge Bundy. *On Active Service in Peace and War.* New York: Harper & Brothers, 1947.

Stuart, Graham H. *The Department of State.* New York: Macmillan, 1949.

Sulzberger, C. L. *A Long Row of Candles. Memoirs and Diaries, 1934-1954.* New York: Macmillan Co., 1969.

Truman, Harry S. *Mr. Citizen.* New York: Random House, 1960.

————. *Year of Decisions.* Garden City: Doubleday and Co., 1955.

————. *Years of Trial and Hope.* Garden City: Doubleday and Co., 1956.

Truman, Margaret. *Harry S. Truman.* New York: Simon and Schuster, 1973.

Ulam, Adam. *The Rivals: America and Russia Since World War II.* New York: Viking Press, 1971.

————. *Stalin, The Man and His Era.* New York: Viking Press, 1973.

Vandenberg, Arthur H., Jr. *The Private Papers of Senator Vandenberg.* Boston: Houghton Mifflin, 1952.

Werth, Alexander. *France, 1940-1955.* London: Robert Hale, 1956.

Wheeler-Bennett, John W. *King George VI: His Life and Reign.* London: Macmillan, 1958.

———— and Anthony Nichols. *The Semblance of Peace. The Political Settlement After the Second World War.* London: Macmillan, 1972.

Williams, Francis. *A Prime Minister Remembers.* London: Heinemann, 1961.

Yergin, Daniel. *Shattered Peace, The Origins of the Cold War and the National Security State.* Boston: Houghton Mifflin Company, 1977.

ARTICLES

Bernstein, Barton J. "The Quest for Security: American Foreign Policy and International Control of Atomic Energy, 1942-1946." *Journal of American History,* 60 (March 1974), 1003-44.

Bidault, Georges. "Agreement on Germany: Key to World Peace." *Foreign Affairs,* 24 (July 1946), 57.

Campbell, John C. "The European Territorial Settlement." *Foreign Affairs,* 26 (October 1947), 196.

Dean, Vera Micheles. *Saturday Review of Literature,* 29 (26 October 1946), 16.

Hess, Gary. "The Iranian Crisis of 1945-46 and the Cold War." *Political Science Quarterly,* 89 (March 1974), 117-46.

Lippmann, Walter. "A Year of Peacemaking." *Atlantic Monthly,* 30 (December 1946), 36-38.

"Man of the Year: James F. Byrnes." *Time,* 49 (6 January 1947), 25.
Nicolson, Harold. "Peacemaking at Paris: Success, Failure, or Farce?" *Foreign Affairs,* 25 (January 1947), 190.
Schlesinger, Arthur M., Jr. "Origins of the Cold War." *Foreign Affairs,* 46 (October 1967), 22-52.

UNPUBLISHED MATERIAL

Herken, Gregg. "American Diplomacy and the Atomic Bomb." Ph.D. dissertation, Princeton University, 1973.
Jarvis, Bertrand Fox. "The Role of the Small Powers in the Development of the Western Bloc at the 1946 Paris Peace Conference: A Study in the Origins of the Cold War." Ph.D. dissertation, University of Alabama, 1973.

PERIODICALS

Atlantic Monthly, May 1945-January 1947.
American Mercury, May 1945-January 1947.
Colliers, May 1945-January 1947.
Commonweal, May 1945-January 1947.
Current History, May 1945-January 1947.
Life, May 1945-January 1947.
Nation, May 1945-January 1947.
New Republic, May 1945-January 1947.
Newsweek, May 1945-January 1947.
Time, May 1945-January 1947.
U.S. News and World Report, May 1945-January 1947.

INDEX